Travel & Tourism

2nd edition

Christine King • Andy Kerr • Malcolm Jefferies

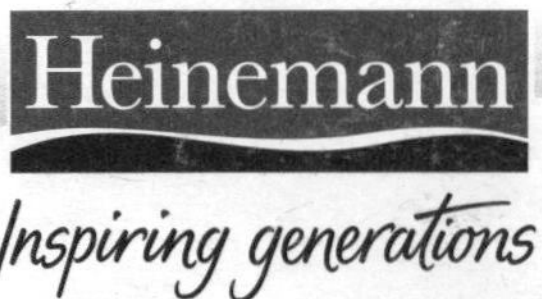

Heinemann Educational Publishers
Halley Court, Jordan Hill, Oxford OX2 8EJ
Part of Harcourt Education

Heinemann is the registered trademark of
Harcourt Education Limited

First published 2006

10 09 08 07 06
10 9 8 7 6 5 4 3 2 1

British Library Cataloguing in Publication Data is available from the British Library on request.

10-digit ISBN: 0 435 40219 6
13-digit ISBN: 978 0 435402 19 8

Edited by Caroline Low, Virgo Editorial
Designed by Wooden Ark
Typeset and illustrated by Saxon Graphics Ltd, Derby
Original illustrations © Harcourt Education Limited, 2006
Cover design by Wooden Ark
Printed in the UK by Scotprint
Cover photo: © Jupiter Images
Picture research by Catherine Bevan

Websites
Please note that the websites suggested in this book were up to date at the time of writing. We have made all weblinks available on the Heinemann website at www.heinemann.co.uk/hotlinks. When you access the site, the express code is 2196P.

Contents

Acknowledgements

The author and publisher would like to thank the following individuals and organisations for permission to reproduce photographs:

AIGA pp**71**; Alamy Images pp**1**, **14**, **55**, **97**, **115**, **145** bottom, **258**, **308**; Alamy Images/Jeff Greenberg pp**61**; Alamy Images/Jon Arnold Images pp**144**; Alamy Images/BananaStock pp**188**; Arnos Design Ltd pp**171**, **197**, **202**, **218**, **219**, **220**, **255**, **312**; BAA pp**32**, **58**, **79**; British Airways Museum pp**25**; Brittany Ferries pp**74**; Corbis pp**8**, **17**, **26**, **139** top, **145** top, **147**, **284**; Corbis/Ashley Cooke pp**91**; Digital Vision pp**11**, **28**, **63**; Eyewire pp**243**; First Choice pp**132** top, **180**; Getty Images pp**35**, **320**; Getty Images/PhotoDisc pp**21**, **30**, **38**, **67**, **72**, **131**, **132** bottom, **140**, **195**, **232**, **234**, **299**; Getty Images/Stuart Franklin pp**304**; Getty/Hulton pp**19**; Harcourt Education Ltd/Debbie Rowe pp**88**, **95**, **185**, **260**, **289**, **291**, **300**; Harcourt Education Ltd/Martin Sookias pp**129**; Harcourt Education Ltd/ Devon Obugenga Shaw pp**213**, **250**; Inghams pp**138**, **183**, **253**; International Hotel Groups plc pp**47**; National Express pp**7**; National Geographical Data Centre pp**44**; P&O Ferries pp**139** bottom; Qantas.com pp**29**; Rex Features pp**110**, **135**, **324**; The Brighter Group pp**167**; Thomson Holidays Ltd pp**59**, **77**; Virgin Atlantic pp**12**, **34**; Visit Wales pp**199**; Zooid Pictures pp**261**; Visual Image Photographic Services tel: 01904 631933 pp**96** screen grab photos.

Every effort has been made to contact copyright holders of material reproduced in this book. Any omissions will be rectified in subsequent printings if notice is given to the publishers.

About this book

The travel and tourism industry is one of the fastest growing industries in the world. Employing thousands of people in the UK and millions around the world, it generates millions of pounds in the UK and billions worldwide. Most people participate in its activities, whether it is going for a day trip to a theme park or shopping centre, or spending two weeks at a beach resort. There is no doubt that working in the industry can be tiring, and dealing with such a variety of customers and situations can sometimes be frustrating; however, it can also be tremendously rewarding, offering job satisfaction and helping people to make the most of their trip. By working in the industry you may also get the opportunity to travel yourself and experience a variety of cultures and destinations.

What's in this textbook?

The *BTEC First Diploma in Travel and Tourism* is certificated by Edexcel, one of the country's leading awarding bodies for vocational qualifications. This textbook covers all of the core and specialist (optional) units you will need to study to complete your course and achieve your qualification.

Assessment

You will be assessed by a series of assignments. You will need to demonstrate your understanding of a number of learning outcomes.

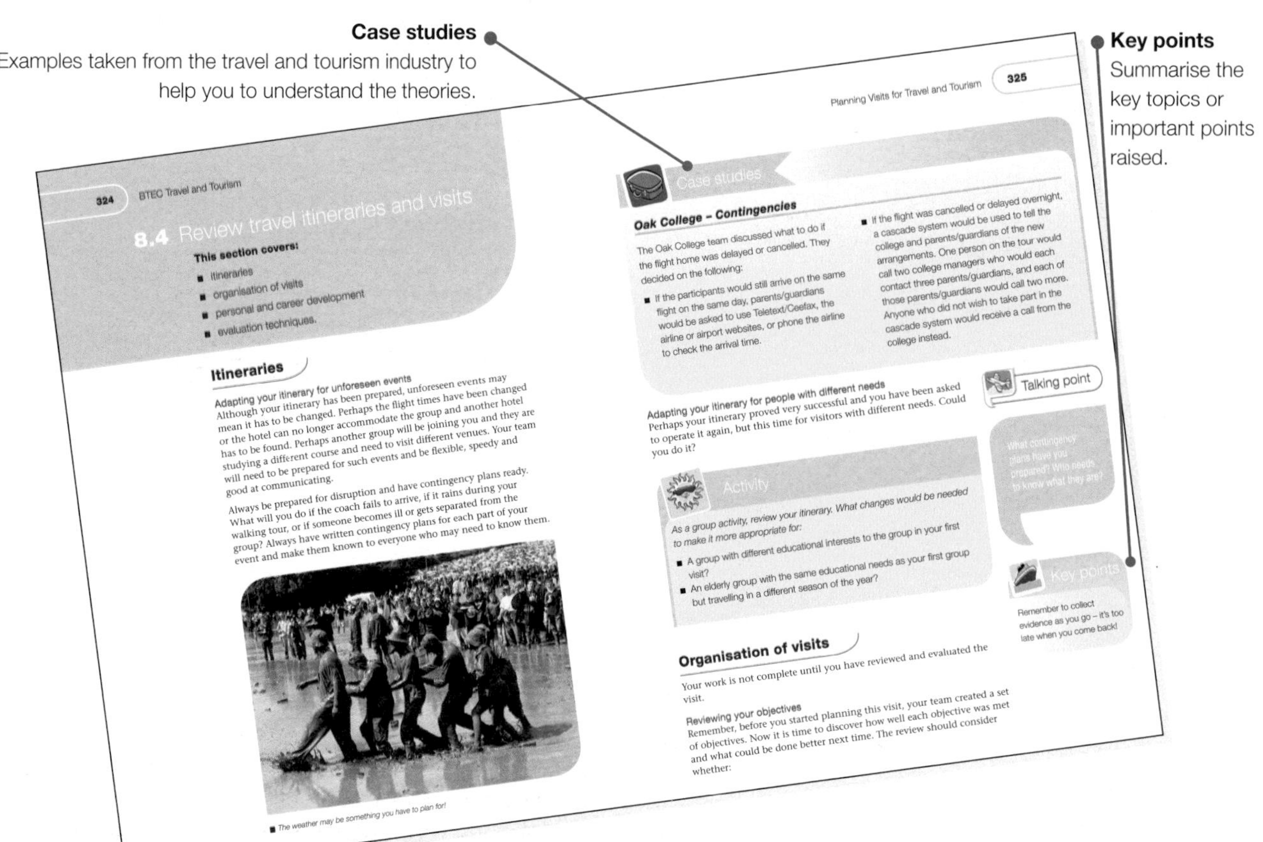

Case studies
Examples taken from the travel and tourism industry to help you to understand the theories.
Key points
Summarise the key topics or important points raised.
324 BTEC Travel and Tourism
8.4 Review travel itineraries and visits
This section covers:
itineraries
organisation of visits
personal and career development
evaluation techniques.
Itineraries
Adapting your itinerary for unforeseen events
Although your itinerary has been prepared, unforeseen events may mean it has to be changed. Perhaps the flight times have been changed or the hotel can no longer accommodate the group and another hotel has to be found. Perhaps another group will be joining you and they are studying a different course and need to visit different venues. Your team will need to be prepared for such events and be flexible, speedy and good at communicating.
Always be prepared for disruption and have contingency plans ready. What will you do if the coach fails to arrive, if it rains during your walking tour, or if someone becomes ill or gets separated from the group? Always have written contingency plans for each part of your event and make them known to everyone who may need to know them.
The weather may be something you have to plan for!
Planning Visits for Travel and Tourism 325
Case studies
Oak College – Contingencies
The Oak College team discussed what to do if the flight home was delayed or cancelled. They decided on the following:
If the participants would still arrive on the same flight on the same day, parents/guardians would be asked to use Teletext/Ceefax, the airline or airport websites, or phone the airline to check the arrival time.
If the flight was cancelled or delayed overnight, a cascade system would be used to tell the college and parents/guardians of the new arrangements. One person on the tour would call two college managers who would each contact three parents/guardians, and each of those parents/guardians would call two more. Anyone who did not wish to take part in the cascade system would receive a call from the college instead.
Adapting your itinerary for people with different needs
Perhaps your itinerary proved very successful and you have been asked to operate it again, but this time for visitors with different needs. Could you do it?
Talking point
What contingency plans have you prepared? Who needs to know what they are?
Activity
As a group activity, review your itinerary. What changes would be needed to make it more appropriate for:
A group with different educational interests to the group in your first visit?
An elderly group with the same educational needs as your first group but travelling in a different season of the year?
Key points
Remember to collect evidence as you go – it's too late when you come back!
Organisation of visits
Your work is not complete until you have reviewed and evaluated the visit.
Reviewing your objectives
Remember, before you started planning this visit, your team created a set of objectives. Now it is time to discover how well each objective was met and what could be done better next time. The review should consider whether:

Each unit may be assessed by one or a series of small assignments. These will cover the grading criteria published by Edexcel and will be available for you to check your progress against.

Each unit has a Pass, Merit and Distinction grade. You will need to provide evidence for:

- each of the criteria at Pass grade to obtain a Pass
- all of the Pass grade and the Merit grade criteria to obtain a Merit grade
- all of the Pass, Merit and Distinction grades to obtain a distinction.

As well as reading this book and completing the exercises, you should try to be aware of all the information available to you in the media. There are a number of television programmes, such as *Wish you were here* and *Airport*, which are made for prime-time television but which also give you an insight into the industry. Look at the travel supplements of weekend newspapers, visit as many different kinds of attractions as you can with a 'professional eye', and look at brochures, posters and guides. The more aware you are of all the many and varied ways of being a 'tourist', the easier you will find it to obtain the higher grades and the more you will enjoy learning about this vibrant and exciting industry!

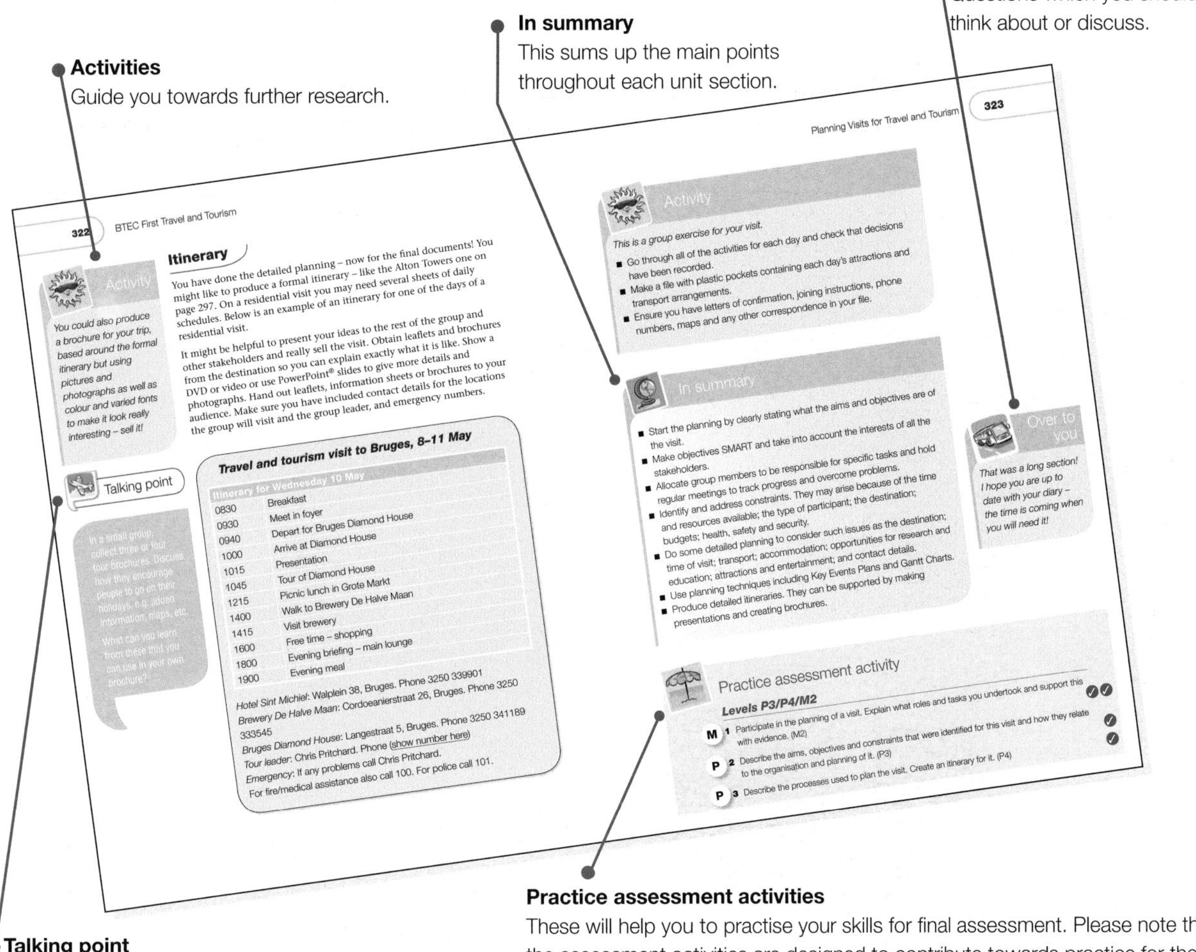

Over to you
Questions which you should think about or discuss.
In summary
This sums up the main points throughout each unit section.
Activities
Guide you towards further research.
Talking point
Questions for you to discuss in your group.
Practice assessment activities
These will help you to practise your skills for final assessment. Please note that the assessment activities are designed to contribute towards practice for the candidates' assessment but should not be used as exemplar assignment briefs.

322 BTEC First Travel and Tourism

Activity

You could also produce a brochure for your trip, based around the formal itinerary but using pictures and photographs as well as colour and varied fonts to make it look really interesting – sell it!

Talking point

In a small group, collect three or four tour brochures. Discuss how they encourage people to go on their holidays, e.g. images, information, maps, etc.

What can you learn from these that you can use in your own brochure?

Itinerary

You have done the detailed planning – now for the final documents! You might like to produce a formal itinerary – like the Alton Towers one on page 297. On a residential visit you may need several sheets of daily schedules. Below is an example of an itinerary for one of the days of a residential visit.

It might be helpful to present your ideas to the rest of the group and other stakeholders and really sell the visit. Obtain leaflets and brochures from the destination so you can explain exactly what it is like. Show a DVD or video or use PowerPoint® slides to give more details and photographs. Hand out leaflets, information sheets or brochures to your audience. Make sure you have included contact details for the locations the group will visit and the group leader, and emergency numbers.

Travel and tourism visit to Bruges, 8–11 May

Itinerary for Wednesday 10 May	
0830	Breakfast
0930	Meet in foyer
0940	Depart for Bruges Diamond House
1000	Arrive at Diamond House
1015	Presentation
1045	Tour of Diamond House
1215	Picnic lunch in Grote Markt
1400	Walk to Brewery De Halve Maan
1415	Visit brewery
1600	Free time – shopping
1800	Evening briefing – main lounge
1900	Evening meal

Hotel Sint Michiel: Walplein 38, Bruges. Phone 3250 339901
Brewery De Halve Maan: Cordoeanierstraat 26, Bruges. Phone 3250 333545
Bruges Diamond House: Langestraat 5, Bruges. Phone 3250 341189
Tour leader: Chris Pritchard. Phone (show number here)
Emergency: If any problems call Chris Pritchard.
For fire/medical assistance also call 100. For police call 101.

Planning Visits for Travel and Tourism 323

Activity

This is a group exercise for your visit.

- Go through all of the activities for each day and check that decisions have been recorded.
- Make a file with plastic pockets containing each day's attractions and transport arrangements.
- Ensure you have letters of confirmation, joining instructions, phone numbers, maps and any other correspondence in your file.

In summary

- Start the planning by clearly stating what the aims and objectives are of the visit.
- Make objectives SMART and take into account the interests of all the stakeholders.
- Allocate group members to be responsible for specific tasks and hold regular meetings to track progress and overcome problems.
- Identify and address constraints. They may arise because of the time and resources available; the type of participant; the destination; budgets; health, safety and security.
- Do some detailed planning to consider such issues as the destination; time of visit; transport; accommodation; opportunities for research and education; attractions and entertainment; and contact details.
- Use planning techniques including Key Events Plans and Gantt Charts.
- Produce detailed itineraries. They can be supported by making presentations and creating brochures.

Over to you

That was a long section! I hope you are up to date with your diary – the time is coming when you will need it!

Practice assessment activity

Levels P3/P4/M2

M 1 Participate in the planning of a visit. Explain what roles and tasks you undertook and support this with evidence. (M2)

P 2 Describe the aims, objectives and constraints that were identified for this visit and how they relate to the organisation and planning of it. (P3)

P 3 Describe the processes used to plan the visit. Create an itinerary for it. (P4)

Springboard Charitable Trust

Springboard Charitable Trust is pleased to endorse this book. It provides up-to-date and industry-relevant materials which are essential for any student following this vocational course. The authors recognise the need to prepare young people appropriately for their potential entry into the travel and tourism jobs market through providing case studies and lists of key points that illustrate the structure and future development of the sector.

Springboard recognises the vital importance of working closely with employers and industry partners, and encourages teachers to develop close links with Springboard's local and national activities which are designed to excite and inspire the sector workforce of tomorrow.

Details of the website address for Springboard and other related sites have been made available at www.heinemann.co.uk/hotlinks. Enter the express code 2196P.

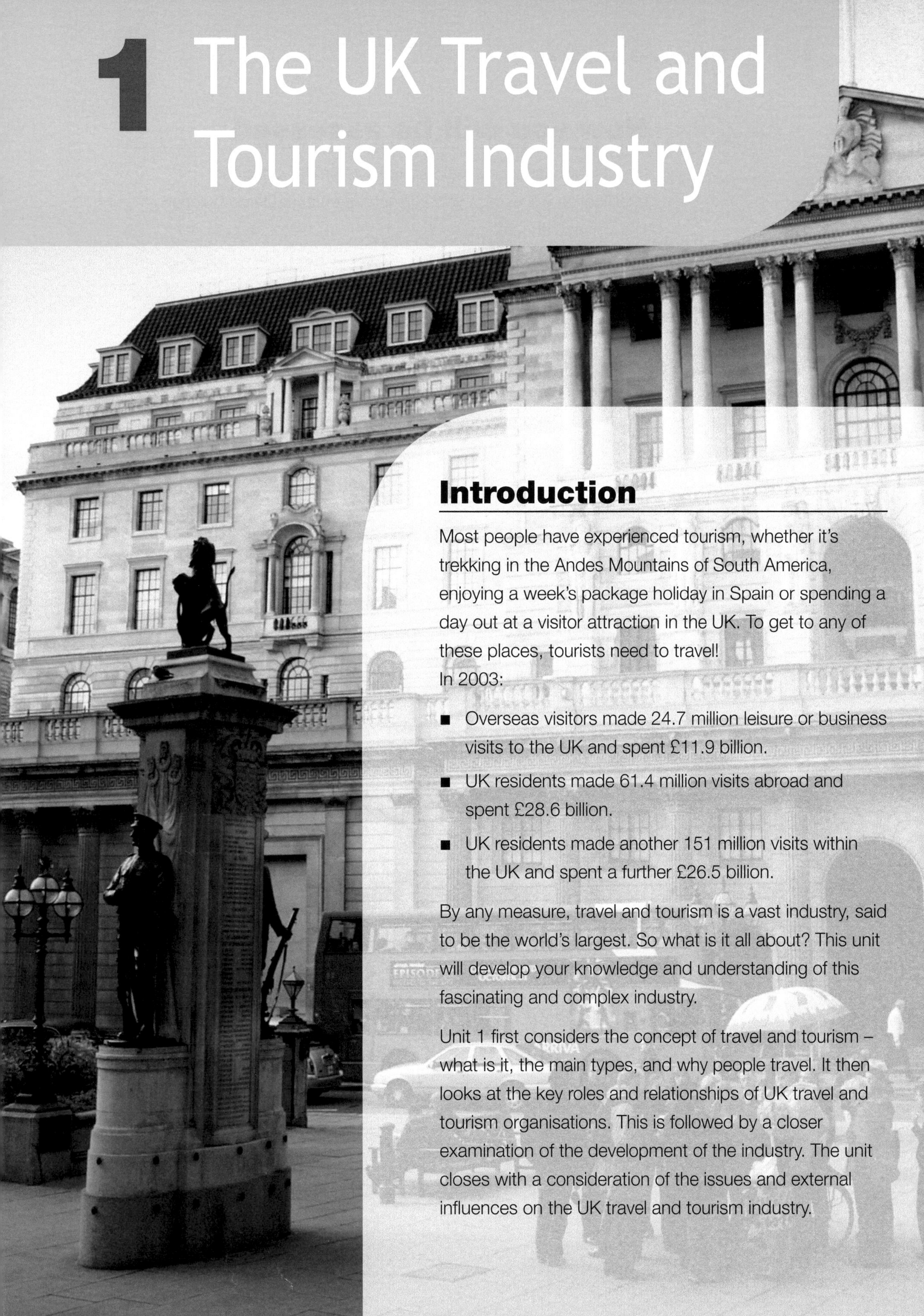

1 The UK Travel and Tourism Industry

Introduction

Most people have experienced tourism, whether it's trekking in the Andes Mountains of South America, enjoying a week's package holiday in Spain or spending a day out at a visitor attraction in the UK. To get to any of these places, tourists need to travel!

In 2003:

- Overseas visitors made 24.7 million leisure or business visits to the UK and spent £11.9 billion.
- UK residents made 61.4 million visits abroad and spent £28.6 billion.
- UK residents made another 151 million visits within the UK and spent a further £26.5 billion.

By any measure, travel and tourism is a vast industry, said to be the world's largest. So what is it all about? This unit will develop your knowledge and understanding of this fascinating and complex industry.

Unit 1 first considers the concept of travel and tourism – what is it, the main types, and why people travel. It then looks at the key roles and relationships of UK travel and tourism organisations. This is followed by a closer examination of the development of the industry. The unit closes with a consideration of the issues and external influences on the UK travel and tourism industry.

How you will be assessed

Unit 1 is assessed internally so the Centre delivering the qualification will assess you against the criteria. On completion of this unit you should:

1.1 understand the concept of the travel and tourism industry

1.2 know the roles and relationships of organisations within the UK travel and tourism industry

1.3 understand the development of the UK travel and tourism industry

1.4 understand the impact of legislation and other issues on the UK travel and tourism industry.

Assessment grades

The Edexcel Assessment Grid for Unit 1 details the criteria to be met. In general, to gain a Pass (P) you are asked to identify or describe; to gain a Merit (M) you are also asked to explain and analyse; and to gain a Distinction (D) you are also asked to evaluate.

1.1 The concept of the travel and tourism industry

This section covers:

- main types of travel and tourism
- reasons why people travel.

Main types of travel and tourism

Key definitions

Travel involves getting from one place to another, and there are a variety of means – by air, rail, road or sea.

Tourism is a service-based industry – there are few real products for tourists to take away with them, just souvenirs, photos and memories. What the travel and tourism industry provides, most of the time, are dreams and experiences. The World Tourism Organization defines tourism as:

> 'The activities of persons travelling to, and staying in places outside their usual environment for not more than one consecutive year, for leisure, business and other purposes.'

People who travel

All types of travellers engaged in tourism are described as **visitors**. Visitors can be distinguished as:

- **Tourists**: visitors who stay away from home for at least 24 hours.
- **Day-visitors** or **excursionists**: visitors who do not stay overnight.

Activity

How many different methods of transport have you used? List as many types as you can think of – some you may have paid for, others may have been free.

Over to you

What is the difference between travel and tourism?

A refinement of the definition of 'tourist' which is sometimes used is that they must be at least 160 kilometres (100 miles) from the person's usual environment.

Main types of tourism

- **Domestic tourism** is undertaken by visitors within their own country.
- **Outbound tourism** is undertaken by visitors travelling outside their own country.
- **Inbound tourism** is undertaken by visitors coming into a country from another country.

Reasons why people travel

Day-visitors or tourists travel for one of three main reasons:

- **Leisure**: they are away from home during their free time for a variety of reasons such as a holiday or a shopping trip.
- **Business**: they are away from home or their usual workplace and are undertaking work while away. They may be attending a business meeting, trade fair or conference, or be on a sales trip. Of course, a business tourist may become a leisure tourist during his or her visit.
- **Visiting friends or relatives**; this is known as VFR.

Other reasons

Although sometimes considered as part of the Leisure grouping, this category includes those away from their home for such reasons as to participate in or watch sporting events, attend religious events, go on an educational course or have health treatment.

In summary

- The travel and tourism industry is very large and complex.
- Tourists stay away from home for at least one night.
- Tourism is either domestic, outbound or inbound.
- Tourism is for leisure, business purposes, visiting friends and relatives, or for 'other' specific reasons.

Practice assessment activity

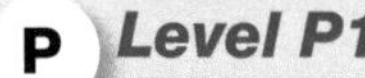

P ***Level P1***

Describe the main reasons why people travel, giving examples for each reason.

1.2 Roles and relationships of organisations in the UK travel and tourism industry

This section covers:

- roles and sectors in the UK travel and tourism industry
- domestic, outbound and inbound organisations, and organisations that support the UK travel and tourism industry
- relationships between organisations in the travel and tourism industry.

Roles and sectors in the UK travel and tourism industry

Roles

Many types of organisations in the travel and tourism industry work together to provide visitors with the products and services they desire. This includes providing advice and booking services as well as providing transport, accommodation, catering, attractions and entertainment etc., plus ancillary features like providing passports and visas, insurance, foreign currencies and health services. Some of these organisations exist to provide products and services to the rest of the industry rather than directly to the customer.

Sectors

There are three sectors to the industry:

- The **public sector** is non-commercial. That means it does not aim to make a profit but rather to provide a service or to educate. Central, regional or local government form the public sector and sometimes own (and run) attractions such as parks, gardens and museums. Tourist boards, whether national or local, are public sector organisations. In some countries, governments own, or have a stake in, rail companies, airlines, etc.
- The **private sector** is the commercial part of the industry that exists to make a profit for its owners or shareholders. This sector makes up the bulk of the travel and tourism industry and includes sub-industries such as airlines, tour operators, travel agents, accommodation providers and some visitor attractions.

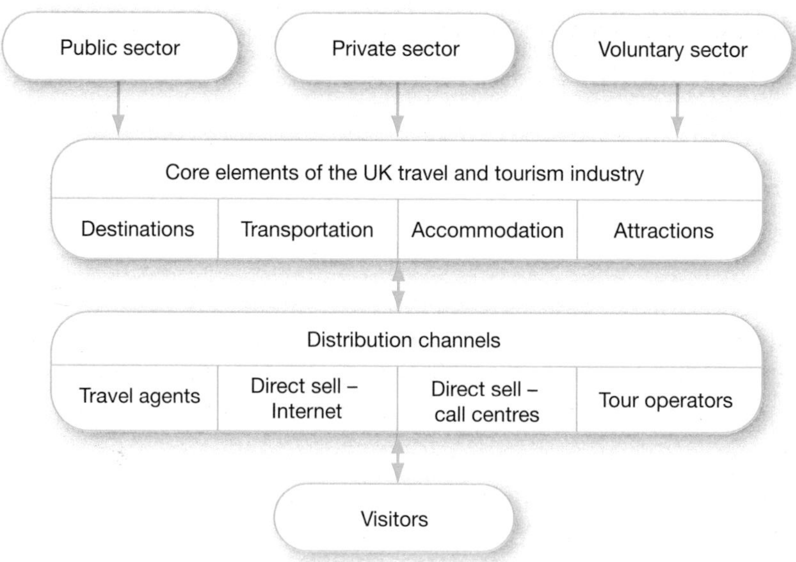

■ *Sectors in the travel and tourism industry*

The travel and tourism industry is divided into three sectors:

- public
- private
- voluntary.

- The **voluntary sector** is non-commercial and includes organisations such as the National Trust, English Heritage and the Youth Hostel Association. These organisations rely on members' subscriptions and sponsorship as well as admission charges (in some cases) as a means of funding.

Activity

1. *Contact the leisure and tourism department of your local council and discover what services it owns or runs. What information can you find on their website?*
2. *Visit English Heritage's website and discover what properties they own in your area – a link to this website has been made available at www.heinemann.co.uk/hotlinks. Enter the express code 2196P.*

Domestic, outbound and inbound organisations, and organisations that support the UK travel and tourism industry

Now you will look more closely at the organisations involved in the travel and tourism industry. These can be categorised as:

- domestic (for those travelling within their own country)
- outbound (for those travelling outside their own country)

- inbound (for those travelling to your country from abroad)
- organisations that support the travel and tourism industry.

You will also consider the importance of the relationships between these organisations.

Domestic organisations

Domestic tour operators

Tour operators bring together different components of the travel and tourism industry, such as transportation and accommodation, and package them to sell at an inclusive price to tourists. This is where the terms 'package holiday' and 'inclusive holiday' come from. Tour operators either sell their products direct (personal callers, over the telephone, via the Internet) or through travel agents to whom they pay commission.

Domestic tour operators arrange holidays in the UK for UK residents. These include anything from holiday centres (such as Butlins and Center Parcs) to coach holidays (such as Shearings) to hotel breaks (such as Superbreak and Highlife).

Domestic transport providers

- **Rail**: rail travel provides a popular and generally convenient form of transport, suited to most distances that people need to travel in the UK. UK rail transport is experiencing major change and upgrading to enable it to compete with road and air travel and to compare favourably with other countries' rail systems.
- **Coach**: there are many scheduled coach services operated within the UK by companies such as National Express, which operates to approximately 1,000 UK destinations and carries around 16 million

A National Express coach

passengers a year. Several companies offer inclusive holidays by coach. These either stop at a number of different points for a day or two each or take you straight to your destination to stay for a number of days. Many companies offer day excursions within the UK.

- **Air**: air travel is well suited to domestic journeys over approximately 150 miles (240 kilometres). In 2003, 22.7 million passengers flew on UK domestic flights.
- **Car hire**: Companies such as Avis and Hertz provide self-drive cars for tourists, enabling them to have greater freedom and better access to their destinations. Chauffeur-driven cars are also available.
- **Own-car tours**: another road option is to use your own car but follow a route itinerary arranged by a tour operator, with all your accommodation pre-booked.

Over to you

Make a list of the different types of accommodation where you could stay in the UK. Then name some companies which provide each type of accommodation.

Domestic accommodation

There is an enormous range of accommodation in the UK, of many different types.

Accommodation isn't just a bed. What else might it include?

Perhaps you thought of hotels, motels, guest houses, serviced apartments, bed-and-breakfast accommodation, farmhouse accommodation, inns, self-catering apartments and cottages, university campus accommodation, youth hostels, mobile and static caravans, chalets and campsites, and staying with friends or relatives.

Domestic catering

Visitors need food. This may be provided as part of the transport, accommodation or visitor attraction experience, but it may also be a 'stand-alone' facility. The choice of catering is enormous as it forms an important part of most visitors' enjoyment. It can range from formal dining in a hotel or restaurant to eating at a street-side stall. Many countries have rating schemes for their catering establishments. Catering is not only important at the visitors' destinations but also during their travelling, so airports, seaports, train and coach stations often have a range of catering outlets. Transport companies may provide refreshments or meals during the journey, for which they may charge.

Domestic visitor attractions

A visitor attraction can be natural or man-made. Natural attractions are part of the environment, like the Yorkshire Dales and Chesil Beach, Dorset. Some areas of the UK have been designated as National Parks or Areas of Outstanding Natural Beauty (AONB). Man-made attractions range from those that have been built specifically to attract visitors like theme parks or museums, to those that were built for other purposes, such as cathedrals and castles. Some attractions have tourist guides who provide information on the venue and may take visitors on a guided tour of it. (You will read more about Guiding Services on page 13.)

Activity

In your group, look at a map covering a 20-mile (32-km) radius from your home town. Identify three locations or attractions where guides may be used. What services would they be providing?

Outbound organisations

These organisations cater for those travelling to destinations abroad.

Outbound tour operators

Tour operators offer a range of inclusive holidays overseas, such as beach, lakes and mountains, winter sun or winter sports. Thomson, Airtours, Thomas Cook and First Choice are often referred to as the 'Big 4'. Between them they take more than 10 million people on holiday each year, which is nearly 50 per cent of the inclusive holiday market.

■ *The logos of the 'Big 4' (Reprinted with kind permission)*

Some tour operators specialise in holidays of a particular type or to a particular destination. Examples of European destination specialist operators include Mundi Color (Spain) and Citalia (Italy). Long-haul specialists include Kuoni Travel and Bales Worldwide. Specialist product tour operators include Sunsail (sailing) and Neilson (skiing). Club 18–30 and Saga cater for specific age groups. Some specialist tour operators are owned by the 'Big 4'.

You read earlier that two of the main components of an inclusive holiday are transport and accommodation. In addition:

In a small group, collect a selection of travel brochures. Compare the facilities offered. What type of guest might be interested in staying in each type of accommodation? What forms of transport are offered?

- Tour operators may also offer services to attract clients, like pre-booking of seats on the aircraft, in-flight meals and an escorted transfer service between the airport and the hotel.
- A holiday representative will either be based at the accommodation or visit it, to ensure that their customers are happy and that any problems are solved. The holiday representative's role includes offering guidance and information, and organising and selling excursions.
- Most tour operators offer the option to buy travel insurance from them; in fact, many companies make this compulsory.
- Tour operators may also arrange car hire at competitive rates. By pre-booking car hire in the UK, customers have greater control over their holiday budget.

Travel agents

The travel agent provides the link between the customer and the principal (airline, tour operator, hotel, etc.). Travel agents assess the needs of their customers and sell the right product to them. In return, they receive commission (payment) from the principal, although you will read later of changes in how travel agents get paid for their efforts. Although the majority of their work, particularly for leisure travel agents, is for customers going overseas, they can also sell domestic products.

There are four categories of travel agent:

- *Multiples*: agents that generally have at least 50 branches; these include companies such as Thomson, Going Places, Thomas Cook and First Choice. Some of these companies have more than 600 UK branches.
- *Miniples*: agents that have between 5 and about 50 branches, usually located in one region, e.g. Althams Travel has around 30 branches across Lancashire and Yorkshire.
- *Independents*: agents with up to about 5 branches in one particular area.
- *Online*: these travel agents interface with their customers via the Internet. Some multiples, miniples and independents operate online in addition to their branches, whilst other 'virtual' travel agents only

work through the Internet (e.g. Last Minute.com; Expedia – a link to these websites has been made available at www.heinemann.co.uk/hotlinks. Enter the express code 2196P).

Key points

There are four types of travel agent:

- multiple
- miniple
- independent
- online (Internet-based).

Transport providers

- **Ferries**: about 15 UK ports provide ferry services to other countries, such as Spain, France, Belgium, the Netherlands and Ireland. Journeys range from less than an hour to over 30 hours, depending upon the route and type of ship. On some of the longer sea crossings, for example, between Portsmouth and Bilbao in Spain, the journeys are sometimes referred to as 'mini-cruises' and some people make the round trip for the pleasure of the voyage. This form of transport is particularly suitable for people wanting to take their own car and drive to their holiday destination from the port.
- **Rail**: since the Channel Tunnel opened in 1994, the Eurotunnel service has been a serious competitor to the car ferry operators, particularly on the Dover to Calais route, as people are able to drive their car on to a train and arrive in France in little over half an hour. Passengers without a car can travel by the high-speed Eurostar service from London Waterloo (St Pancras from 2007) and Ashford, to destinations such as Paris, Disneyland Paris, Lille and Brussels. High-speed rail connections are then available to other towns and cities in Europe and beyond.

Eurostar speeds travellers to Europe

Activity

Locate your nearest rail station. In pairs, work out which rail routes from your local station would enable you to connect with Eurostar to take you to Paris.

- **Airlines**: there are two main types of airline:
  - *Scheduled airlines* operate to a published timetable and must fly regardless of how many passengers are booked on a flight. Airlines

such as British Airways and Virgin Atlantic are known as full-service airlines. Ryanair and easyJet are budget airlines offering a basic service.

- *Charter airlines* charter their aircraft to a person or organisation paying for its exclusive use. This might be as an *ad hoc* charter (a one-off arrangement), a series charter (several journeys between the same points) or a time charter (an aircraft which is chartered for a given period of time).

You will explore the different types of airline later in this unit (see pages 29–31).

Case studies

Planning a holiday

The Montague family wants to take a summer holiday in August. Pam and Dennis have two children, 11-year-old Victoria and 3-year-old Andrew. They live in Cambridge and want to visit Pam's family in Zurich and then continue to a beach resort. They don't want a package holiday.

1. What questions would you ask the Montagues?
2. What suggestions would you make to them about transport and accommodation?
3. What other services might you offer them?

Inbound organisations

Inbound tour operators

Inbound tour operators deal with holidays in the UK for overseas visitors. They organise tours and accommodation to meet the needs of these tourists. Tourwise of London (for Globus Tours) and Miki Travel are two operators in this category. (Visit UKinbound's website for further information on inbound tour operators. A link to this website has been made available at www.heinemann.co.uk/hotlinks. Enter the express code 2196P.)

Key points

There are three categories of tour operator:

- domestic
- outbound
- inbound.

Coach operators

There are many UK coach operators providing UK tours for foreign visitors either as part of an inclusive holiday or for the independent tourist. Some foreign coach companies provide the transport element of inclusive holidays to the UK for overseas visitors. The Eurotunnel has made this option more common. There are also scheduled coach services to and from the continent, e.g. by Eurolines.

Guiding services

Guiding is an invaluable feature of tourism. There are many types of guide, meeting a range of visitor needs. A good guide, whether travelling on a two-week coach tour or on a day excursion, or offering town or city guided walks, or working at a historic building or museum, can add considerably to the visitors' experience.

Guides are available both within the UK for domestic and overseas visitors and also for UK visitors visiting other countries. Tourists on inclusive holidays are often encouraged to take day excursions which frequently have a guide. Coaching holidays may have a guide travelling with the coach party for the entire holiday.

Guides must be knowledgeable, friendly and good communicators. They should have knowledge both of their clients' language(s) and of the country they are in. The national standard guiding qualification in the UK is the Blue Badge. Blue Badge guides have a wide range of specialities and interests. They have detailed knowledge of their location and subject and are skilled in presenting.

Activity

Look at the Institute of Tourist Guiding website. (A link to this website has been made available at www.heinemann.co.uk/hotlinks. Enter the express code 2196P.) What is their role? What are the criteria for becoming a qualified guide?

Organisations that support the UK travel and tourism industry

It won't be a surprise to discover that, given the size and scope of the industry, there are many organisations providing support services.

Tourist Boards

Some support organisations exist primarily to promote and provide information about their geographical area. This includes Tourist Boards and Tourist Information Centres. These may represent a country, e.g. Austria National Tourist Office; a region, e.g. Highlands of Scotland Tourist Board; or a city/town, e.g. Belfast Visitor and Convention Bureau.

■ *Tourist Information Centres are a good source of information*

VisitBritain markets Britain to the rest of the world and England to those in the UK. It is funded by the Department of Culture, Media and Sport and is the official tourist office for those visiting Britain. (You can find out more about VisitBritain by visiting their website, which you can access by going to www.heinemann.co.uk/hotlinks and entering the express code 2196P.)

Trade associations

The travel and tourism industry has a number of trade associations to support its members and ensure they provide a professional service, and to provide advice and protection to consumers.

The largest in the UK is ABTA, the Association of British Travel Agents (a link to this website has been made available at www.heinemann.co.uk/hotlinks. Enter the express code 2196P). The association represents over 6,300 travel agency outlets and over 1,000 tour operators in the UK. Part of ABTA's responsibility is to ensure that all bookings through any of its members are financially secure, although the organisation introduced some restrictions to that responsibility in recent years. It also provides an arbitration service for customers who are in dispute with their travel agent or tour operator.

AITO, the Association of Independent Tour Operators (a link to this website has been made available at www.heinemann.co.uk/hotlinks. Enter the express code 2196P), represents about 160 specialist tour operators in the UK. The aim of AITO members is to provide the highest level of customer satisfaction and to promote responsible tourism.

Activity

Visit the websites of these organisations by visiting www.heinemann.co.uk/hotlinks and entering the express code 2196P:

- *Federation of Tour Operators (FTO)*
- *Guild of Travel Management Companies (GTMC)*
- *UKInbound*

Which sectors of the travel and tourism industry do they represent? How many members do they have? What is their aim?

Regulatory bodies

Any organisation has legislation to adhere to, such as the Data Protection Act 1998 or the Health and Safety at Work Act 1974. However, the travel and tourism industry has a number of regulatory bodies which establish regulations and codes of practice for segments of the industry. These include the Association of British Travel Agents (ABTA) which represents and regulates UK tour operators and travel agents, and the Civil Aviation Authority (CAA) which regulates airlines but also some of the tour operators' functions. (You will explore this more in Section 1.4 of this unit.)

Other support organisations

Other organisations also serve the travel and tourism industry, for example, travel insurance companies, taxis, the Post Office (passport application checks) and bureaux de change. Many government departments perform travel and tourism related activities including the Foreign and Commonwealth Office, Passport Office, Department for Culture, Media and Sport, HM Customs, HM Immigration and embassies.

Talking point

A business woman is travelling to Japan and South Africa. In what ways might she find the Foreign and Commonwealth Office useful?

Activity

Discover how the functions of the government departments below relate to the travel and tourism industry:

- *Foreign and Commonwealth Office (a link to this website has been made available at www.heinemann.co.uk/hotlinks. Enter the express code 2196P).*
- *Department for Culture, Media and Sport (a link to this website has been made available at www.heinemann.co.uk/hotlinks. Enter the express code 2196P).*

Relationships between organisations in the travel and tourism industry

The many sectors of the travel and tourism industry are dependent upon each other to enable them to efficiently provide the best products and services to customers. Relationships between the organisations are important. For example:

- Tour operators establish relationships with providers of accommodation, transport and other services, as well as travel agents and tourist boards, to ensure the design, availability, marketing, sale and operation of their holidays goes well.
- Coach operators, visitor attractions, local tourist boards and guide services need to work together to provide excellent coach tours and visits.
- Additionally, as you will learn in Section 1.3 of this unit, some organisations have become integrated, e.g. a tour operator may own an airline and travel agency chain, to provide maximum efficiency and market share.

In summary

- The main objectives of the travel and tourism industry are to provide products, services and information both to the customer and to other sectors of the industry.
- There are three sectors: public, private and voluntary.
- Domestic organisations serve the needs of domestic visitors.
- Outbound organisations cater for visitors going to other countries.
- Inbound organisations meet the needs of visitors coming into the country.
- Organisations that support the industry include tourist boards, trade associations and regulatory bodies.
- Relationships across the industry are key to providing what the customer needs.

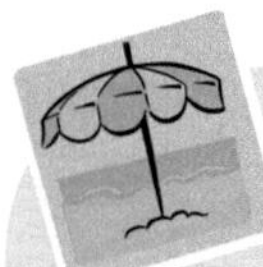

Practice assessment activity

P **_Level P2_**

Describe the roles of the different types of organisations in the travel and tourism industry

P **_Levels P3 and M1_**

Identify three examples of relationships between sectors of the industry. (P3)

M Explain the relationships – how do they work and why are they important? (M1)

1.3 The development of the UK travel and tourism industry

This section covers:

- the development of package holidays and travel agents
- horizontal and vertical integration
- technological developments
- developments in the airline industry
- other developments in transport
- changes in tourism habits post-1945.

The development of package holidays and travel agents

A history of travel and tourism

There was little passenger transport until the introduction of the stage-coach in the mid-eighteenth century. Before then, it was rare for people to travel any further than the nearest town in their entire life. Imagine what that would be like! You would have no knowledge of what other people were like or of different scenery to that around your home. Even

■ *An eighteenth-century stagecoach*

in the eighteenth century, travelling was only for the privileged few and was probably a once-in-a-lifetime journey.

The stagecoach

Stagecoach journeys were tough, with nausea, mishaps and highway robbery. Journeys were advertised as 'If God permits'. They were slow and expensive – it took over two days to get from London to Birmingham and cost 21 shillings, approximately £1,000 in earnings at today's rates. Nevertheless, in the peak years, over 250 stagecoaches left London every day, for a wide range of destinations.

Trains and cars

In 1825, Robert Stephenson's *Locomotion Number One* signalled the arrival of the steam train and, by 1850, the end of the stagecoach. In the following century the railways grew rapidly and, by the Second World War (1939–45), the railway network covered nearly every town and village in Britain.

The car was close behind: Mr Daimler and Mr Benz are usually recognised as being most responsible for that breakthrough in 1886. By the turn of the century, their invention was being used for public transport. The massive growth in private motoring in the 1950s meant tremendous losses for the railways and the network was substantially reduced in the early 1960s.

Ships and aeroplanes

Shipping only became a major form of passenger transport in the nineteenth century as people started to venture abroad. In the first half of the twentieth century, almost everyone leaving the UK had to do so by boat.

The child of the twentieth century was the aeroplane. The first commercial flight from the UK was to Paris in 1919, but flying remained very expensive until well after the Second World War. In 1956, for the first time, more travellers left the UK by air than by sea. The introduction of the Boeing 747 'Jumbo' jet in 1970 brought the unit-costs of flying down dramatically and opened the doors to mass tourism.

Passenger shipping turned to cruising for its future. Aviation grew rapidly but now faces congestion and environmental challenges. Road transport continues to grow substantially but is beginning to be strangled by congestion and pollution.

Why did people travel?

Before the nineteenth century few people travelled for pleasure but today it is the main reason given for travel. Some wealthy people went on 'The Grand Tour', travelling around Europe largely for educational purposes, but travel was generally still only for trading or religious purposes.

So, in just over a century, there were major changes in why and how people travelled. How did these changes shape the travel and tourism industry?

Development of package holidays

Thomas Cook (1808–1902) is often hailed as the 'father of tourism'. The Industrial Revolution in the mid-nineteenth century brought with it some appalling conditions for the working classes and, despite their poverty, many were driven to drink. This horrified Cook whose Baptist faith drove his encouragement of temperance. Temperance meetings were held throughout the country and it was this and the advent of the railways that prompted him to charter a train to take temperance supporters from Leicester to Loughborough for a meeting on 5th July 1841. The enormous response prompted him to arrange an increasing number and range of excursions to destinations in the British Isles, including seaside resorts, to give people a temporary escape from the drudgery of their daily lives. In 1855, his first group ventured abroad to visit Belgium, Germany and France, with all arrangements made by him.

Although leisure time and disposable income remained limited, the interest in travelling grew in the first half of the twentieth century, particularly within the UK. Coastal resorts like Brighton and Bournemouth became popular. In 1931, Harry Warner opened his first holiday camp on Hayling Island, followed by Billy Butlin at Skegness in 1936. Holidaymakers enjoyed accommodation in basic but bright chalets, three meals a day and entertainment for an all-inclusive price. These holidays grew in popularity and, in 1972, Butlins took a record one million bookings.

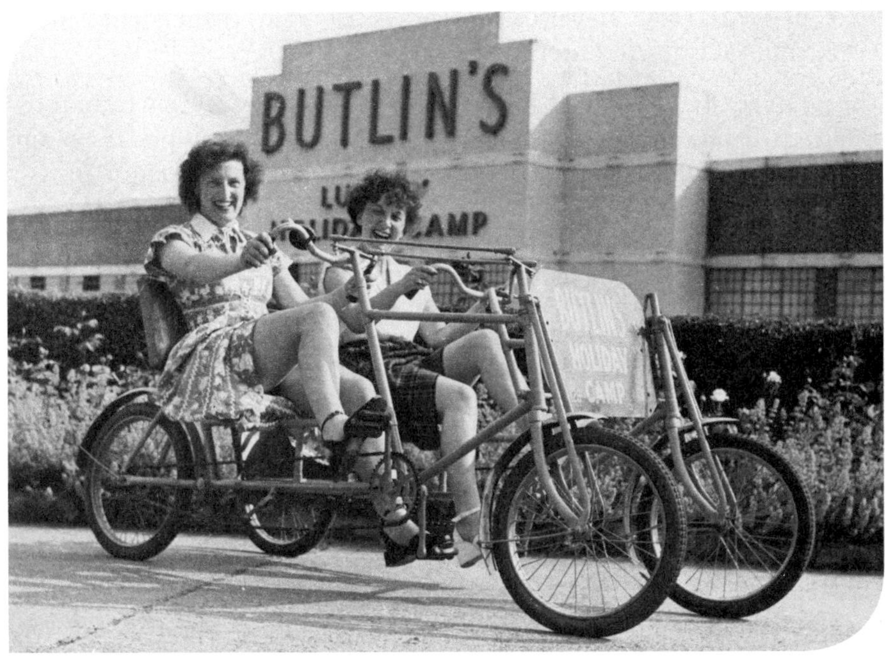

■ *A Butlins holiday camp in the 1950s*

Activity

Look at the Butlins website (a link to this website has been made available at www.heinemann.co.uk/hotlinks. Enter the express code 2196P). What products do they offer now? How are they similar or different to 50 years ago? (To find out more visit the website for Butlins Memories by going to www.heinemann.co.uk/hotlinks and entering the express code 2196P.)

The Holidays with Pay Act 1938 made it a legal requirement for employers to provide holidays with pay which helped pave the way for major growth in the travel and tourism industry. After the Second World War (1939–1945) there was a greater interest in travelling abroad, influenced by soldiers returning from overseas. Vladimir Raitz, who founded Horizon Holidays, organised the first overseas package by air, taking a group to Corsica in a DC3 aircraft in 1950. By combining the transportation, ground transfers and accommodation into a package holiday (now more commonly known as an inclusive holiday) tour operators encouraged people to take their first holidays abroad. By the early 1960s, millions were doing so, many heading for the sunny beaches of Spain.

Several major tour operators started business or were created by mergers in the 1960s and 1970s, including the Thomson Travel Group. Some became very large but failed spectacularly together with their associate airlines in later years, including Clarksons Holidays/Court Line (which failed in 1974), Laker Travel/Laker Airways (Skytrain) (which failed in 1982), and Intasun/Air Europe (which failed in 1991).

The popularity of travel and tourism grew particularly rapidly from the 1960s, partly because of technological advances – for example, faster and larger aircraft, improved transport networks and the introduction of computerised booking systems – but also because of the changes in leisure time and disposable income. People tended to work fewer hours and most were entitled to a minimum of four weeks' paid annual leave. Earnings increased which meant that more people were able to afford holidays; also, holidays were becoming cheaper as a result of volume sales and advances in technology leading to reduced costs.

By the 1990s, people were becoming more sophisticated and more demanding in their holiday choices. Many tourists looked for new destinations, so long-haul holidays in places like America and south-east Asia were increasingly offered. All-inclusive holidays based at resorts were introduced, with everything, including sports facilities and pool-side drinks, included in the price. Holidaymakers wanted to have new experiences and learn new things, so the popularity of specialist holidays also grew.

Shipping, having lost its point-to-point traffic to the airlines, turned to cruises, and became one of the fastest growing sectors of the market. In the closing years of the twentieth century, people wanted to take more holidays and this led to the popularity of short-stay holidays, often city-breaks, to places like Paris, Amsterdam and Prague.

Development of travel agents

In addition to Thomas Cook, other people who created travel agencies in the late-nineteenth century included Dean and Dawson (absorbed into Thomas Cook in 1960) and Sir Henry Lunn (whose company merged into Lunn Poly, the UK travel agency arm of TUI).

In 1926, Thomas Cook opened its prestigious headquarters in fashionable Berkeley Street in London. The cost of travel in the first half of the twentieth century meant travel agents were not numerous and were often sited in wealthy areas. Mass travel and package holidays in the second half of the twentieth century created an enormous growth in travel agents with several located in almost every UK high street. Many of these agencies were, or became, the retail outlets for major travel companies like Thomas Cook, First Choice, Going Places and Thomson.

Leisure travel agents

Leisure travel agents are usually found in the shopping centres of towns and cities. Their customers are leisure tourists who are mostly booking inclusive holidays and who are likely to need advice on the destinations and components of the package holiday.

Business travel agents

Business travel agents, or business travel management companies, handle and manage the travel accounts of businesses. Business travellers tend to make the majority of their bookings by telephone or email, so business travel agencies do not need highly visible shops to attract customers in the same way as leisure travel agencies do. They will often have offices away from the high street and may even be located within their clients' offices. Normally, companies pay for their employees' business travel arrangements. Many business clients travel frequently, so it is important that the travel consultant builds a good relationship with them.

Business travel agencies include such companies as BTI UK and Portman Travel. Sometimes they are divisions or subsidiaries of larger travel organisations, for example, American Express and Carlson Wagonlits.

Have part of your group use the Internet or other resources to research at least one business travel agency and identify the facilities they offer. The other part of the group should carry out the same research but for at least one leisure travel agency.

- Compare your research with the other group. What are the similarities and differences in the facilities offered by each type of travel agency?

Travel agents' products and services

Travel agents offer a wide range of products and services. Whether a leisure agent or a business agent, the range is similar but the product mix is different.

- Leisure agents rely on sales of inclusive holidays to maintain their business, which may account for more than 70 per cent of their sales.
- Business agents rely on the sale of air tickets, accommodation and car hire, and will sell very few inclusive holidays.

■ *Products offered by travel agents*

To survive in a very competitive market some agents also sell tickets for scheduled coach services, excursion tickets, and tickets for theme parks such as Disneyworld or Universal Studios. With many principals (airlines, tour operators, hotels, etc.) reducing the amount of commission they pay to the travel agent, some agents are diversifying and sell travel accessories such as guide books and suitcases.

Travel agents provide other important services and information to their customers, including:

- passport, visa and health information
- country information and advice
- foreign currency exchange.

A passport allows travellers to leave and re-enter their own country. Visas may also be required by visitors to enter certain countries.

Horizontal and vertical integration

Horizontal integration

Horizontal integration exists when an organisation owns two or more companies on the same level of the buying chain (see diagram below). For example, the First Choice group of companies owns First Choice Travel Shops and First Choice Holiday Hypermarkets, both of which are retail travel agents and on the same level of the buying chain. One advantage to the First Choice group of owning these two travel agent companies is that it can increase its market share by having two types of outlet in the same city. Sometimes companies merge into one. Travel agents Pickfords Travel and Hogg Robinson merged in 1993 to become Going Places

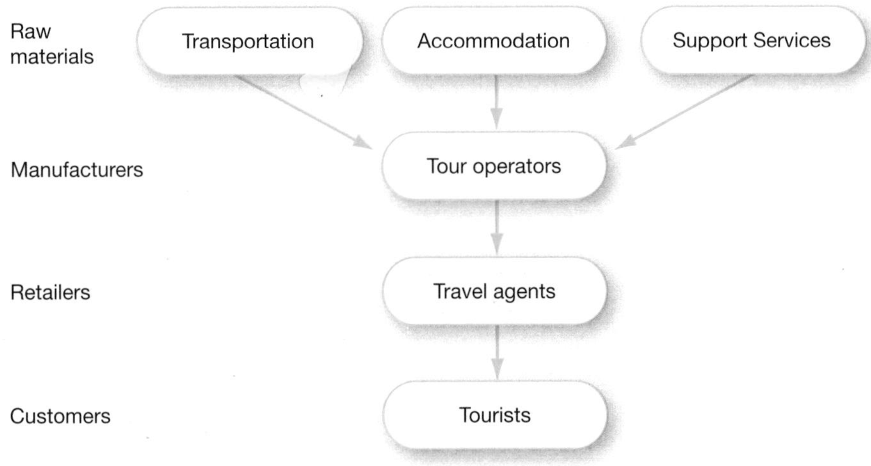

■ *The travel and tourism industry buying chain*

Vertical integration

Vertical integration exists when an organisation owns companies on two or more levels of the buying chain. For example, each of the 'Big 4' travel companies (Airtours, Thomas Cook, Thomson and First Choice) are vertically integrated, with each owning an airline, a tour operator and travel agency. Going Places, which was mentioned earlier, itself became the retail distribution arm of the MyTravel Group, which owned MyTravel Airways and tour operator Airtours. Until recently, some of these companies used different names for their airline and travel agency.

However, they are now 'power branding' (using the same name throughout the organisation) so it is easier for the customer to see exactly who they are booking and travelling with. A good example of this is TUI UK, the UK's largest holiday company, which has re-branded its companies using the Thomson name (see table below).

	2004	2005
Airline	Britannia Airways	Thomsonfly
Tour operator	Thomson	Thomson
Travel agent	Lunn Poly	Thomson

Key points

- Horizontal integration is when an organisation owns two or more companies on the same level of the buying chain.
- Vertical integration is when an organisation owns companies on two or more levels of the buying chain.

Vertical integration allows an organisation to control the market and to retain more of the profits. For example, if a customer books a Thomson holiday that uses a Thomsonfly flight through a Thomson travel agency, the commission that Thomson pays to the travel agency stays within the organisation. The company might also be able to negotiate better rates with its own airline and, of course, the customer may also buy goods on board the aircraft and contribute to the overall profits of the company in that way.

The First Choice Group of companies is a good example of development through horizontal *and* vertical integration. First Choice was founded in 1973 as Owners Abroad. Through the 1980s it acquired other tour operators and set up its own airline, Air 2000. The company re-branded as First Choice in 1994 and formed its retail arm (Travel Choice) in 1998. Now, the tour operator, airline and travel agency are all branded as First Choice.

Case studies

Using the First Choice website (a link to this website has been made available at www.heinemann.co.uk/hotlinks. Enter the express code 2196P), access the Corporate Information section then select History and click on Key Events. Look for and make notes on:

- evidence of horizontal integration
- evidence of vertical integration
- evidence of power-branding.

Technological developments

The incredible growth seen in the travel and tourism industry would not have been possible without major technological developments.

Computer reservations systems

Until the mid 1960s, even major airlines did not have computerised reservation systems but recorded and controlled bookings by writing details on flight lists and passenger record cards. This was a laborious exercise and prone to error. It could not handle the potential growth in passenger numbers which was possible with the increase in the numbers of flights and size of aircraft. Basic computer systems were being introduced by the mid-1960s, which have grown to the sophisticated systems that are used today.

■ *British European Airways BEACON reservations system in the mid-1960s* (*Source*: British Airways Museum)

This technology had a major effect upon how well airlines manage their yields – the amount of revenue per flight. Huge databases track the past booking pattern of flights. With that historic data, the airline is able to forecast how many seats will be sold by any date prior to the date a specific flight operates, and can adjust the fares on it to get the best revenue result. This is very valuable to the airlines and has particularly aided the growth of budget airlines. Such systems are now used by most sectors of the industry, e.g. hotels, car hire and cruises.

The Internet

In 1998 it was estimated that 2.3 million UK households (9 per cent) had access to the Internet from home and 1.4 million people used it to purchase tickets. By 2005, 12.9 million UK households (52 per cent) had Internet access and the market research organisation Mintel reported that more people would be booking their holidays independently than by taking a pre-arranged package tour. The Internet is dramatically changing the way many people book holidays.

Changes in the way tour operators and travel agencies work

E-commerce

Most tour operators and travel agents now have their own websites to capture the increasing Internet market. A new type of travel agent has emerged, specialising in e-commerce (electronic business), e.g. Expedia and ebookers, who offer customers the facility to book accommodation, travel and car hire, etc. online. One advantage of this to tour operators is that they do not have to pay commission to travel agents for holidays booked directly by customers through their website, so they tend to offer such clients online discounts. Some tour operators use call centres to handle bookings for customers who prefer not to visit a travel agent's shop or who do not have the time to do so.

Holiday cypermarket shops enable potential clients to surf the web for travel deals before making a booking. Holiday cybermarkets have interactive screens in the shops showing video footage of hotels and resorts, making clients feel as though they are there. Potential clients can 'chat' with a travel agent on the interactive TV while looking at maps, images and video clips of the destinations. Visitors to tour operators' websites, for example, the First Choice website, can 'leaf through' an e-brochure, make bookings, order foreign currency and read its magazine.

Technological advances have enabled staff to become homeworkers, accepting calls and making bookings on their home computers, thus creating virtual travel agencies rather than the need for large call centres.

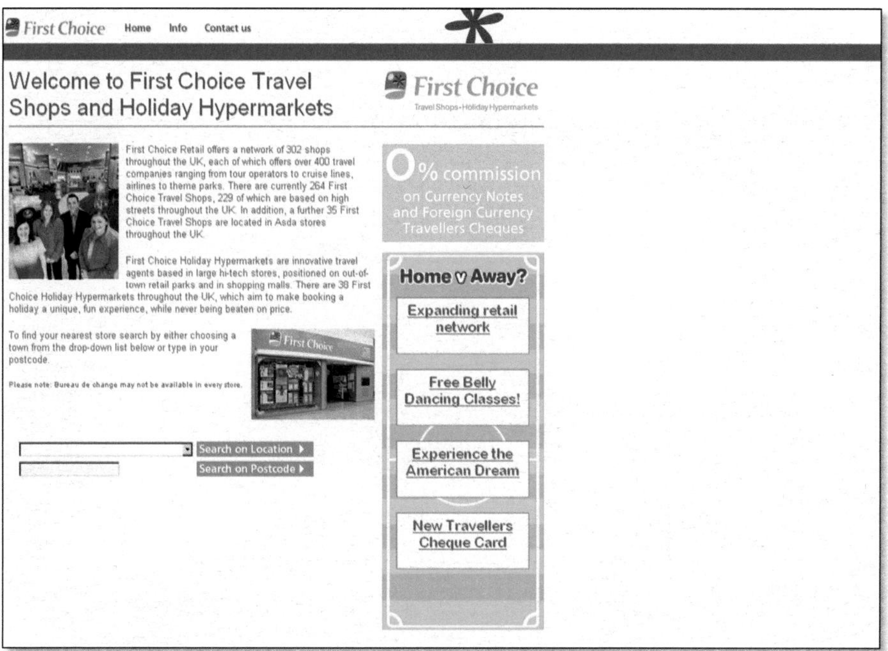

■ *An Internet travel shop and holiday hypermarket (Reprinted with kind permission)*

Teletext and digital TV channels devoted to holidays are designed to make the buying process simpler for the customer and enable travel agents and tour operators to keep up with today's lifestyle.

Technology helps the agent make bookings and handle administration. Their in-house booking systems link with that of tour operators so that transaction times can be quicker. Back-office systems automatically make diary entries to check that customers' holidays have been paid for and that tickets have been received.

Activity

In pairs, visit your local travel agent's shop or visit a tour operator on the Internet. Look for evidence of recent technological changes. What are they? What other technological advances do you think could be made to benefit their clients?

Self-help technology

Tourists can also visit websites to obtain guidance and information which sometimes give virtual tours of the destination, etc. They can also use other technological advances such as audio/visual presentations at historic houses and museums.

Developments in the airline industry

Technological developments

Technology is often the entry point to changes in the airline industry.

Faster journey times

The introduction of the jet engine in the 1950s made long-haul journeys less of a long haul (it cut the London to New York flying time from 17 hours to 8 hours). Supersonic Concorde started to fly commercially in 1976, cutting the London to New York journey time to just over 3 hours, enabling business people to fly to New York for a day's work and return to London the same day.

Larger aircraft

The size of aircraft also grew substantially.

- The Boeing 707 was the dominant aircraft operating across the Atlantic in the 1960s, with a typical seating capacity of around 140 seats.
- The 747 'Jumbo jet' came into operation in 1970 with up to 450 seats and paved the way for mass tourism at a reasonable cost. Later versions of the 747 provided greater range and size, although the introduction of more passenger services and three- or four-class cabins brought the typical seating configuration down to around 325.
- The giant double-deck Airbus A380 is due to enter service in 2006. It could carry up to 800 passengers but, with a typical three-class seating configuration, it is likely to carry around 550. Customers include Virgin Atlantic, Qantas, Singapore Airlines and Emirates. Some airlines may have shops or boutiques and play areas on board.

Changes to flight products and services

Flight products and services have also changed in recent years. Airlines need to cater for both the business traveller and the leisure traveller, so scheduled 'full-service' airlines may offer as many as four classes of service: first, business, premium economy and economy. The price of the ticket and the level of service vary depending upon the class in which passengers travel.

- When travelling in a class other than economy, the amount of legroom, known as the seat pitch, and the width of the seat, are greater.
- First- and business-class cabins on many long-haul airlines have sleeper seats which recline to form beds.

■ *The Airbus A380 (Source:* quantas.com*)*

- Passengers in first- and business-class cabins are likely to be offered superior quality meals, drinks, toiletry kits, newspapers and gifts.
- Those travelling at higher fares will generally have greater flexibility to change their flights. This is particularly valuable for the business traveller who may need to change arrangements at short notice.

Advances in technology have enabled airlines to offer in-flight entertainment on seat-back screens so that every passenger is able to make their own choice of entertainment. This may include the latest movie releases, electronic games, live external views from the aircraft and a comprehensive selection of audio channels.

Different airlines, different flights

Full-service airlines

These airlines normally provide a choice of cabin class, seat allocation. free in-flight catering and in-flight entertainment, and will through check transfer passengers and their bags so that they do not have to check in again at their transfer airport.

Budget airlines

Low-cost airlines, known as budget airlines, are a comparatively recent innovation although they were preceded by Freddie Laker's low-cost Skytrain which operated from London to New York from 1977 to 1982. Budget airlines predominantly operate short-haul routes. Fares can be very low, sometimes less than £1 plus taxes, although the fare varies by the demand for the flight and by the closeness of its departure time, such that budget airlines are sometimes more expensive than 'full-service' airlines. However, most budget airlines:

- charge extra for food, drinks and in-flight entertainment
- charge for any baggage which has to go in the aircraft hold
- will not allocate specific seats, so the first on board get the best seats

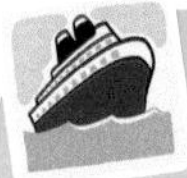

Key points

- Long-haul flights: an imprecise term meaning flights longer than three to four hours.
- Short-haul flights: an imprecise term meaning flights shorter than three to four hours.
- Domestic flights: flights within your own country.

DINNER

A selection of canapés

Starters

Tiger prawn cocktail
Provençale tart with a sour cream and garlic dressing
Chicken and mushroom soup
Fresh salad leaves with your choice of balsamic vinaigrette or lemon and chive mayonnaise
A selection of warm breads

Main

Grilled veal medallions with sage and wild mushrooms
Pan-fried sea bass with XQ sauce
Fresh pasta with your choice of carbonara sauce or tomato and basil sauce
Tandoori chicken on Greek salad

Snacks

Bacon roll served with tomato ketchup
Chicken and mushroom soup with a side salad
Char-grilled chicken sandwich with honey Dijon relish
A selection of finger sandwiches
A selection of cheese and fruit

Dessert and Cheese

Fresh fruit and Scottish shortbread served with whipped cream
Warm sherry and Mascarpone pancakes
A selection of cheese
A bowl of fresh fruit
Your choice of
Esprésso, cappuccino, coffee, decaffeinated coffee, tea or herbal tea

A sample menu for first-class passengers

- may fly to airports that are further from the city centre than those used by full-service airlines
- will only provide 'point-to-point' facilities, i.e. they will only accept passengers and their baggage to the destination of the first flight; passengers with onward flights have to check themselves and their baggage in again at the transfer airport, which can be a lengthy and tiring process. If the delivering airline is late and passengers miss their onward flights, the airlines are unlikely to accept responsibility and the passengers may have to buy new tickets for their onward flights.

For all these reasons, budget airlines are often called 'no-frills' airlines. On the plus side, budget airlines provide low-cost fares and routes to and from many regional airports, many of which have seen major growth as a result. Ryanair and easyJet are the largest of the UK budget airlines.

Charter flights

Charter flights are mostly used by tour operators who sell the seats to the public as part of their inclusive holiday programmes. Some tour operators charter a complete aircraft to operate a flight to a particular destination; others (generally smaller tour operators) buy seats on a charter flight to suit the needs of their holiday programme. Thomsonfly and First Choice Airways are examples of charter airlines owned by tour operators.

Recently, the distinction between types of airline has become blurred, particularly on European routes. To compete with the budget airlines, some scheduled (full-service) airlines have been changing their products, for example, introducing Internet fares which match or beat budget airline fares. Some airlines, like Aer Lingus, no longer offer free food and drink on board but retain other aspects of full service like passenger and baggage interlining facilities. Many charter airlines sell 'seats only' on their charter flights to the public, through travel companies. Some, like Monarch, operate scheduled flights as well as charter flights. Passengers should check carefully what their chosen airline will and will not provide.

Case studies

In pairs, research and compare the products and services provided by the three airlines:

- British Airways
- Ryanair
- Monarch Airlines.

The growth in airports

Airports have also been growing to meet the demand for air travel.

- Atlanta airport in the USA is the busiest airport in the world, with 84 million passenger movements (arrivals plus departures) in 2004.
- London's Heathrow has more international passengers than any other airport. It has grown from just 60,000 passengers through one tented terminal when it opened in 1946, to a forecast of over 70 million in 2006 through four terminals (see chart below). In 2008 the fifth Heathrow terminal will open with the potential to handle a further 30 million passengers a year.

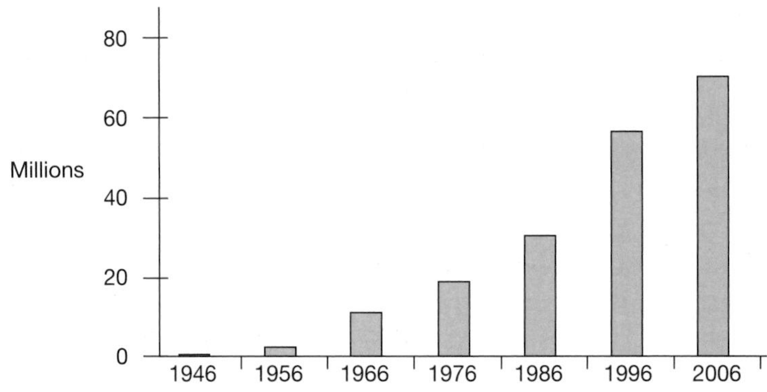

■ *London Heathrow airport passenger volumes, 1946–2006*

■ *Heathrow's fifth terminal is due to open in March 2008*

Activity

Discover all you can about the fifth terminal at Heathrow Airport. How many aircraft parking stands will it have? How many terminal buildings will there be? What new facilities will it offer?

A government White Paper published in 2003 identified proposals for the development of air transport and airports over the next 20 years. It supported a number of development proposals around the UK including a further runway at Stansted and a third runway at Heathrow.

The Airbus A380 is so large that airports will have to make adjustments to departure gates to accommodate it. Heathrow demolished a pier at Terminal 3 and built a new one that will allow passengers to offload and board on both levels.

Improving customer care

Airports and airlines around the world continually seek ways to improve the passengers' experience and reduce queues at airports. Many passengers can now check in remotely, perhaps at a town terminal, or by phone, fax or Internet. Those who check in at the airport can do so at self-service machines. Local innovations also improve customer service:

in Barbados, a Virgin Atlantic vehicle visits key hotels and passengers can check in there and dispose of their baggage, enabling them to enjoy more time on the beach before their evening flight.

Airports may have one-third or more of their passengers transferring between flights. London Heathrow, Paris Charles de Gaulle, Frankfurt and Amsterdam are major transfer airports and compete fiercely to keep that traffic. Airports work closely with the airlines, concessionaires and regulatory bodies to provide smooth processes and excellent facilities like shops, children's play-areas, catering outlets, business lounges and showers.

Other developments in transport

The rail industry

Rail travel provides a popular alternative form of transport. UK rail transport was privatised in 1996 and is experiencing major change and upgrading to enable it to compete with road and air travel and to compare favourably with other countries' rail systems. At the time of writing, there are 26 train operating companies in the UK. Most of them operate regional and local routes, for example, Merseyrail and Island Line, but others operate trunk routes or in major areas of the country, for example, First Scotrail and Virgin Trains. In addition, there are private railways operated as visitor attractions.

A trunk route is a major route carrying many passengers between large centres, for example, London to Glasgow.

Train companies seek to win customers by providing regular and punctual services on routes which meet the customers' requirements, with a range of add-on facilities at stations and on the train, at fares which customers feel meet their needs.

- Virgin Trains has introduced its Pendolino 'tilting' trains, capable of travelling at 140 miles (225 kilometres) per hour. Pendolino routes include the west coast line from London to Scotland. These luxurious trains offer an audio system with a range of channels; power points for laptop computers and mobile phones; a shop selling food, drink, magazines, books and toiletries; a quiet zone; and special seats and tables for disabled passengers. (To find out more about the Pendolino trains, visit the photo gallery at the company's website, select *Travelling with us* then click on the *Pendolino 360° virtual tour* link. (A link to this website has been made available at www.heinemann.co.uk/hotlinks. Enter the express code 2196P.)
- First Scotrail operates sleeper trains between London and Scotland and lounges at some stations.
- Transpennine Express and others carry bicycles free.
- Heathrow Express has large baggage storage areas and onboard TV.
- The opening of the Eurotunnel between England and France means passengers can either travel with their coaches or cars to France, or travel on Eurostar from London to Paris or Brussels in about 150 minutes.

■ *Virgin Train's Pendolino 'tilting' train*

Talking point

Research the Internet for ferry companies operating international routes from the UK. Discover what types of ship(s) they operate, how frequent and fast the journeys are, and what on-board facilities there are.

Compare your findings with other members of your group. Why do you think different types of ships are used by the companies you compared? What similarities and differences are there in the on-board facilities?

Train companies offer a range of fares to suit the needs of their passengers. These may include first-class, advance purchase, group, off-peak, student, senior citizen and disabled persons' fares, Rover tickets, and season tickets. It is also possible to arrange inclusive holidays by rail.

Sea travel

Sea travel is also experiencing change. In 2004, there were 25.8 million international sea journeys to or from the UK, with a further 3.6 million domestic sea journeys within the UK (e.g. to/from the Channel Islands and Northern Ireland) (Source: Office for National Statistics, 2005). There was a slight downward trend over the previous five years, possibly influenced by the Eurotunnel and budget airlines.

Sea travel companies compete on price, speed and facilities. Speed improved with the introduction of the hovercraft in 1962, followed by hydrofoils and other high-speed craft. Most sea routes from and within the UK are operated by car ferries. The Irish Sea routes boast the largest ferry in the world – Irish Ferries' *Ulysses*, which stands 12 decks high and weighs 50,938 tonnes, with almost 3 miles of parking space for 1,342 cars or 240 articulated trucks and room for up to 2,000 passengers and crew. Ferries have improved substantially with many providing a range of catering facilities, entertainment, business lounges and cabins.

Cruise ships

Cruising is increasing in popularity. In 2004, over 1 million UK residents chose cruising holidays. Major companies are building magnificent ships to cope with the increasing demand. Cunard's 150,000 tonne *Queen Mary 2* (*QM2*) is the world's largest, longest and

tallest ocean liner, carrying over 2,600 passengers and 1,250 crew. In a few years' time, Cunard plans to introduce another new ship, the *Queen Victoria*.

Cruises can be considered as inclusive holidays: the ship provides the transport, accommodation, catering and entertainment. Apart from the pleasure of visiting different ports, excursions are provided from those ports at an extra cost. It could be argued that cruising is the original all-inclusive holiday!

The main cruising areas for UK tourists are the Mediterranean, Scandinavia and the Caribbean. Many take advantage of fly-cruises. By flying to near the cruising area, for example, Miami for the Caribbean, and transferring by coach or taxi to the cruise ship, passengers can save several days compared with the time taken if they had taken the cruise from a UK port.

Road travel

Coach companies

Scheduled coach companies offer a wide range of competitive fares, including for young persons, senior citizens, overseas visitors and families, as well as advance purchase and special promotions. On-board services include TV with headsets, comfortable seats and toilet facilities. Some coach holiday companies provide a door-to-door service collecting their customers by minibus from their home and taking them to a central location for the coach journey.

Car hire

Self-drive car hire is popular, particularly for business travellers and overseas visitors. Companies like Budget and Alamo have offices across much of the world. The companies offer different sizes of cars at a range of rates. Incentive rates are offered to frequent hirers, those hiring for longer periods and those who have travelled on an airline with whom the car hire company has a partnership agreement.

Activity

What are the advantages and disadvantages of travelling by each type of transport discussed so far in this unit? How could each be improved?

To avoid waiting in long queues and having to give the same information every time they hire a car, regular hirers can join the company's frequent customer club. Quoting their membership number enables the company to refer to existing information held about the customer, for example name, address, driving licence and credit card details, car preferences, etc. This means the documentation and car keys can be ready when the customer comes to the fast-track counter at the pick-up location.

Another form of car hire is chauffeur-driven. This may be for business people or those who wish to treat themselves to some luxury (for example, stretched limousines), or those who are travelling in small groups and require chauffeur-driven people-movers.

Changes in tourism habits post-1945

In the decade following the Second World War (1939–45), people had little disposable income and holidays were usually for a week or fortnight. Purpose-built resorts in the UK run by companies like Butlins, Pontins and Warners provided good-value inclusive holidays for families.

More holidays abroad

In 1960, UK residents took over 30 million domestic holidays but just 3.5 million holidays abroad. (In 2000, this had grown to 106 million domestic holidays and 36.7 million holidays abroad.) The 1960s were a boom time for people making their first trips abroad. Being a new experience, most turned to tour operators for inclusive holidays, which had all the arrangements packaged for them. This was a major growth time for tour operators but it meant that traditional one- or two-week holidays at the seaside in the UK declined. The era of mass tourism had arrived. Spain led the explosion in overseas holidays and supply had difficulty meeting the demand in the 1960s and 1970s. Long-haul travel remained expensive, with few inclusive packages available. Even in 1970, the cheapest return air fare from London to New York was £113, the equivalent to £1,057 at 2006 rates! (In 2006, it was possible to travel on a scheduled 'full-service' airline for one fifth of this price.)

To combat the relative decline in domestic holidays, some regions promoted themselves as theme destinations, e.g. Brontë Country; Lorna Doone Country. This was helped by the interest in TV drama series set in particular locations, such as Yorkshire for *Emmerdale*, Cornwall for *Doc Martin*.

More adventurous tastes

Having tasted overseas travel and with greater disposable income, people became more adventurous. Some tour operators withdrew their holiday representatives from some resorts, perhaps because holidaymakers became more confident and individualistic.

Despite improved holiday entitlements, many people were tending to work harder and longer, so wanted to enjoy several, shorter holidays. The reduction in the cost of air travel prompted by the arrival of budget airlines, and the increasing familiarity with the Internet, meant that people were prepared to make their own arrangements for short-haul trips, only using tour operators and travel agents for the less familiar, long-haul trips.

These changes mean that, today, more people are 'unpackaging' the traditional package holiday by booking their flights and accommodation separately. Although more holidays are being taken (a 3 per cent increase to 41 million in 2003), the proportion of package holidays fell to 47 per cent of the holidays taken. The disadvantage for customers is that, by doing so, they do not have the protection of ATOL or ABTA bonding if the tour operator or any of its suppliers, like an hotel or airline, goes into liquidation. With an ABTA or ATOL bonding, arrangements will be made for the holiday to be completed and for the travellers to get back to the UK (although in 2006, ABTA introduced limits to its protection).

Most airlines and tour operators have reduced or stopped paying commission to travel agents for booking flights and inclusive holidays, so many travel agents now charge their clients fees for making their travel arrangements.

Key points

- ATOL = Air Travel Organisers' Licensing.
- ABTA = Association of British Travel Agents.

Over to you

What are the effects on travel agents if more people decide to book their own holidays?

Catering for different needs

Since the mid-1980s, all-inclusive resorts and hotels have developed. These offer all meals, drinks and sports facilities at an inclusive price. This helps holidaymakers budget their holiday spending much more easily before leaving the UK – they may only need to take money for some excursions and souvenirs.

Families with young children now take overseas holidays in their stride, but holiday providers realise they must meet their needs with such facilities as kids clubs, buggy provision, children's meals and babysitting facilities.

In the closing decade of the twentieth century, sitting on the beach for two weeks was no longer the sole purpose for taking holidays. There was growing interest in cross-channel shopping, short city break holidays, country leisure activities and new experiences like photo-safaris in Africa, extreme sports in New Zealand and eco-tourism in the Far East. These new activities were partially created by the growth of two markets: gap-year students and retired folk with longer life expectancy and greater disposable income than previous generations.

Activity

Using the Internet and other information sources, discover the significance of some of the key travel and tourism events listed in this section. Why are they so important? What other developments have these led to/will they lead to?

Sports tourism is also growing, with some participating and many travelling to watch international sports events. In 2004, Greece had 14.2 million visitors, some of whom came for the 2004 Olympic Games, and this publicity played a major part in increasing the number of visitors to Greece by approximately 14 per cent in 2005 (*Source*: *Wikipedia* – a link to the Wikipedia website has been made available at www.heinemann.co.uk/hotlinks. Enter the express code 2196P). China expects a massive tourism boom when they host the 2008 Olympics; Britain should also experience an incredible tourism boost when it is the host in 2012.

Not all tourists are leisure tourists. Many are business tourists, with their own needs and expectations. They may, for example, want a quiet airport lounge to work in and a comfortable hotel with 24-hour room service, a business centre and Internet connections in the room.

Over to you

What of the future? People are living longer, filling their leisure time better, having more disposable income, and travelling more and further. Richard Branson has announced plans for space travel as early as 2007/8, with spacecraft taking five passengers on a three-hour flight at a cost of around £100,000.

- What travel and tourism changes might you see in your lifetime?

■ *Will we be sending tourists into space in 2007?*

In summary

- The development of tourism was encouraged by the work of Thomas Cook and others in the nineteenth century.
- Domestic inclusive holidays became popular with the introduction of holiday camps in the 1930s/1940s and later. Overseas inclusive holidays started their substantial growth in the 1960s, aided by technological advances in computers and aircraft.
- Tour operators and travel agencies grew substantially in the second half of the twentieth century and many amalgamations created horizontal and vertical integration.
- Technological advances are a major cause of change for the industry. Tour operators and travel agents are particularly experiencing changes in the way they must work.
- Changes such as new runways and airport terminals need to be planned many years in advance.
- The industry continually has to provide a higher and wider range of services to meet the increasing demand of customers.
- The general public are becoming more confident in making their own travel arrangements, more independent and adventurous, and more comfortable with using technology.
- Tourism habits continue to change, with increasing disposable income and desire to use leisure time to the full.

Practice assessment activity

P

Level P4

Describe how the travel and tourism industry has developed in the Tour Operator and Travel Agency sectors. ✓

P M

Level P5/M2

Describe the key changes in tourism habits since 1945. (P5) Select two major developments and analyse their impact on travel and tourism organisations. (M2) ✓ ✓✓

D

Level D1

Evaluate the importance of the influence of lifestyle changes on the structure of the travel and tourism industry over the last century.

1.4 The impact of legislation and other issues on the UK travel and tourism industry

This section covers:

- legislation and regulatory bodies which affect the travel and tourism industry
- issues that have affected the industry.

Activity

Part of the Development of Tourism Act 1969 required the establishment of four organisations. What were they?

Legislation and regulatory bodies which affect the travel and tourism industry

Some legislation has a particular impact upon the travel and tourism industry; examples are described below.

Annual leave

Pressure on employers and governments in the nineteenth and twentieth centuries gradually brought about legislation entitling workers to paid holidays; for example, the Bank Holidays Act 1871, Holidays with Pay Act 1938 and Working Times Regulations Act 1998. Legislation on working hours also resulted in the concept of weekends off, although recent times and the Sunday Trading Act 1994 have seen a substantial move towards a 24/7 style of living.

Access to the countryside

The Countryside and Rights of Way Act 2000 introduced a new right for people to walk across areas of open countryside and registered common land in England and Wales.

Activity

In pairs, visit two local travel and tourism venues.

- *Note what provision they have made for disabled people.*
- *Note any further provisions you feel they could usefully provide for disabled people.*

Discuss your findings with your main group. What were the most common facilities that were provided and which further provisions could usefully be provided?

Disability

The Disability Discrimination Act was introduced in stages. The stage covering goods, facilities and services came into effect in 2004. From then, organisations had to ensure reasonable adjustments had been made to any physical barriers preventing disabled people from using the service provided. This might include improved lighting and signs, ramps and handrails, induction loops, seating, and lower reception desks for those in wheelchairs.

Consumer protection

There are several pieces of legislation and industry requirements which provide consumer protection:

EU Directive on Package Travel

This piece of European Union legislation applies to package travel whether it is for holidays or business, or any other reason. In many respects it brings together laws and industry codes of practice which already existed. It is a very important Directive which had a major influence on the industry.

The UK enacts this Directive through the Package Travel, Package Holidays and Package Tours Regulations 1992. It is designed to protect consumers. The main parts cover:

- misleading descriptive matter
- accuracy of brochures
- information which the organiser must provide to the client, e.g. on passport and visa requirements, health formalities, how client's money is being safeguarded and arrangements for repatriation in the event of insolvency
- the requirement for a written contract covering specified subjects
- the circumstances under which transferring bookings to other dates, destinations or people can be made
- changes in price
- client's cancellation rights
- organiser's responsibility in the event of failure to provide services
- liability for proper performance of contract: this is a particularly significant part of the Directive – the organiser is responsible for all obligations of the contract, even though the services may be provided by third parties
- security in case of insolvency.

Activity

Look at two tour operators' brochures. Identify at least four examples of them meeting the requirements of the EU Directive on Package Travel.

Air travellers

In 2005, the EU introduced further protection for air travellers, including those on charter flights.

Activity

Obtain a copy of the EU leaflet on air passenger rights and read the legislation on denied boarding, cancellations, delays and downgrading (to access the leaflet, go to the EU website, click on en, then click on Transport *in the 'What the European Union does by subject' area, then click on* Air transport *in the 'A comprehensive guide to European law' area. Finally, click on* Denied-boarding compensation system. *A link to the EU website has been made available at www.heinemann.co.uk/hotlinks. Enter the express code 2196P). List the amount of compensation due under each of the circumstances contained in this Directive.*

Civil Aviation Authority (CAA)

The CAA is the UK's independent regulatory body for aviation matters. Amongst other responsibilities, it regulates the finances and fitness of travel organisers selling flights and package holidays in the UK. It manages the UK's largest system of consumer protection for travellers, known as the Air Travel Organisers' License (ATOL), which is required by all who sell packages which include flights. Applicants must show they are fit to hold an ATOL and have adequate financial arrangements. The CAA requires a guarantee, called a bond, to be lodged with them. If a firm goes out of business, the CAA will make a refund to the passengers or, if the passengers are still abroad, arrange for them to finish their holiday and fly home. However, in 2006 there was a proposal to have travellers bear the cost of refunds and repatriation through a Consumer Protection Charge.

Over to you

Read the customer comments at the end of the report on EuJet's failure in 2005, accessed on ATOL's website. A link to this website has been made available at www.heinemann.co.uk/hotlinks. Enter the express code 2196P. What are your views?

Association of British Travel Agents (ABTA)

Bonding for those organising packages without an air carriage component is provided through the ABTA Bonding scheme. Non-ABTA members can also arrange packages without bonding. However, they are required to take out insurance to protect their clients' money or hold it in a separate account. Local Authority Trading Standards officers monitor these arrangements.

Issues that have affected the travel and tourism industry

Economic

In recent decades, apart from a few downturns, people have generally had more disposable income than previous generations, unemployment has been at a relatively low level and international business has developed. All these factors encourage travel for both business and leisure reasons. Nevertheless, some travel organisations have gone out of business.

Rising fuel costs

The availability and cost of fuel is of increasing concern and many in the transport industry are working hard to achieve fuel efficiency and to become more environmentally friendly.

Political factors

The influence of the EU is increasingly being felt. It has been at the forefront of deregulation, prohibition of subsidies, protection for travel and tourism consumers, and negotiations with the United States regarding transatlantic airline freedoms. Whilst tourism is becoming more easy to some parts of the world, for example, China, it is becoming more difficult to others, such as the Middle East.

Availability of visas

Some countries require travellers to have visas. The main types are:

- **Entry visas**, permitting the traveller to enter the country. These may restrict the number of days the traveller can stay, the number of times the traveller can enter on that visa, and the purpose of visiting the country. These visas are usually available from that country's embassy or consulate in the traveller's home country. They may also be available through the Internet or even on arrival in the country. Many travel agents will obtain visas (and passports) on behalf of their clients. For a fee they will check a customer's application form and supporting documentation before submitting them on behalf of the customer.
- **Exit visas**. A few countries require visitors to obtain a visa to leave the country they are visiting. This might be done at the airport before leaving the country. A very few countries even require their own citizens to have exit visas before they can leave their own country.

It is important that tour operators and/or travel agents alert their clients to visa requirements.

Major incidents

War and terrorism

War and terrorism has put some countries off-limits for tourists and has deterred people from travelling to certain areas or by some methods of transport, for example, by air. The 9/11 attack on the New York World Trade Center in 2001 damaged the airline industry considerably, with several airlines failing, and it has taken more than two years for confidence to be re-established.

Natural disasters

Natural disasters have been to the fore so far this century. The Asian tsunami of 2004 killed hundreds of thousands of people and devastated the tourist areas of many of the affected countries. They have embarked upon a road to recovery which is likely to create change and take a long while. However, in many parts of the world there is an increasing awareness of the need for environmentally-friendly, sustainable tourism which considers and supports the needs of the local community and habitat; everyone who travels must play a part in supporting this.

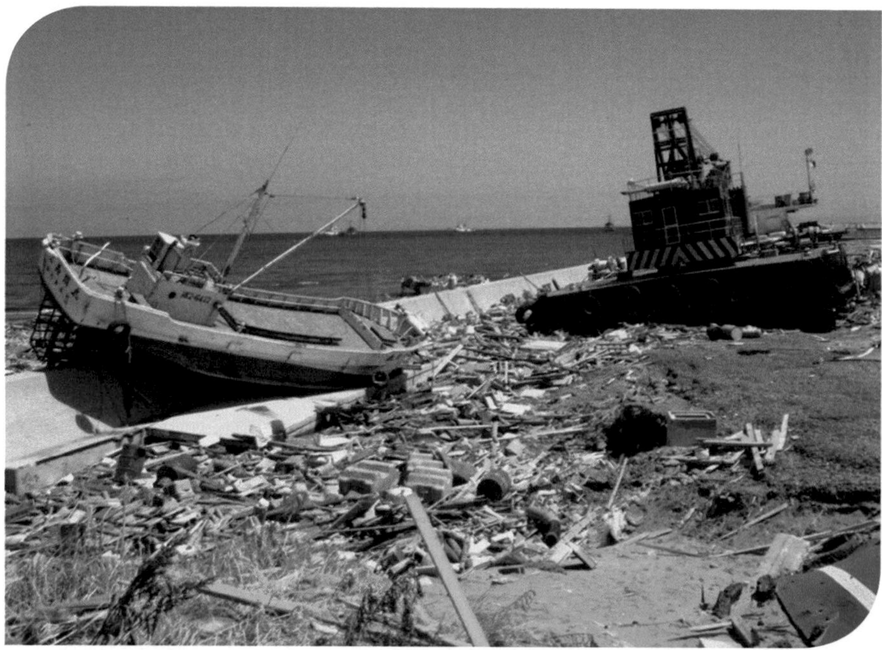

■ *Tourist areas affected by the Asian tsunami of 2004 are likely to take a while to recover*

Activity

Health scares have recently caused concern for tourists. Research the following events to discover what areas of the world they affected and what the tourism implications were:

- SARS
- UK foot and mouth outbreak
- Avian influenza (H5N1 virus).

In summary

- Some generic legislation has had a major impact upon the travel and tourism industry.
- EU legislation is becoming more evident.
- Economic and political issues and natural disasters impact upon the industry.
- There is a trend towards more responsible tourism.
- There are many challenges ahead!

Practice assessment activity

P M

Level P6/M3

Describe two pieces of legislation and two issues that have affected the travel and tourism industry since 1945 and explain their effect.

Level D2

Select two further issues that have affected the industry in the last ten years and evaluate how the industry has responded to them.

Test your knowledge

1. There are three sectors in the travel and tourism industry. One is the private sector. What are the other two?
2. What is the difference between a tourist and a visitor?
3. Name the 'Big 4' tour operators.
4. What is a miniple?
5. Name six products a leisure travel agent might sell.
6. What is the difference between a charter airline and a scheduled airline?
7. What are the main cruising areas for UK holidaymakers?
8. What are the two recent main competitors to Channel ferries?
9. Name the English National Parks.
10. Name four trade organisations. What are their roles?
11. When did the Boeing 747 make its first commercial flight and why did that aircraft have such an effect on the industry?
12. Give an example of (a) horizontal integration and (b) vertical integration.
13. What are the two main components of an inclusive holiday?
14. Why has Heathrow had to demolish a pier?
15. Who will Cunard name a future cruise ship after?
16. Name two EU Directives affecting the travel and tourism industry.

2 Exploring Customer Service in Travel and Tourism

Introduction

Travel and tourism is about people, all of whom have customer service needs. When you meet those needs, or better still exceed them, customers will want to return to you again and again. Customers will also tell others how good (or bad!) you are.

Whether you work directly with customers or behind the scenes, you will be involved in the challenging, exciting and satisfying world of providing excellent customer service. This Core unit examines what customer service is; the different customer service approaches used by organisations; different types of customer and their needs; and the skills needed to provide it. Completing the unit will help you to understand and provide excellent customer service.

How you will be assessed

Unit 2 is assessed internally, so the Centre delivering the qualification will assess you against the criteria. On completion of this unit you should be able to:

2.1 understand different approaches to customer service in different travel and tourism organisations

2.2 understand the needs of different types of customers in the travel and tourism industry
2.3 know the skills and techniques needed to provide good customer service in the travel and tourism industry
2.4 demonstrate customer service and selling skills and techniques in travel and tourism situations.

Assessment grades

The Edexcel Assessment Grid for Unit 2 details the criteria to be met. In general, to gain a Pass (P) you are asked to describe or demonstrate; to gain a Merit (M) you are also asked to compare, explain or deal with situations; and to gain a Distinction (D) you are also asked to evaluate and make recommendations.

2.1 Understand different approaches to customer service in different travel and tourism organisations

This section covers:

- what customer service is
- organisations
- processes
- resources
- policies.

What is customer service?

In this section you will consider organisations, their policies, processes and resources, and how these affect the customer service they provide. But first you need to ask an important question: what is customer service?

Every day, you experience customer service. It may be when you buy something in a shop, travel on a bus or go to a swimming pool; it may even be when you go to the dentist. Most of the time, you probably don't even notice it. Sometimes you will, either because the customer service you receive is particularly bad or because it has been especially good.

Please refer to the Talking point on this page. Did your group suggest any of the words in the diagram below when you brainstormed good customer service?

■ *Examples of good customer service behaviours*

Talking point

In a small group, brainstorm as many words and phrases as you can to describe good customer service. Then, brainstorm as many words and phrases as you can to describe bad customer service.

Review the words and phrases you have chosen and, in one sentence, write a definition of customer service.

The diagram below shows some of the words and phrases your group might have suggested for bad customer service.

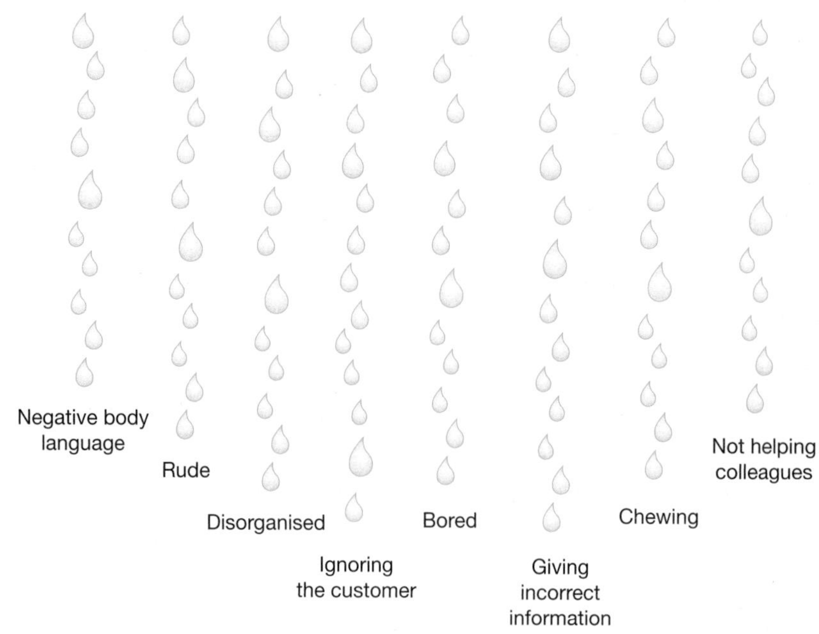

■ *Examples of bad customer service behaviours*

Case studies

Going the extra mile!

Passenger Agent Maria had a tricky situation at Toronto airport. An elderly couple who had been visiting their son and his family were checking in to return to the UK. Their son drove them 100 miles (160 kilometres) from his home, left them at Toronto airport and set off home again. When the couple tried to check in, they discovered they had left their passports in his car!

Maria could have taken the easy way out by telling them they could not travel until they had their passports. However, she wanted to help the distraught couple. Their son did not have a mobile phone so she asked if he had the car radio on. He had, and they remembered the programme he was listening to. Maria called the radio station and asked them to put a message out to the son, to return to the airport. The son heard it and drove back to the airport just in time for his very relieved parents to catch their flight! Maria had gone the extra mile and had delighted the couple and their son.

- Write down as many reasons you can think of as to why customer service is important.
- Discuss your reasons with someone else in your group.

Customer service is difficult to define, partly because it is the customer who will decide what it is. The Institute of Customer Service defines customer service as:

> 'The sum total of what an organisation does to meet customer expectations and produce customer satisfaction.'

So, everyone in an organisation (whether or not they have direct contact with the customer) should aim at satisfying the customer. However, if you only 'meet' customer expectations, they may feel that the customer service is alright but nothing special. What you must do is delight every one of your customers so that they will remember you, enjoy dealing with you, come back to you again and tell other people about you.

Customer service is important because…

- You must ensure that customers are so pleased with doing business with you, they will keep returning to you.
- You have to keep your customers away from your competitors.
- It costs five times as much to win a new customer as it does to keep an existing one.
- Dissatisfied customers tell others of their bad experiences and those people will avoid using your organisation.
- Your organisation needs to be able to compete on value rather than just price, i.e. customers are prepared to pay more for your product or service.
- Your organisation needs to be secure and able to develop, and so do you.
- You want the buzz you get out of providing excellent customer service!

Over to you

A customer bought a £1.00 loaf of bread from her supermarket. How much is that customer worth to the supermarket? Just £1.00? Give reasons for your answer.

Case studies

Ryanair will send staff to charm school

Ryanair's famously outspoken boss Michael O'Leary has performed the biggest U-turn of his career – by ordering his staff to be nice to his airline's frazzled passengers … At two meetings in London, Ryanair executives revealed plans to focus on providing a kinder, softer approach to its customers … James Freemantle of the Air Transport Users Council said: 'The slide show and presentation was strongly focused on punctuality, behaviour by staff towards customers and a greater emphasis on understanding air travellers' needs. It's not just about cost anymore.'

(*Source:* Based on an article by Jerome Reilly, ©Jerome Reilly. *Sunday Independent* (Ireland), 8 August 2004. Reprinted with the kind permission of the author)

Key points

- Customer service can be defined as: 'The sum total of what an organisation does to meet customer expectations and produce customer satisfaction.'
- The customer decides what is good customer service.
- Customer service is important for many reasons, the most important of which is that you must ensure that the customer is so pleased doing business with you, he or she keeps returning to you!

Organisations

The travel and tourism industry ranges from giants with integrated businesses to small independent companies, and from those which supply the main goods and services to those which supply the support services. These include:

- transport operators – air, sea, rail, road
- accommodation – hotels, villas, campsites, holiday centres, etc.
- attractions – theme parks, heritage sites, activity centres, etc.
- secondary services – insurance, airport representatives, tourist offices, passport offices.

As you will have read in *Unit 1: The UK Travel and Tourism Industry*, some organisations (for example, tour operators) integrate services vertically and horizontally. This gives them control over each level of the products they market but leads to an underlying consistency in customer service across that integrated group. People operating small private companies may have a niche market and know many of their clients as regular customers, which helps give a more personal style of customer service. Large organisations may depend more upon systems to help provide customer service but, with the right approach and by selecting and training staff who have a real desire to provide excellent care to their customers, such organisations can also provide a personal style of service.

The same principles apply whether the organisation is privately owned, a public service or a voluntary organisation.

Processes

Organisations' processes require documentation. Documentation may include booking forms, customers' records, tickets, invoices, receipts, communications with customers and contractors, feedback forms and customer databases. Additionally, processes are needed to run the business, such as contracts of employment, pay and training records, and health and safety documentation. While many of these are computer-based, some remain paper-based. Documentation and record keeping require great care and accuracy. Much of it is required, or affected by, legislation, for example, the Health and Safety Act 1974 and the Data Protection Act 1998. (You can learn more on this subject in *Unit 6: Business Skills for Travel and Tourism*.)

Resources

Every organisation needs resources to be able to provide customer service. The initial resource may be finance, from loans and profits. This funds other resources, like accommodation, equipment and systems, all of which will go toward establishing the style, level and quality of service. However, as this industry is a people business, the prime resource will be an organisation's staff. Care must be taken to provide sufficient staff who have a keen interest in providing customer service and who have the abilities, experience and qualifications to do so. How many staff are needed if there are peaks and troughs in the workload each day, or across the week or year? What might the customers expect the staff to be able to do? Are the staff able to speak a foreign language? Do they understand how to meet the needs of a disabled person? Can they get to work for a shift starting at 0430 hours? Do they have the right to work overseas?

Policies

Mission statements and objectives

Many organisations have a **mission statement** which describes their purpose, strategy, standards of behaviour and values. **Objectives** state what the organisation, or departments within it, specifically aim to achieve; how success will be measured; and the timescale for achievement. Specific targets may then be quoted, for example '5 per cent improvement in punctuality compared with the previous year'.

Mission statements have a major influence upon the levels and styles of customer service of an organisation; for example, an airline with the mission of being a computer-led business with minimal staff contact with passengers may decide to only accept Internet bookings and have self-service check-in at airports. This would require a different customer service approach to, for example, an airline with the mission of being the friendliest airline with staff available at every point of the passengers' travels. The first airline would invest in technology and procedures which enable the passengers to do things without human help; the latter airline would invest in selecting and training customer-caring staff, with procedures to support them. This does not mean one is better than the other; it merely identifies that there is more than one way to meet customers' needs.

Discuss in your group the similarities and differences between the mission statements of easyJet and Virgin Atlantic. What impact might these mission statements have upon the levels and styles of customer service?

Here are the mission statements of two UK airlines:

> 'To provide our customers with safe, good value, point-to-point air services. To effect and to offer a consistent and reliable product and fares appealing to leisure and business markets on a range of European routes. To achieve this, we will develop our people and establish lasting relationships with our suppliers.' (*easyJet*)

> 'To grow a profitable airline which people love to fly and where people love to work.' (*Virgin Atlantic*)

Responsive and proactive approaches

Just as it is important for individuals to be proactive and responsive to customers, so it is for organisations. They must anticipate changes and developments in their business and their customers. They must be alert to external changes (sometimes known as PEST – Political, Economic, Social and Technological) and take advantage of them. They also need to be aware of internal changes to the organisation. Many companies, such as Boeing and British Airways, conduct surveys to discover their staff's opinions. Issues might cover views on:

- how well the organisation supports them in giving customer service
- what is being done well
- what they would like more/less of
- their concerns.

Organisations must respond to the information so that customers and staff know action is being taken to improve its customer service.

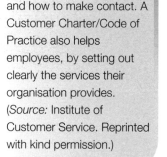

A Customer Charter tells customers the standards of service to expect, what to do if something goes wrong, and how to make contact. A Customer Charter/Code of Practice also helps employees, by setting out clearly the services their organisation provides. (*Source:* Institute of Customer Service. Reprinted with kind permission.)

Customer Charters

Many organisations describe their customer service policies in Customer Charters. These might include:

- what information the organisation will provide, how it will provide it and when
- the performance levels they will aim for (e.g. punctuality, quality)
- their payment and refund policies
- what they will do in the event of a disruption to arrangements (e.g. delays, cancellations)
- the compensation they will provide.

Activity

Explore some travel and tourism organisations' websites. Have they published customer service charters (often found in the website menu under Customer service *or* About us*)? Example organisations include Ryanair, United Airlines, South West Trains, Butlins (student pack), but there are many others.*

- Compare several customer service charters.
- Are they specific enough and measurable, so that there can be no doubt what will be done for their customers?
- Is there anything which you feel is missing from any of them?

Procedures

How an organisation expects its customers to buy and use its products and services also affects the style of customer service it provides and the amount of human interaction it has with its customers. For example, rather than visit a travel agent's shop, many customers use the Internet to research what is available and book their arrangements; organisations must therefore design dependable, user-friendly websites. Many passengers make their bookings on the Internet and take a reference number to the departure terminal, rather than obtain a paper ticket, to enable them to board. This is known as e-ticketing.

■ *E-ticketing helps travellers to avoid the queues*

Talking point

In your group, discuss why and how e-ticketing may affect the style and level of customer service given to passengers.

Meeting consumers' individual needs

Passengers have a much wider choice between organisations and processes nowadays. Some budget ('no frills') airlines may offer a limited choice of methods to check-in. Other airlines may offer a choice of check-in methods, for example, at a check-in desk, using a self-check-in machine or via the Internet. Such differences between budget and full-service airlines do not mean that passengers should not receive good customer service. Passengers make a value judgement when they decide whether to travel on a budget airline or a full-service airline, but the human element should exist on both. The US budget airline Southwest is famous for the humour and friendly service given by its staff.

Hotels offer different styles and levels of service. Business people want fast check-in and check-out. Computer databases build information on customers' needs and preferences, so that they can be taken into account each time a customer buys from the organisation. This personalises the experience. The preferred room might be pre-allocated, with the key ready to hand over at a special desk in exchange for a booking reference and presentation of a credit card. Guests can check their bill on their in-room TV prior to check-out, and just drop their key at the desk as they depart.

Training

Customer service doesn't just happen! The organisation needs to put much into place and adopt particular styles and behaviours to deliver it well. Part of this is continuous investment in its staff, to ensure they are *able* to give excellent service and *want* to give it. That means caring for staff, including providing training which will develop their customer service skills – just as this course is aiming to do for you.

Encouraging loyalty and providing rewards

Customers must feel the organisation is a great one to do business with. The organisation must do everything they can to keep all of its customers and should reward them for their loyalty. There are many ways to do so. Some organisations run 'Clubs' for their loyal customers which provide facilities like priority booking, special phone numbers, guaranteed seat selection, cabin or car upgrades, airport lounges, club magazines and discounts on future bookings. Membership is earned by the amount of money spent, the number of bookings made or the number of journeys taken. The greater the amount of business given by the customer, the greater the rewards might be.

Activity

Explore the websites of tour operators, airlines, coach operators, train operators, cruise and ferry companies. Discover those which offer loyalty schemes to their customers. Compare them. Look for common themes and unique ideas.

Feedback

Every organisation should have policies and procedures to gather feedback from its customers. How else could it learn what its customers like and dislike and how else can it be given the opportunity to put things right if they go wrong? You shall look further at gathering and using feedback later in this unit (see pages 81–2).

In summary

- Organisations may be small, large, independent, integrated, private, public or voluntary.
- Organisations need policies which start with a mission statement declaring what they wish to achieve and measurable objectives to aim for.
- Such statements have a direct impact on the level and styles of customer service each organisation wishes to deliver. They determine the approaches organisations have to:
  - being responsive and proactive
  - developing customer charters and procedures
  - developing their staff
  - encouraging customer loyalty
  - obtaining customer and staff feedback.
- Processes like record keeping are essential to meet the needs of the business and legal requirements.
- Every organisation needs resources, often obtained by finance. A key resource in the travel and tourism industry is its staff.

Practice assessment activity

P *Level P1* ✓

Working in pairs, visit two local travel or tourism organisations. Obtain copies of their missions and objectives. Observe how they provide customer service. Seek evidence of their procedures, processes and training.

Levels P1/M1/D1

Make a presentation to the rest of the group:

- **P** describing how the two organisations approach customer service in terms of policies, processes and resources (P1) ✓
- **M** comparing the two organisations' customer service policies, processes and resources in respect of the customer service they provide (M1) ✓✓
- **D** evaluating the customer service provision of the two organisations and making justified recommendations for improvement (D1). ✓✓✓

2.2 Understand the needs of different types of customers in the travel and tourism industry

This section covers:

- different types of customers
- different types of needs.

Different types of customers

To work in travel and tourism you must be willing and able to meet the needs of a wide range of customers.

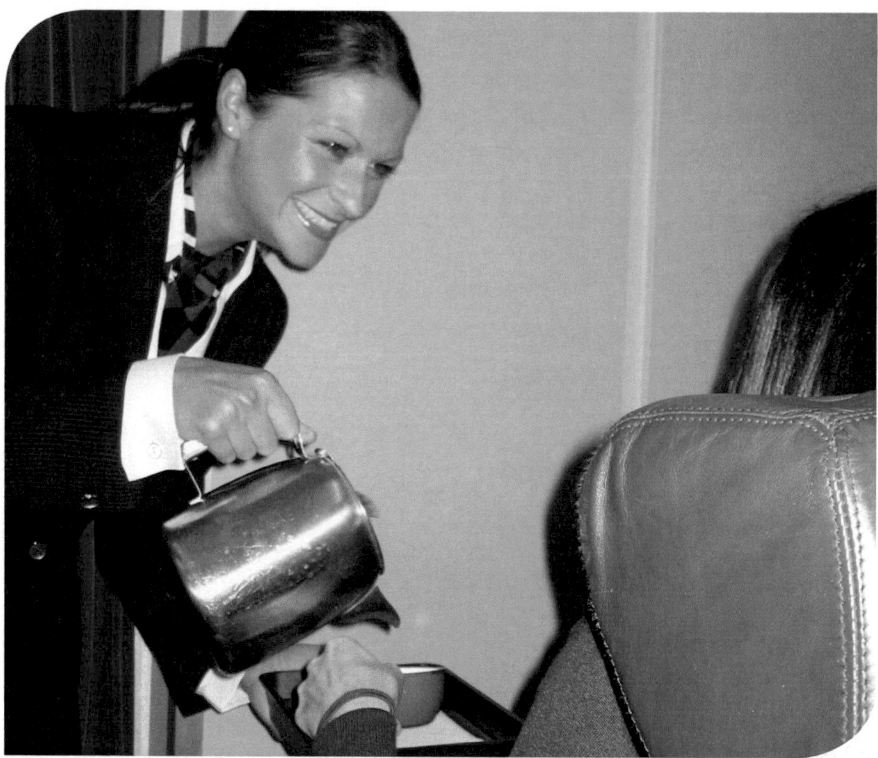

Segmentation

Whether you call your customers clients, visitors, guests or passengers, their needs must be understood. To do so, you need to segment them. **Segmentation** is the grouping of people who have common characteristics (see also *Unit 5: Exploring Marketing in Travel and Tourism*, pages 172–3). The spider diagram below shows some of the customer categories which could be segmented.

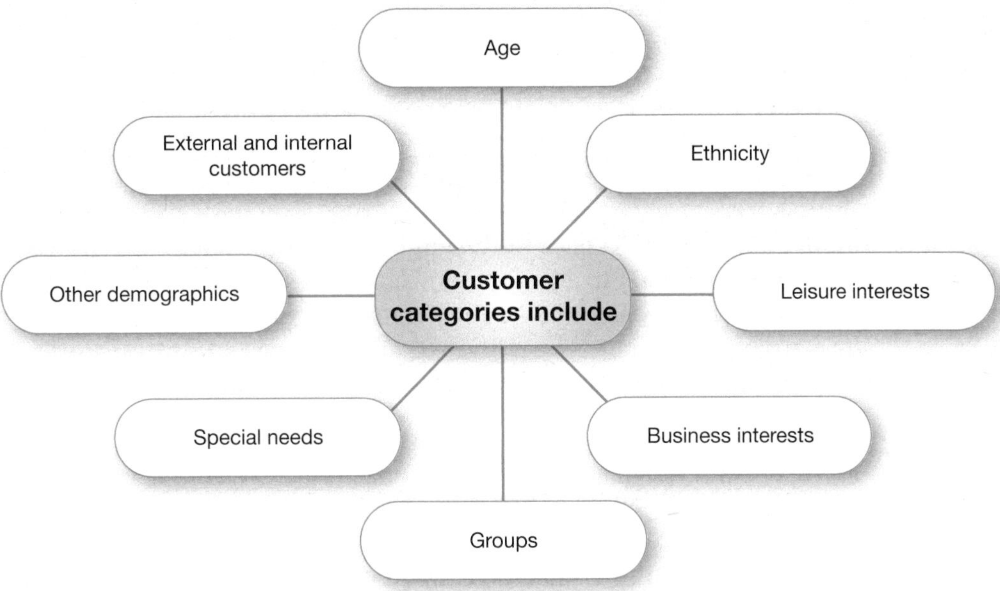

Age

Many customers are children. They want to enjoy themselves but they might find their experiences a bit daunting, so they will be delighted to have someone they can relate to and who can give them help and assurance at the appropriate times. Facilities such as kids clubs in hotels, play areas at airports and in travel agencies are great for children but also meet a customer service need for adults who can be relieved from looking after them. Some adults without children may also appreciate 'child-free' zones.

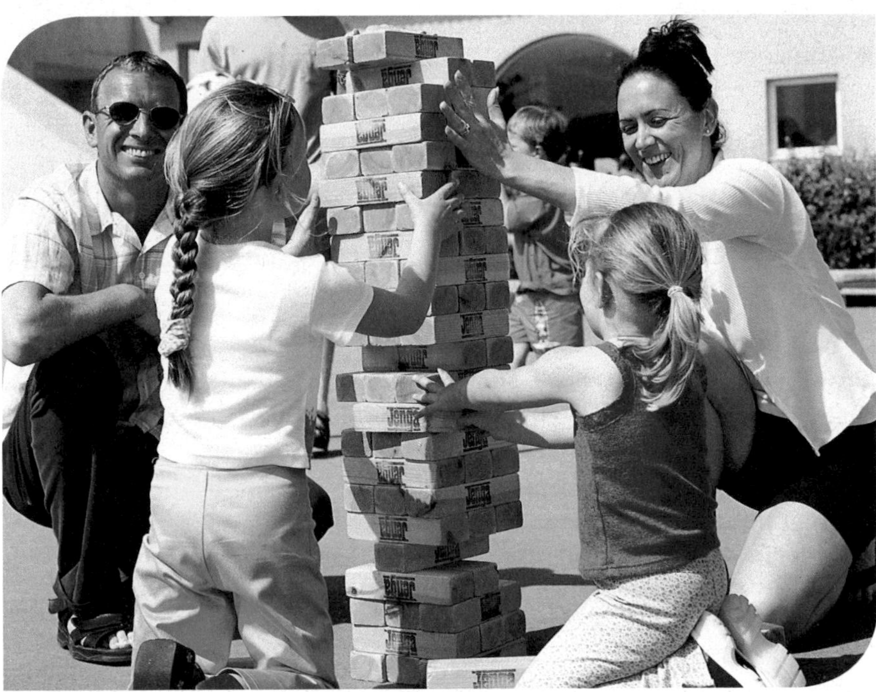

■ *Kids clubs meet both children's and adults' needs*

The fastest growing segment of the UK population travelling overseas is the over-54 age group. The number of overseas visits made by this age group in 2000, compared with 1993, increased by 98 per cent (compared with 63 per cent increase for the 0–54 age group). With such growth, it is important that you learn how to give the older age groups customer service they value. The older generation generally prefers a more formal approach and welcomes the recognition that they have experienced more than younger generations. Don't assume that elderly clients are losing their mental faculties or physical abilities – Saga Holidays caters for those over 50 years. Its 'Go for it' range includes learning to scuba dive among the coral reefs of Borneo, wine tasting in South Africa and horse riding on a ranch in Arizona!

Key points

- Muslims and Jews do not eat pork.
- In much of Asia, it is offensive to pat the head, as this is seen as the most sacred part of the body. Cabin crew should therefore be careful not to pass anything over people's heads.
- In northern Europe, greetings are quite formal, for example, a handshake. In southern Europe, a greeting is more likely to include hugging and cheek kissing.

Ethnicity

Each person has beliefs, practices, traditions, languages and preferences which influence their way of life. These become the norm for that person, but they may not be the norm for other people, especially those with different cultures. Religion is often a strong feature of culture and can be a particularly sensitive issue. You should respect, learn about and respond to other people's cultures so that you understand their customer service needs and avoid causing offence.

Leisure interests

Why, where and how people travel, and the style of customer service they want, is influenced by the interests they have. Some will look for organised activities and entertainment. Some will want excitement; others will want a relaxing time. Some people will want to learn new things, whilst others will simply want to be with their family and friends.

- Someone interested in historic buildings may appreciate an expert on the subject who recognises the customer's interest and knowledge.
- Someone on a surfing holiday may want a guide with local knowledge to tell them where the good surfing conditions are, warn them of the dangers and share experiences with them.
- Someone on a gastronomic tour may expect knowledgeable, good-quality staff at fine-dining locations.

Business interests

Business people want speedy, efficient service. They need to have the facilities and support normally available at their home or office. A calm airport lounge with newspapers, computers and communication facilities would be welcome. Hotels providing communication and Internet links, same-day laundry facilities, 24-hour room service, and express check-in and check-out are valued. However, even business people need to relax, so they may become leisure tourists as well and want customer service appropriate to leisure tourists.

Each sector of the industry seeks ways to meet the needs of their customers, so the types of customer service will be different, depending upon the market segment.

Groups

Members of organised groups, such as orchestras and youth clubs, often already know each other. They usually have a group leader who may share with you the responsibility for communicating with the group. However, although there will be common needs, each member still has his or her own concerns and it is important to relate to them.

The other type of group is formed by circumstance, for example, the people in the group all happen to be on the same inclusive holiday or are all taking a guided tour. They probably will not know each other and will not have a group leader. You will probably be asked more questions by such a group as there is a wider range of needs and no group leader to help you. This can be challenging; you need to be alert to their individual needs and ensure they are met.

Customers with special needs

All customers have needs which are individual to them, but some have additional needs beyond those of most customers. These might arise because the customer:

- has a physical limitation such as being unable to walk or having a hearing or sight impairment
- has a learning disability
- has a severe language limitation

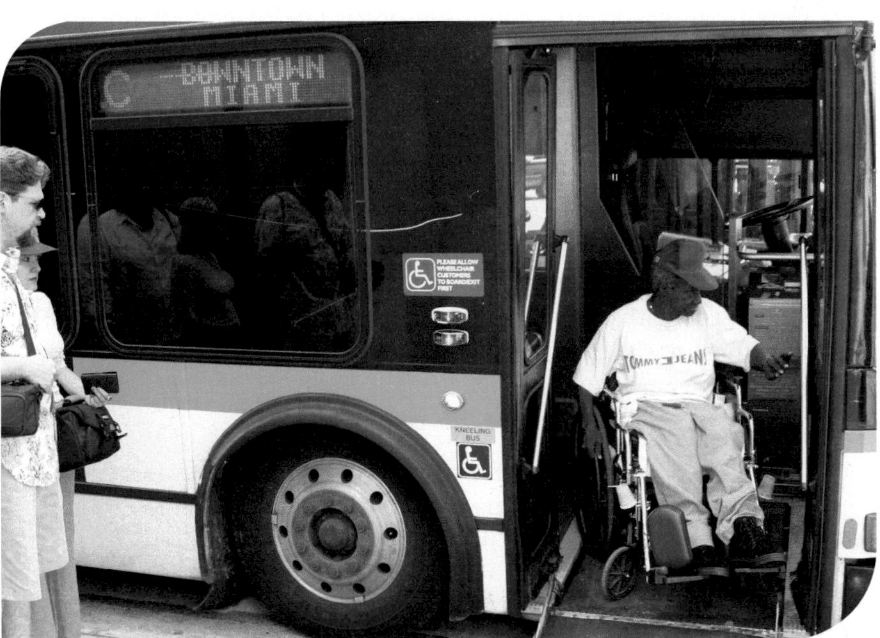

Travel destinations in various parts of the world provide suitable facilities for those who have a disability

Talking point

In small groups, brainstorm what facilities and style of customer service would be appropriate for:

- young travellers on an activities holiday in Australia
- families on a beach holiday in Spain
- retired couples on a Christmas cultural weekend in Vienna
- women on a health spa break
- a businessman at a two-day meeting, night-stopping in a foreign city.

- is a child travelling on his or her own
- is a woman travelling with a baby and/or young child
- has special dietary needs or preferences.

All staff can help such customers, with care, empathy and a clear understanding of their specific needs. Some staff may be given training to help those with special needs; for example, learning sign language or how to assist wheelchair users or escort sight-impaired passengers. When caring for a customer with special needs, ensure you introduce them to the next person who will look after them, and explain what is needed.

Here are some examples of caring for customers with special needs:

- A ferry has a special car parking space for people with physical disabilities. It is next to a lift to the cabin deck, rather than stairs. A wheelchair is kept by the parking space. A trained staff member meets the passenger to assist them to cabin level.
- An airline has unaccompanied minor escorts at airports and during the flight. There is a special airport lounge with videos, soft drinks, nibbles and games. In flight, the children are given comics, games and tuck boxes.
- A holiday hotel has staff to look after and entertain children in exclusive 'kids zones' and to babysit.

Other demographics

Other demographic factors also influence the customer service needed. There are different needs between single people and families; women and men; children and adults. Sometimes, you may look after a VIP (very important person) like a film star or the chairperson of a major international company. These are very influential people and you may need to look after them in a particular way.

External and internal customers

External customers are those who purchase and/or use your organisation's products and services. The distinction between those who buy your product or services (the purchasers) and those who use them (the consumers) is important. Think of the parent with a child in a shop. The child pleads with their parent to buy some sweets. The parent is the purchaser and the child is the consumer. Both are important customers and can influence buying decisions.

Internal customers are those who work for the same organisation as you and who may need your services. That includes departments that need timely and accurate information from you, so that they can meet the needs of the customer and the organisation. Everybody in an organisation, whether they are in finance, operations, catering or any other department, is directly or indirectly serving the customer, so they deserve excellent customer service from you. They need you to be approachable, understanding, supportive, effective and efficient. Unless the whole organisation is working as one, with the customer at the heart of all that it does, the customer will lose and you will therefore lose the customer.

Different types of needs

Information, advice, instructions

As the travel and tourism industry is a people business, you will spend much of your time giving information, advice and instructions to customers.

> The customer's lament:
> *Hey, I'm ME!*
> *I'm not the last customer you had.*
> *I'm not the next customer you will have.*
> *Please treat me as an individual with my own needs.*
> *I'm ME!*

■ *Remember that each person is an individual*

Activity

For each of the following jobs, list three pieces of information that are likely to be asked for frequently:

- travel agent
- theme park ride assistant
- on-board train manager
- historic house guide
- hotel receptionist.

Discuss your list with someone else in your group.

How did you do? You probably thought of questions specific to the job, for example, a historic house guide might frequently be asked 'Who painted that picture?' but don't forget the many types of non-job specific questions such as 'Where is the cafeteria?'

Increasingly, technology is used to provide information to staff and customers; for example:

- tour operators' computers provide information and booking facilities for their inclusive holidays
- transport organisations use computers to make reservations and to provide 'real time' information on arrival times
- heritage locations use visual and audio aids to provide information to visitors.

Health, safety and security

The Health and Safety at Work Act 1974 requires employers and employees to ensure a healthy, safe and secure environment for the public and employees. You should always be observant and report anything which could be a hazard, for example, a loose carpet in a hotel or trailing cables in an office.

Customers will seek advice on overseas health arrangements. During the SARS outbreaks in 2002–03, industry staff needed up-to-date information on the situation and preventative measures. They obtained much of this information from various government and medical organisations, communicated particularly by the Internet and leaflets.

Weather can affect health, safety and security, for example, hurricanes can result in flights being delayed or cancelled, hotels being changed and holiday arrangements being altered. Tour operators and airlines have emergency procedures and support systems which they activate when such emergencies happen. Staff must be well trained, calm and able to use their initiative to assist holidaymakers who are at or are due to visit the destination, and those who are concerned about relatives. World concern regarding international security and terrorism has heightened in recent years. Everyone in the travel and tourism industry has to be alert to security risks and ensure customers are briefed and given reassurance.

Assistance

Different customers need different levels of assistance. This may range from giving directions or carrying someone's bag, through to helping customers like parents and disabled travellers, who may need greater assistance than normally required.

Expectations

Remember that the customer will define customer service. This is due to factors such as their own experience, ethnicity and circumstances. However, all customers share one set of needs. They want you to:

- make them feel important – that means valuing them, treating them as an individual and anticipating their needs; using the person's name is one way to make the customer feel valued
- know your products or services
- listen and show empathy (understand how they feel).

In summary

- There are many different types of customer, who can be categorised in a number of ways.
- Each customer segment will have its own set of customer service needs.
- Each person within a segment also has his or her own needs.
- It is as important to give good customer service to the internal customer as it is to provide it to the external customer.
- Needs may be generic, e.g. directions, or specific to the job, e.g. babysitting.
- Customers may need information, advice and instructions.
- Employers and staff have legal responsibilities to customers and colleagues for their health, safety and security.
- Customers have different expectations but all expect customer service staff to make them feel important, know the products and services, listen and show empathy.

Practice assessment activity

P Level P2

Work on this activity in groups of three or four. You are the passenger agents dealing with the following situation and are face to face with the customers.

> It's a foggy day at the airport. The flight to Milan is delayed overnight. It has 150 passengers. Hotel accommodation has to be arranged as well as transport to and from the hotels. Some passengers have people meeting them at Milan. Some passengers should have been making connections to other flights at Milan to continue to their destination. There are some families with young children and babies. There are 35 members of a Welsh male-voice choir due to sing in Milan tomorrow night.

In your group, decide:

a) what different types of passenger you may encounter

b) what their needs may be.

2.3 Skills and techniques needed to provide good customer service in the travel and tourism industry

This section covers:

- communication methods and skills
- selling skills
- presentation skills and personal presentation
- ways of measuring customer service.

Communication methods and skills

Effective communication is a major factor in customer service. This section considers types of communication and the skills and techniques useful in communicating well.

Case studies

Moments of truth

Jan Carlzon was the Chief Executive Officer of Scandinavian Airlines System (SAS). He realised that the reputation and success of SAS depended upon how highly the passengers judged their communication with SAS staff. That communication could be at any time in their dealings with the airline. It could be for any reason and by any method, lasting for several minutes or just a few seconds. He called these contacts, 'Moments of truth'. He realised the airline had to do everything to ensure those 'moments' were highly successful. He said:

> 'These "Moments of truth" are the moments that ultimately determine whether SAS will succeed or fail as a company.'

- What did Jan Carlzon mean by a passenger's 'Moment of truth'?

Why do people communicate?

People communicate with others to:

- inform
- instruct
- seek information
- motivate.

Activity

You have just taken a phone call from Ahmed. He wants Caroline to discuss the complaint from Mrs Harrison in his office at 11.30am. She is to bring all the paperwork about the complaint. She must call Ahmed by 11am on extension 2403 if she cannot make the meeting.

- Write a suitable message for Caroline.

Inform

You may be a holiday representative and need to leave a written message for a colleague or want to tell your customers verbally about the resort.

How did you do? Your message to Caroline should say who it is from, who it is to, when the message was taken, give the accurate detail of the message and state what Ahmed's extension number is.

Instruct

This may be a verbal safety instruction given by cabin crew. It may be a notice to passengers telling them what they cannot carry in their hand-baggage.

Activity

You work in a three-storey tour operator's office. Your manager has left you a note:

> *'I've had the Fire Service here this morning. They've told us to get signs up about fire evacuation, pronto. Something about what to do if a fire is found, how to get out, where to go, what to do, what not to do. Apparently it's got to be clearly phrased and understood. Sort it out by this afternoon!'*

- Create a written instruction which meets the needs set out by your manager. Your instruction must be eye-catching, clear and logical.

Seek information

Some of your verbal communication will be to seek information from a customer, so that you can respond to his or her needs. You may need to write a letter asking for information. A common type of written communication seeking information is a customer service questionnaire (see page 81).

Motivate

You may want to verbally encourage your customers to go on an excursion. You may want to compliment an employee on their good work, in writing.

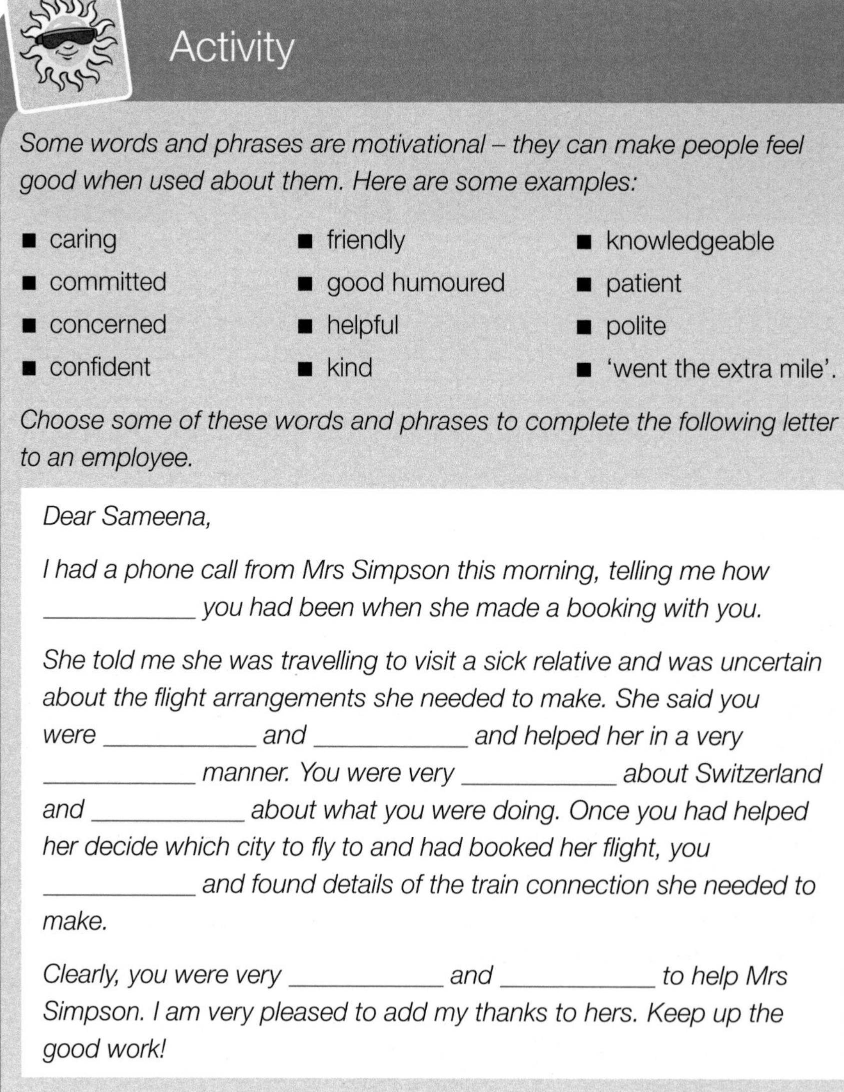

Activity

Some words and phrases are motivational – they can make people feel good when used about them. Here are some examples:

- caring
- committed
- concerned
- confident
- friendly
- good humoured
- helpful
- kind
- knowledgeable
- patient
- polite
- 'went the extra mile'.

Choose some of these words and phrases to complete the following letter to an employee.

Dear Sameena,

I had a phone call from Mrs Simpson this morning, telling me how __________ you had been when she made a booking with you.

She told me she was travelling to visit a sick relative and was uncertain about the flight arrangements she needed to make. She said you were __________ and __________ and helped her in a very __________ manner. You were very __________ about Switzerland and __________ about what you were doing. Once you had helped her decide which city to fly to and had booked her flight, you __________ and found details of the train connection she needed to make.

Clearly, you were very __________ and __________ to help Mrs Simpson. I am very pleased to add my thanks to hers. Keep up the good work!

The style of communication

People use different styles of communication depending upon whether they are talking or writing to a friend, a tutor or a grandparent. Sometimes your style will be formal, sometimes informal. Different customers and situations also require different styles.

Over to you

How would you talk to a client:

- during a happy holiday experience
- who had a complaint
- if the hotel was on fire?

How do people communicate?

People communicate with each other face to face, electronically (for example, by telephone) and in writing.

Whichever way you communicate, the same process occurs:

- *Stage 1*: The sender wants the receiver to understand a message.
- *Stage 2*: The sender puts the message into a logical language and style.
- *Stage 3*: The message is transmitted.
- *Stage 4*: The message is received.
- *Stage 5*: The receiver 'decodes' (interprets) the message.
- *Stage 6*: The receiver understands the message and may respond.

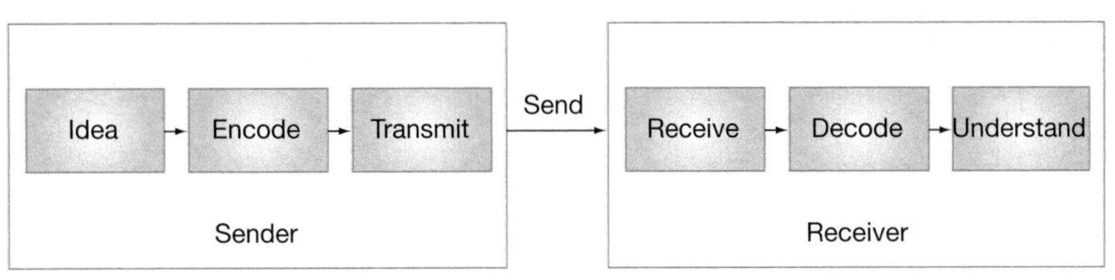

The communication process

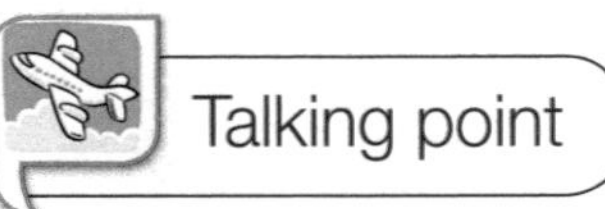

Talking point

Communicating isn't just about sending messages. It is also about receiving them. People waste a lot of time and create bad impressions by talking when they should be listening. If people listened more, they would gain more information more quickly and demonstrate greater respect for their customers. Everybody has been given two ears and one mouth – they should be used in that proportion!

Communicating face to face

People tend to think that the important thing to do when communicating is to say the right words. In truth, the 'words' that are used are only one part of communicating – and it is this part which has the least impact!

- The words that people use account for around 10 per cent of the impact of communication.
- 30 per cent of the impact comes from the pitch and tone of the voice – this can be called 'the music'.

Words – what we say

Music – pitch and tone of our voice: how we say things

Dance – our body language

■ The part which has the most impact – 60 per cent – is body language; this can be called 'the dance'.

Words

Customers gain their main impression of you in the first few seconds of communication. These are powerful 'Moments of truth'! 'Hello', 'Good morning', 'Can I help you?' are common opening statements but try to find ways to personalise the greeting. Use the customer's name as soon as you know it (it may be on their ticket, their baggage label or credit card).

Case studies

Feargal Quinn founded the supermarket chain Superquinn. He believes in spending time with the customers. Once, he was assisting staff when a man and woman, with their son, came to the check-out desk. He bagged their goods and said, 'Thank you Mrs Connolly for shopping at Superquinn.' Minutes later, the customer returned to ask Feargal to explain to her husband that they had never met before. He happily did so, and was asked how he knew the wife's name. He explained that he had noticed the boy's name on a nametag on his scarf. How's that for observation!

Be aware that an older person may prefer formality and like to be addressed by courtesy title and surname, for example, Mrs Green. A young person may prefer to be addressed by his or her first name.

Activity

Write down opening remarks you might make to personalise your communication in the following situations:

- You are a coach escort. Among the passengers joining the coach is a woman with a young child eating an ice cream.
- You are a hotel receptionist and a woman wearing a wet raincoat and shaking water off her umbrella approaches you to check in.
- A man checks in at your desk with a lot of baggage. You notice the name Maurice Wesson on a label on one of the bags.

What opening remarks did you suggest? Here are a few you might use:

- 'Hello, are you enjoying your ice cream?'
- 'It looks as though it's raining pretty heavily. Let's get you checked in to your room quickly, so that you can change into some dry clothes.'

- 'You've got a lot of bags with you, Mr Wesson. Are you going away for a long time?'

The travel industry uses lots of jargon, for example, hotac, no-show, ETA. Don't use it when communicating with customers. They may not understand it and it is discourteous; so is the use of slang.

Key points

- HOTAC = hotel accommodation.
- no-show = passengers or guests who fail to arrive for their flight or booking.
- ETA = estimated time of arrival

Overcoming language barriers

Sometimes people assume that others can (and should!) speak their language. This shows disrespect to customers. Be patient, listen and look for clues as to what the customer is saying. Be careful to use clear diction (speak clearly) and not to speak too quickly. Use your body language, or even quick drawings, to communicate. A useful aid to language is the use of symbols. These are often universal, so will be understood in any country.

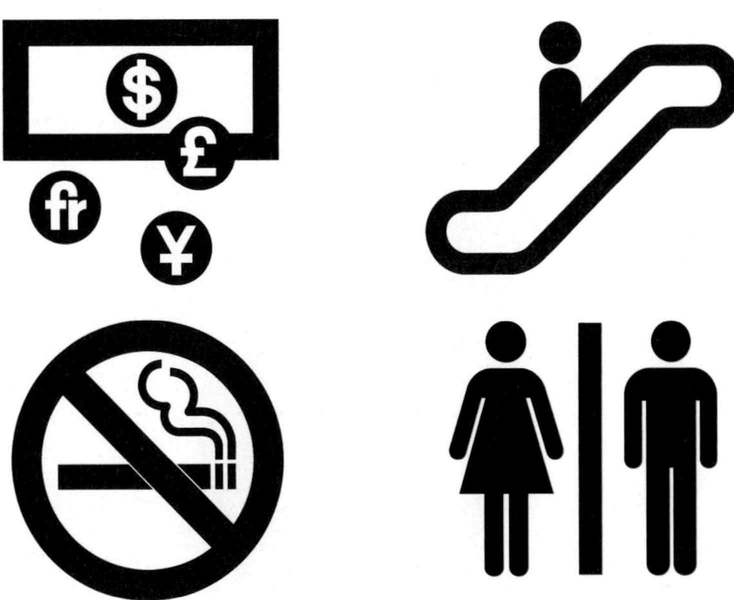

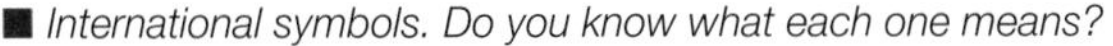

International symbols. Do you know what each one means?

Throughout your communication, think about what you want to say and how you will say it. Structure helps you manage the communication and demonstrates knowledge and confidence.

Pitch and tone

This is the 'music' of communication. The effectiveness of your verbal communication is powerfully altered by the pitch and tone of your voice. Varied pitch and tone demonstrates interest and enthusiasm. Flat pitch and tone demonstrates disinterest and boredom. You can vary the volume of your voice to create an effect. You might use a loud voice to communicate an instruction in an emergency, or a quiet voice to encourage a calm atmosphere.

Body language

This is the important 'dance' of communication. Look around you. What does the body language – the non-verbal communication – of others in the room tell you? Do you see enthusiasm, boredom, anger, puzzlement or happiness?

- How would you feel if the escort on your excursion leant against the coach door, legs crossed and arms folded? This person would be presenting a 'closed' style. You might assume that he or she is bored, not interested in you and not about to give you a fun journey.
- What if the cabin crew member greets you on board with good eye contact, a smile and is standing upright? This person is presenting an 'open' style. You will probably feel that he or she is demonstrating interest, warmth and confidence, and that this should be a good flight.

■ *Is this person interested or bored?*

A useful technique with young children is to crouch down to their level and talk to them about something of particular interest to them, for example, their teddy's name. This has a 'halo effect' – while you have established an exclusive zone for you and the child to talk within, those outside your zone will see you are relating to the child and recognise your caring approach.

Mannerisms

Think about how you speak and what your body is doing. Ask a friend if you have any mannerisms. You may be surprised. Do you 'um' and 'er', or use slang phrases like 'Gotcha!' or 'Y'know'? Do you put your hand in front of your mouth or stand on one leg? Stop doing it!

Non-face-to-face communication

Written communication

The same principles apply to written communication as they do for verbal communication. Think about what you want to communicate and who you are communicating with, and choose an appropriate communication style.

Electronic communication

You cannot use body language when using a telephone, so you must be skilled in using the remaining 40 per cent which comes from the words used and the pitch and tone of your voice. Standing or sitting comfortably, upright and alert, will affect the way you speak.

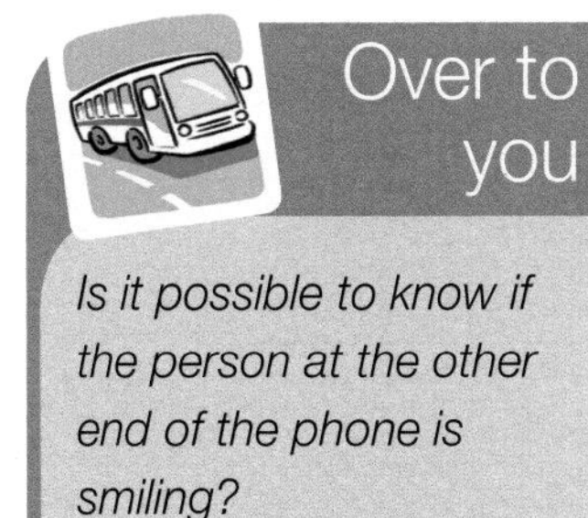

Is it possible to know if the person at the other end of the phone is smiling?

Confidentiality and accuracy

Customers expect organisations to treat information about them in confidence. That means not discussing any details about them or their arrangements with others unless for valid business reasons. This would include discussions about bookings they make, contact details and credit card information.

Do not make casual remarks about customers or release information to people asking about them. Airline staff are sometimes asked if a certain person is on a flight. The caller might say he is the passenger's husband and she has asked him to meet her at the airport. Staff will not release the information. That might seem unfair, but how do they know the caller is really her husband or that she wants her husband to know where she is?

Customers' confidentiality is protected in law. The Data Protection Act 1998 protects individuals from the misuse of computer data which is held about them. They have the right of access to that data, rights of compensation for inaccuracies or wrongful disclosure, and the right to have inaccuracies corrected.

Accuracy is very important. If you need to record or say anything which is supposed to be factual, make sure it is correct. Grammar and punctuation can easily change the meaning that you originally intended. Email is convenient and speedy; however, emails are not confidential and they can be misinterpreted, with the reader assuming a much tougher, less polite message than the sender intended. Learn email etiquette; this includes how to structure what you want to say and how to phrase sentences so that they cannot be misunderstood and demonstrate the appropriate style (for example, formal/informal, happy/concerned).

In summary

- People communicate to inform, instruct, motivate and seek information.
- Remember to *listen*!
- Electronic communication needs to be used carefully to ensure the appropriate style and content is communicated.
- The impact of communication comes from the words, the pitch and tone of the voice, and through body language – together, these make the words, music and dance of communication. Body language is by far the most powerful of these.
- There are many techniques you can use when communicating.
- You must be accurate and confidential when recording or using information.

Selling skills

Selling is not just about having a customer buy and pay for a product – for example, an inclusive holiday, a guided tour, a train journey. It is a key part of customer service and is part of promoting your organisation, which will encourage the customer to buy from you.

■ *Shopping on board a ferry*

The eight stages of selling

The eight stages of selling are described below.

1 **Create an image**. Make sure you and your environment are creating the right image to attract the customer.
   - Is your appearance smart?
   - Is your office clean and your desk tidy?
   - Are the goods you want to sell or the brochures you want to offer in good condition and easily available?

2 **Establish a rapport**. Create a favourable first impression. Be warm and sincere. Personalise the experience. Pay attention to how you communicate, including your body language. Don't get distracted.

3 **Investigate needs**. Find out what a customer wants by asking appropriate questions.
   - Start with **open questions** (i.e. questions which start with *what, why* and *how*). These will give you a lot of information; for example, 'What interests does your daughter have?'
   - Continue with **leading questions**. These will narrow down the subject to give you more information; for example, 'If she likes travelling, where does she like to go?'
   - Move on to **closed questions**. These will give you specific information or confirm something; for example, 'Has she been to France?'

4 **Actively listen**. Demonstrate that you are listening and have understood what has been said. Use your body language, for example, by nodding. Repeat key words and statements, for example, 'You said you like cruises, but only if they call at a different port every day.' Say encouraging things, such as 'Since you have already taken a cruise on the *QE2*, you know how enjoyable cruises can be.'

5 **Present the product/service**. By now, you should know your customer's needs and preferences. Make sure you know your products/services. Select one or more suitable ones to offer your client. Choose two or three features which you feel will particularly appeal to the customer. Sell the benefits; for example, 'You said you like calling at a different port each day. This ship is a bit smaller, so it can get in to ports which the larger ships can't visit.'

6 **Handle the objections**. Don't tell the customer that he or she is wrong but overcome the objection by finding something positive to say which addresses it; for example, 'I understand why you feel you might be seasick in a smaller ship, but don't worry, because this is a modern ship fitted with the latest design of stabilisers.'

7 **Close the sale**. Watch for clues that the customer is ready to buy; for example, the customer might say 'That seems like the holiday I'm looking for' or 'Do you need a deposit?' When that happens, re-emphasise the benefits to reinforce the customer's comfort about buying and ask how the customer wants to pay.

8 **After the sale**. Ask the customer if there is anything else that he or she would like to purchase. Remind the customer about when the balance is due, or tell him or her about guarantees, etc. Package the purchase well, even if it is only a ticket. Present it with a flourish! Follow up after the customer has used the product, to enquire if all was as he or she had wished, and encourage the customer to think about the next purchase.

Key points

- There are eight stages of selling.
- Good questioning techniques are important, using a range of open, leading and closed questions.
- Customer service skills and techniques are vital aids to successful selling.

Practice assessment activity

Levels P3/P5/M3/D2

In groups of three:

P
- Prepare three copies of a pro forma with the eight stages of selling listed down the page. (P3)

P M
- Take turns in a selling situation. The first person is the customer; the second is the employee; the third is the observer. Agree a selling situation and have the employee sell a product or service to the customer, using each of the eight stages of selling. The observer will complete the pro forma, noting evidence of when and how each stage was used. (P5/M3)

D
- Complete the sale and then discuss what the employee did well. Evaluate your own performance and what you could do to make it even better. (D2)

Rotate roles, think of another selling scenario, and start again until you have performed three different situations.

Presentation skills and personal presentation

Presentation skills

Many employees in the travel and tourism industry speak in public, for example, guides, cabin crew and holiday representatives. These may be formal presentations or informal announcements, to small or large groups. Often they will be made using a microphone; you should therefore seek opportunities on this course and elsewhere to gain experience of using them.

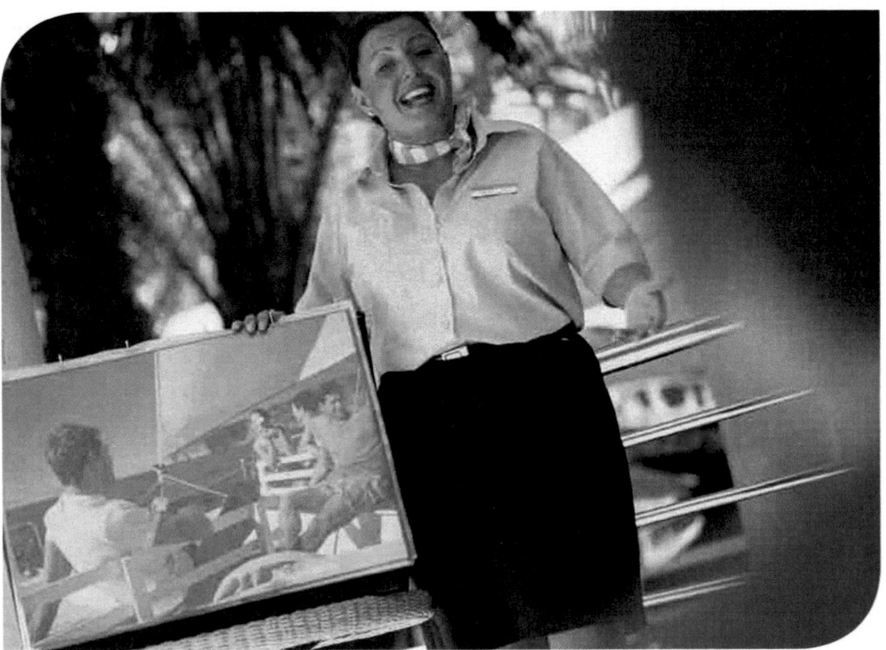

■ *Presenting to customers*

Preparation

Always think about what you are going to say and how you are going to say it.

- Plan a logical structure to your presentation.
- Prompt cards are useful but avoid standing in front of the audience reading them. They want to see your face, not the top of your head!
- Practise your presentation. Ask a friend to give you feedback.
- Check the location is suitable. Are any changes needed to it?
- Make sure you know how to use the equipment and that it works.
- Decide what to wear. Make sure it is clean and smart.

Nerves

- Calm your nerves by rehearsing.
- Have a 'plan B' in case anything goes wrong, for example, the projector fails.
- Take deep breaths.
- Tell yourself you look good and that your presentation will go well.
- Think of the audience as your friends.
- Go out there and enjoy it!

Presentation

- The first few seconds of your presentation will be the most powerful. Make sure your appearance and what you say in your opening sentences creates a positive image. Learn what you are initially going to say off by heart.

- Speak confidently! Make sure you are clear in both what you say and how you say it. Keep your face towards the audience.
- Avoid speech mannerisms.
- Use the pitch and tone – the music – of your voice to keep the audience interested.
- If you are using a microphone, don't put it in front of your face. The audience wants to see you, not a metal stick! Hold it a couple of centimetres below your chin.
- Use your body language to create a confident image. That will impress your audience and have a positive effect on you.
- Scan the audience and make brief eye contact with people in it.

Over to you

When giving a presentation, make sure everyone can hear you. You can do this by asking your audience directly or by looking for body language signs. What might these signs be?

Pace what you have to say. Don't rush it – it can be easy to speed through an announcement, especially if you have made it lots of times. What might happen if you rush a presentation or announcement?

Activity

You are a holiday representative in Barbados. It is 6pm and your clients have just landed after a long flight from Manchester, which arrived two hours late. You are going to make a PA announcement on the coach transferring them to the hotel which must include:

- suitable comment about the flight delay and how they might be feeling
- information about where the coach is going and how long it will take to get there
- information about the meal arrangements tonight.

Work in pairs, one to make the announcement using a microphone, the other to observe. Afterwards, discuss what the speaker did well and what he or she might do to make the presentation better, using the guidelines in this unit. Then swap roles and start again.

Personal presentation

Dress and grooming

Customers will judge you and your organisation on the image you present. Many organisations require staff to wear a uniform. This promotes the organisation and presents a powerful image. The organisation should give a demonstration and written briefing on how to wear the uniform, and rules and guidance about grooming, including information on acceptable hairstyles, make-up, tattoos, jewellery, etc. Look your best by ensuring you and your clothes are clean and smart.

Jacket (male uniform)

- May be worn fully buttoned or fully unbuttoned with uniform.
- Must be fully buttoned when wearing knitwear underneath as a warmth layer.
- Cabin crew in-flight gilet must never be worn underneath the jacket.
- Must not be worn draped around shoulders.
- Must always display relevant name badge and brevet.
- Must always be available whilst on duty.
- Collar must not be worn turned up.
- The 'senior' cabin crew member will make a diplomatic decision on whether it is 'jackets on' or 'jackets off' when boarding and when staff are visible in public places such as airport terminals, hotel lobbies, etc. Once that decision has been made all cabin crew members must present a uniform appearance. It is not acceptable for some crew to be wearing/not wearing the jacket in isolation.
- It is recommended that staff ask their dry cleaner to place metal foil or plastic button protectors over the buttons on their jackets to maintain their appearance.

■ *British Airways provides staff with a uniform guide*
(*Source:* British Airways, Uniform Wearer Standards. Reprinted with kind permission)

Personal hygiene

Good personal hygiene is essential. Take regular showers or baths. Use deodorants and perfumes appropriately. Make sure your teeth are clean and your breath smells fresh. You may be working in difficult environments, for example, in dusty streets, high temperatures or crowded aircraft cabins, so it is a good idea to take hygiene products with you to use throughout the day.

Body language

Always make sure your body language gives a positive and confident message. A list of body language dos and don'ts is given in the table below.

Body language Dos and Don'ts

✔ DO	✗ DON'T
Lean forward slightly when listening to someone	Stand with your arms folded
Have a ready smile to use at appropriate moments	Place your hands in your pockets
Incline your head to the side to show you are interested	Chew gum
Use appropriate hand gestures	Fiddle with articles like pens, loose change or clothing

Attitude and behaviour

You owe it to your customers, your colleagues, your organisation and yourself to have a positive attitude and behave appropriately. You want people to value and like you. A negative attitude will affect the way that you communicate. Have a positive attitude – it feels so much better!

Ways of measuring customer service

In order to assess the quality of customer service provided, organisations must:

- discover what their customers consider important when they are assessing customer service, so that they know what to measure
- monitor their customer service to ensure that it is both what the customers want and to the level they want it
- encourage feedback from their customers, otherwise they will not learn what has gone wrong and will not get the chance to put it right, so it will keep going wrong.

■ *Typical criteria for assessing customer service*

Gaining feedback

There are informal ways to gain feedback, like having conversations with customers while they are with you or phoning them when they return home, as some travel agents and hotels do.

There are also more formal market research methods. The most common is the customer service questionnaire; this might be distributed during the flight, placed at the exit to the tourist attraction or left in the hotel room. Questionnaires give feedback on how the organisation is doing and also show customers that the organisation cares about them. Kuoni Travel is one example of an organisation which includes questionnaires on its website. (A link to this website has been made available at www.heinemann.co.uk/hotlinks. Enter the express code 2196P.) Once you have accessed the website, click on *Site Map*, then under 'Legal' select *Post Holiday Questionnaires*. Others, like airlines, use market researchers to interview customers as soon as their journey has ended, while their views about the holiday are still fresh in their minds.

When compiling a questionnaire, the outline criteria need to be broken down into specific detail to enable decisions to be made on *what* is to be measured and *how*. For example, cleanliness might include cleanliness of hotel bedrooms; measures might include waste bins empty, carpet clean, windows and mirrors mark-free, facilities replenished. These could be measured by observation. (You will learn more about this subject in *Unit 5: Exploring Marketing in Travel and Tourism*.)

SUNSHINE HOTELS

GUEST SATISFACTION SURVEY

Please rate the following hotel services/facilities:
(5 = excellent, 1 = poor)

1. Hotel lobby

a. Cleanliness	5☐	4☐	3☐	2☐	1☐
b. Attractiveness	5☐	4☐	3☐	2☐	1☐
c. Availability of staff	5☐	4☐	3☐	2☐	1☐
d. Efficiency of check-in to your room	5☐	4☐	3☐	2☐	1☐

2. Your room

a. Cleanliness	5☐	4☐	3☐	2☐	1☐
b. Attractiveness	5☐	4☐	3☐	2☐	1☐
c. Condition of furniture	5☐	4☐	3☐	2☐	1☐
d. Equipment provided (tv, radio, trouser press)	5☐	4☐	3☐	2☐	1☐
e. Lighting	5☐	4☐	3☐	2☐	1☐
f. Condition/cleanliness of bathroom	5☐	4☐	3☐	2☐	1☐
g. Room service and mini bar facilities	5☐	4☐	3☐	2☐	1☐

3. Hotel restaurant

a. Cleanliness	5☐	4☐	3☐	2☐	1☐
b. Attractiveness	5☐	4☐	3☐	2☐	1☐
c. Quality of food	5☐	4☐	3☐	2☐	1☐
d. Range of dishes provided	5☐	4☐	3☐	2☐	1☐

4. Hotel staff

a. Friendliness of staff	5☐	4☐	3☐	2☐	1☐
b. Helpfulness of staff	5☐	4☐	3☐	2☐	1☐
c. Availability of staff	5☐	4☐	3☐	2☐	1☐
d. Promptness of staff in attending to your needs	5☐	4☐	3☐	2☐	1☐

How satisfied were you with your stay at this hotel? (5 = very satisfied, 1 = not at all satisfied)	5☐	4☐	3☐	2☐	1☐

Do you believe our services offered value for money?	Yes ☐	No ☐
Would you stay with us again?	Yes ☐	No ☐
Would you recommend us to others?	Yes ☐	No ☐

■ *A guest satisfaction survey*

Quality and quantity of information

Organisations must check that the correct quality and quantity of information is provided. Examples include:

- hotels that train staff in local knowledge and provide information on local tourist attractions and events
- tour operators that provide essential information regarding customers' inclusive holidays but also supplementary information about the destination, etc., perhaps verbally, in writing or as a video
- holiday representatives who hold briefing meetings with clients after they arrive at the hotel.

Timing of service and information provision

Organisations must ensure that good-quality service and information is provided at the right time. For instance, airport operator BAA needs passengers to know what items are forbidden in cabin baggage. To ensure passengers know this before they pack, it communicates such information through its website and newspaper advertisements. Other organisations may need to ensure that their customers receive notification of any changes to their inclusive holiday sufficiently well in advance, or that delayed passengers are given refreshments at appropriate times.

Appearance of the environment

Organisations must monitor the appearance of the work environment. If you arrived at a hotel where the reception area had flaking paint, an 'out of order' sign on the lift, dirty glasses on a table and last week's newspapers on a shelf, you would probably want to leave as quickly as possible.

Being proactive and responsive

Excellent customer service depends upon being proactive – taking action before the customer asks for it. Watch good shop assistants, cabin crew and waiters – they constantly scan their area, looking for clues that a customer needs attention and then checking with the customers that their needs have been met.

On a larger scale, organisations must show that potential changes in the business environment have been anticipated and ways to overcome or take advantage of them are planned. Customer service is always changing. As the public becomes more sophisticated, has higher disposable incomes and receives 'better' customer service, so it will change its opinion of what excellent customer service is.

To demonstrate reactivity, organisations must create ways to respond to customer and staff comments and ideas, and implement changes as a result.

Training

Organisations should review induction and refresher training, including product, technical and customer service training, to ensure employees can give superb customer service.

Key points

Good organisations:

- anticipate and recognise customers' needs
- provide timely and quality information and service
- ensure the working environment looks good
- are responsive and proactive
- train staff
- gain and act upon performance feedback.

Practice assessment activity

Levels P3/P4/M2

Work on this activity in pairs. Choose two organisations in different parts of the travel and tourism industry. Make a presentation to your group:

P a) describing the communication and presentation skills and techniques those organisations use (P3) 

M b) explaining how those skills and techniques enhance the customer service provided (M2)

P c) describing the ways they do, or could, measure customer service in their organisations (P4). 

2.4 Demonstrate customer services skills and techniques in travel and tourism situations

This section covers:

- customer disposition
- location
- situations.

Customer disposition

A wide variety of customer service situations require skills, techniques and initiative, often in unplanned, fast-moving conditions. Customers will have a range of experiences which affect their moods and attitudes. Great, if they are happy – work with them to keep them that way! Unfortunately, some customers may have different dispositions, so how best to manage the situation?

Aggressive customers

Customers may become angry because something has gone wrong or because they are in a situation which they find frightening or worrying. Anger can turn to aggression, which needs a calm but firm response. Stay in control and get assistance if necessary. If other customers see that staff are in control and looking after the interests of all the customers, they will be more likely to support the staff.

Exceptionally, a customer may behave very aggressively, in an environment which makes the situation very distressing for others and potentially unsafe. Some organisations give advance warning to customers of the potential consequences of such behaviour. British Airways has developed a policy and statement entitled 'Zero tolerance on disruptive behaviour', specifying what action BA will take in the event of a passenger disrupting a flight.

Customers with complaints

However hard you and your organisation try, things will occasionally not be to the liking of the customer. Some customers are less able to handle unexpected situations than others, and they may turn their concerns into complaints. Few people like dealing with complaints but by having the right attitude and using the right skills and techniques, the customer can be satisfied, which will make you feel great. Surveys show that a customer who has been handled well after something has gone wrong can become the most loyal of customers.

Do not take complaints personally. Hopefully, the customer is complaining about a situation rather than about you. However, you represent the organisation with which the customer is dissatisfied, therefore you have to take ownership of resolving the problem.

Dealing with complaints

Adopt a friendly, helpful but assertive manner. Being assertive means explaining your position while respecting the other person's feelings and situation. It enables you both to feel OK and valued.

Initially, the customer will be climbing the 'anger mountain', pouring out to you what went wrong and how appalling your organisation is. It is important to stay quiet at this stage. If you try to interrupt or give reasons or excuses why something happened, the anger mountain is likely to keep growing and the customer will continue to complain angrily, and perhaps heighten his or her demands.

■ *The anger mountain*

Indicate you are listening by your body language, for example, nodding and the occasional 'Ah-ha' or 'I see'. Wait until the customer reaches the top of the anger mountain. By doing so, you will have allowed him or her the opportunity to tell you want went wrong, and to calm down.

Then it is your time to speak. Apologise and make it clear that you aim to find a solution. Ask questions; this demonstrates that you have been listening and also gives you the opportunity to get the detail you need, for example, 'You told me you gave your passport to the passenger agent. Can you tell me at which desk they were sitting?' Put yourself in the customer's shoes. That will help you to understand how he or she feels and to understand how the situation may have arisen.

By now you will have gained most of the information you need so that you can investigate and resolve the situation. Once satisfied that you have the best solution, offer it in a positive fashion to the customer. It can help if you give him or her a choice as this shows that you are trying to meet the customer's needs. It also moves the customer away from thinking about what went wrong to thinking about what choice to make.

If further investigation is needed, take a contact for the customer, so that your organisation can respond later. Make sure that whatever went wrong does not happen again, either to this customer or any other. For example, if a rail passenger complains that a wheelchair is not available at the departure station, tell the staff at the destination so that the customer does not have any further problems, and tell your manager so that he or she can ensure it does not happen to anyone else.

Distressed or concerned customers

Dealing with distressed or concerned customers requires a calm approach, with patience, empathy and gentle questioning to establish what is causing the distress or concern, so that the problem can be resolved.

Section 2.2, on the needs of different types of customers, identified techniques to assist other customers, for example, those in groups or with special needs (see pages 58–65).

Location

Indoors or outdoors?

Different styles of customer service may be required, depending upon whether it is being given indoors or outdoors. For example, a tour guide in a historic house can talk quietly, and conversation between the guide and the visitors is easy. Video displays and hand-held audio guides often supplement the guide. Outdoors, acoustics are generally not so good so the guide must draw the customers close and speak very clearly. If possible, some information can be given in the hotel or on the coach before arriving at the destination.

Crowds and noise

Crowded and noisy environments like airports and railway stations can be a problem for transportation organisations. When there is disruption, passengers sometimes complain that 'it was chaotic and no information was given to us'. That is often because the situation is still evolving and uncertain, but also because face-to-face communication is very limited given the numbers of customers involved. Therefore, there has to be heavy reliance upon display screens and public address announcements, although customers tend to want personal assurance from a staff member that all their concerns have been addressed. Patience wears thin and staff must draw upon their communication skills and initiative to minimise difficulties for the customers. It is important to identify and assist those who are finding the situation particularly difficult, for example, the parent with a baby or other special needs passengers.

Activity

Visit your local airport, ferry terminal, railway station or coach station. Look for customer service communication methods which are:

- face to face with staff
- using public address systems
- using customer self-help equipment
- display screens
- leaflets
- notice boards
- signs and symbols
- other methods.

List each method and note what purpose it is serving. On your return, discuss your findings with your group.

Other factors affected by location

Location doesn't only affect communication, it can also affect how formal or informal a situation might be; how clean the area is; or how busy it is, all of which may affect the type and level of customer service.

Situations

Some situations may be familiar and the customers' queries are easily resolved. Sometimes they can be more unusual or difficult, and initiative will be needed. In this unit you have learned how to give good customer service when handling:

- complaints
- selling situations
- customers needing advice and assistance.

Customers may ask a train operator employee the time of the next train; a travel agent for advice on what excursion to take; an airline passenger agent for help to get a message to a relative; a holiday representative for assistance with an elderly friend. In each case, the customer expects the employee to provide an accurate, honest, knowledgeable and helpful response. Staff should be prepared for the most frequent questions and know where to find the answers to the more unusual. If you are asked a question and do not know the answer, don't guess – ask a colleague or manager.

Problems

Customers' problems are very varied. Some staff give excuses for not helping customers, either because they do not want to bother or because they are not using their initiative. Don't be part of the problem, be part of the solution! It is your job to solve problems. Respond in a positive, interested and helpful manner.

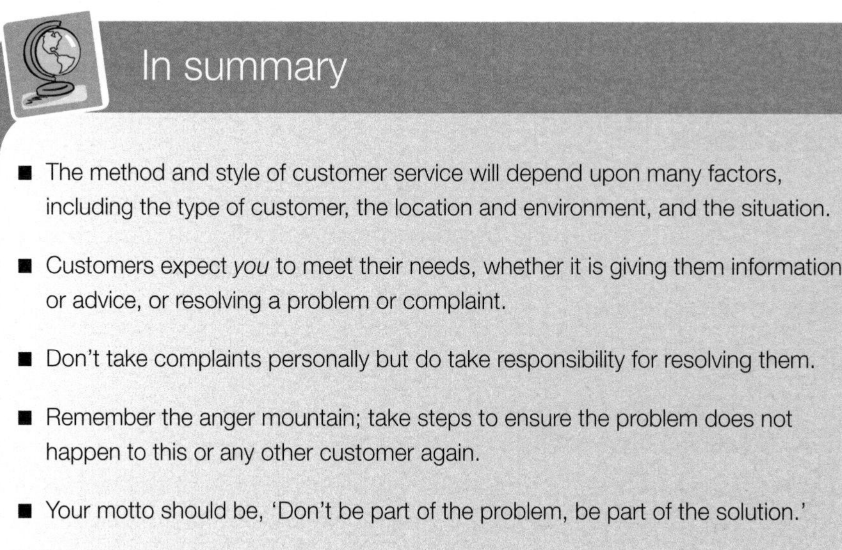

In summary

- The method and style of customer service will depend upon many factors, including the type of customer, the location and environment, and the situation.
- Customers expect *you* to meet their needs, whether it is giving them information or advice, or resolving a problem or complaint.
- Don't take complaints personally but do take responsibility for resolving them.
- Remember the anger mountain; take steps to ensure the problem does not happen to this or any other customer again.
- Your motto should be, 'Don't be part of the problem, be part of the solution.'

Practice assessment activity

Levels P5/M3/D2

In groups of three, work on the following scenarios:

- an angry client has not got a sea view room, which she says she booked; the hotel has no record of this
- a passenger whose child has got lost in the terminal
- a rail passenger waiting for one of your delayed trains, who wants an alternative way to get to his destination at your cost.

Take it in turns to be the customer, the employee and the observer.

P M **1** Role-play the scenarios using the skills and techniques learned in this unit. The objective is to provide realistic and excellent customer service. (P5/M3)

D **2** After 5–10 minutes, discuss how the scenario was addressed, what skills and techniques worked well, and what could be done to improve the performance. (D2)

Change roles and undertake the next scenario.

Test your knowledge

1. Define ‘customer service’.
2. Create a five-item customer charter for your local train company.
3. Discover what methods passengers on three different airlines can use to check in.
4. Consider three types of hotel clients with different needs. What are those needs? How can the hotel satisfy them?
5. Explain four reasons why people communicate.
6. Think of three occasions from the time a holidaymaker checks in for his or her flight to the time this person arrives at the hotel, when staff may wish to communicate with him or her. What would they want to communicate and how would they do so?
7. Describe the eight stages of selling.
8. Recommend three customer service factors which a cruise line should consider.
9. Give four examples of how location can affect customer service factors.
10. What are the three most powerful points you learned about customer service by studying this unit?

3 UK Travel and Tourism Destinations

Introduction

Imagine you were going on holiday tomorrow in the UK – where would you go? Would you prefer a city with a variety of nightlife, or somewhere where you can mountain-bike through forests?

This unit looks at the location of major tourist destinations in the UK and the ways into different regions – the **gateways**. It also explores the appeal of UK travel and tourism destinations for different types of visitors. If you want to find the ideal destination and to travel around the UK, you will need to know when to find information. This unit looks at how to find information from a variety of sources. You will then be able to plan holidays in the UK to meet different and specific customer needs. You will also be in a really good position to be able to plan your own travel!

How you will be assessed

Unit 3 is assessed internally, so the Centre delivering the qualification will assess you against the criteria. On completion of this unit a learner should:

3.1 know the location of significant UK travel and tourism destinations and gateways

3.2 understand the appeal of UK travel and tourism destinations for different types of visitors
3.3 know how to use sources of information to find out destination and travel information
3.4 be able to plan holidays in the UK to meet specific customer needs.

Assessment grades

The Edexcel Assessment Grid for Unit 3 details the criteria to be met. In general, to gain a Pass (P) you are asked to describe, plan and use appropriate sources of information; to gain a Merit (M) you are asked to analyse and explain; and to gain a Distinction (D) you are also asked to make, and justify, your recommendations.

3.1 Know the location of significant UK travel and tourism destinations and gateways

This section covers:

- UK travel and tourism destinations
- airports
- seaports.

UK travel and tourism destinations

Towns and cities

In order to understand UK travel destinations, you will have to know where they are!

The UK is made up of England, Scotland, Wales and Northern Ireland. Each of these countries has a capital city.

Many of the UK's towns and cities have been around for centuries. They have a wealth of history and heritage in their buildings and traditions.

Towns and cities generally have a range of entertainment such as theatres or cinemas, leisure complexes and museums. Shops may range from unusual individual shops to large shopping malls such as the MetroCentre in Gateshead. These destinations will have easy access via trains or coaches, motorways and even airports, and they will also have a range of accommodation available from guest houses to luxury hotels.

London, England's capital city

More tourists visit London, England's capital city, each year than any other destination in the UK. London continues to be one of the most popular cities for overseas tourists with 11.5 million visitors in 2001. It is easily accessible by air, road and rail. Parts of London have been in existence for nearly 2,000 years and visitors can see centuries of different buildings. London is also the commercial and political centre of the UK with thousands of shops and attractions. Unusually, the UK still has its monarchy, and the royal family is a great attraction for many foreign visitors. Palaces, processions and guardsmen hold a fascination for many tourists of any age!

Other UK towns and cities

However, there are many other historical towns and cities throughout the UK which are significant for a variety of reasons, which include universities, castles or spectacular buildings.

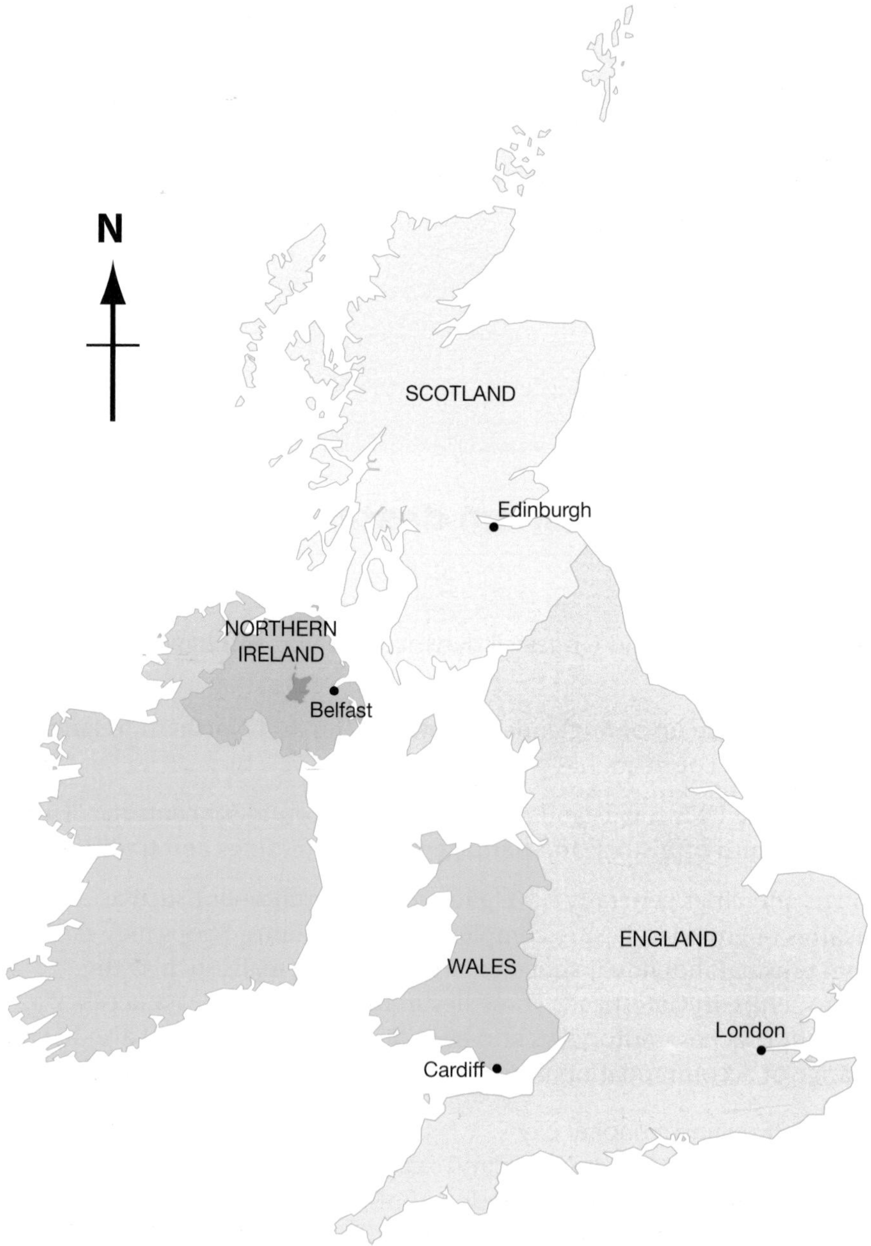

■ *The countries and capital cities of the United Kingdom*

- Spa towns such as Bath, Harrogate and Tunbridge Wells have been the source of healing spa waters for hundreds of years. These were very fashionable in the eighteenth century and even the Romans went to Bath to use the hot springs for spa baths! The mainly Georgian buildings and Roman remains, where the rich and famous went to bathe in the baths and springs, are still very popular with tourists today.
- Oxford, also known as the City of Dreaming Spires, is famous for its university. For over 800 years it has been a home to royalty, politicians and scholars, and since the ninth century an established

■ *Big Ben and the London Eye are popular destinations for visitors to London*

town, although people are known to have lived in the area for thousands of years. The city is also home to a number of museums, galleries and libraries.

- During the last decade, Glasgow has enjoyed steady growth in visitor numbers. In 2003, UK tourists took 2.8 million trips per year to Glasgow. Glasgow has over 20 museums and galleries, each with its own individual collection and events programme, and all with free admission. In 1990, Glasgow was designated the European City of Culture. Today, trips to Glasgow represent around 16 per cent of all UK trips taken to Scotland.

Cultural and historic towns

The UK has always been associated with culture and art. Its writers include Jane Austen, William Shakespeare, William Wordsworth and J.K. Rowling, and Oxford is home to the oldest university in the world. The mix of culture, monarchy and politics has made many areas of the UK historic centres of interest.

- Stratford-upon-Avon is situated in the heart of the English Midlands. A market town dating back to medieval times, Stratford is today most famous as the birthplace of the Elizabethan playwright William Shakespeare (1564–1616).
- Nottingham, the city of 'Robin Hood', offers tourists the chance to follow in the footsteps of this English hero with a trail around the city.
- Edinburgh, the capital of Scotland, is world famous for its castle, university, art and architecture.

Case studies

York

■ *Screen grab from the Jorvik Museum website* (*Source*: Reprinted with the kind permission of York Archaeology and VIPS)

York is the county town of Yorkshire, in the vale of York, at the confluence of two rivers, the Ouse and the Fosse. There has been a city here for thousands of years – the Romans had their settlement of Eboracum and the Vikings built Jorvik on its ruins. The medieval city of York can still be seen in the 'snickleways' (alleys) and 'bars' (gateways) in the Roman-based walls.

Thousands of visitors come to York every year for its history and heritage. The Jorvik Museum can take you back in time to AD 975, on a ride through the sights and smells of the excavated Viking town. This was where the famous York Helmet was found, one of the finest eighth-century Anglo-Saxon helmets discovered in the UK. (You can find out more about The Jorvik Viking Centre by visiting their website, which you can access by going to www.heinemann.co.uk/hotlinks and entering the express code 2196P.)

There are many other heritage attractions in the city such as Clifford's Tower and the Castle Museum, as well as the beautiful York Minster (cathedral). Families can enjoy a trip to the Railway Museum or a boat trip along the river.

There are also many bars and restaurants as well as clubs, and the university and colleges ensure that there is plenty for young people to do as well. There are also individual shops as well as the usual range of department stores. A visit to the tea rooms is a treat not to be missed!

1 List four attractions in York and add who you think would be interested in visiting each of them; for example, children, young people or couples, etc.

2 Locate York on a map and draw in:
- the nearest airport (Leeds/Bradford)
- the main roads to York
- the railway lines to London and Edinburgh.

Activity

Using a travel atlas:

1. *Mark the above towns (see pages 93–96) on a blank map and draw an appropriate symbol for them, such as a castle.*
2. *Then research at least three other tourist towns and find out why people go there. Mark them on the blank map with a suitable symbol.*

Save your map for future activities – you might like to use it again!

Coastal areas

As an island, Britain has thousands of miles of coastline. The National Trust protects over 600 miles (965 km) of coast, keeping it accessible to the public and in its natural state. Thousands of visitors each year walk along long-distance trails, such as the South West Coastal Path.

Seaside resorts

Seaside resorts vary from small villages in coves, such as Porthcurno in Cornwall, to large towns with miles of flat sandy beaches such as Torquay on the English Riviera. There are traditional 'bucket and spade' resorts with piers and candyfloss, crazy golf and arcade games when it rains. Families visit seaside resorts year after year as children can spend hours making sandcastles and paddling in the waves. Visitors find the ever-changing sea relaxing and walks along the 'promenade' can be exhilarating, even in winter.

Activity

Research three more seaside resorts and put them on a blank map.

Talking point

In groups, discuss the UK seaside resorts you have visited and put them on the map.

However, resorts in England find it difficult to compete with the sun of the Mediterranean, so they have developed other ways to encourage tourists. For example, Blackpool has its casinos and illuminations as well as the Pleasure Beach theme park, and Bognor has its 'Birdman' competition to see who can fly furthest from the (broken) pier!

Examples of seaside resorts include:

- Brighton – a sophisticated multi-cultural resort with pebble beaches and conference facilities
- Llandudno – a traditional Welsh resort with a wide sandy bay backed by hills
- Ayr – a Scottish resort, known for its harbour, race course and shopping facilities.

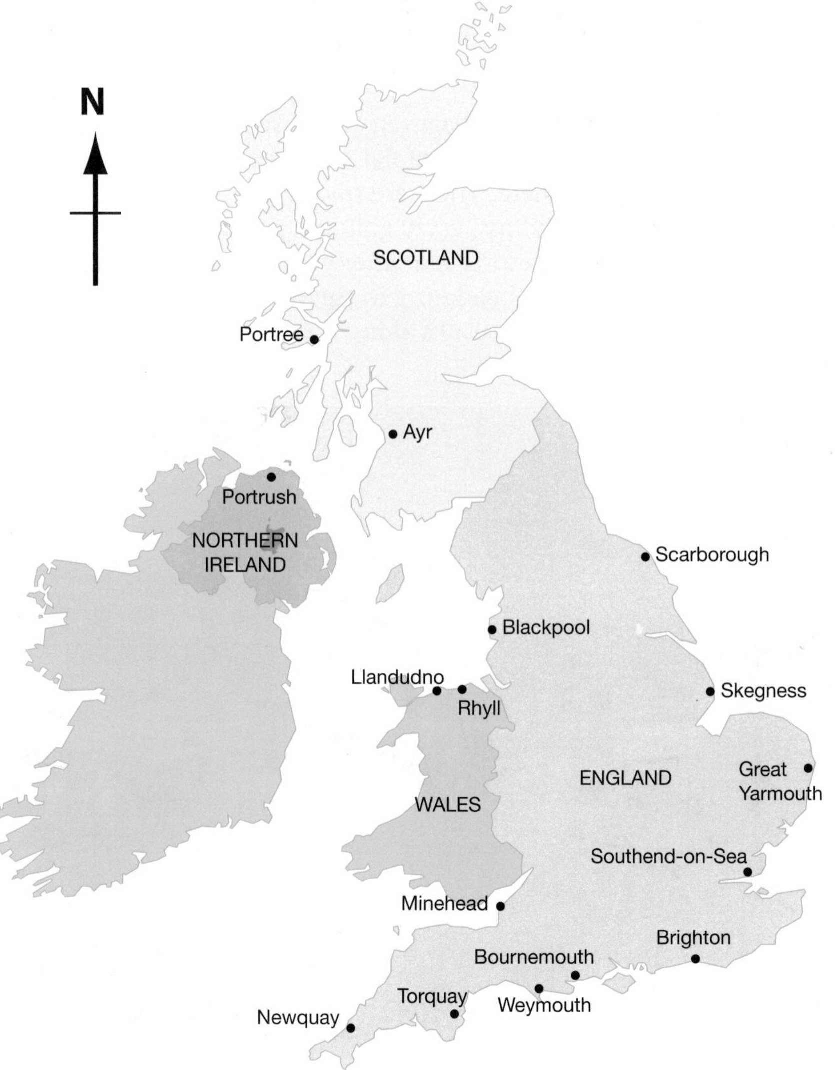

■ *Key seaside resorts of the United Kingdom*

The British countryside

The countryside of the UK is varied and can provide activities for all ages and tastes. There are imposing mountains, such as the Scottish Highlands with its ski resorts; there are rolling hills such as the Cotswolds; there are peat marshes, such as Romney Marsh. Visitors come to 'get away from it all' and to pursue leisure activities such as horse riding and hiking.

National parks

The UK is densely populated and guards its countryside areas against development. One of the most effective ways of ensuring that underdeveloped areas remain that way is the National Park System. There are nine National Parks in England, three in Wales and two in Scotland. Much of the land is still privately owned, but it is protected by legislation against unsuitable building projects, the use of insecticides, etc. The Parks are also required to encourage visitors so that everyone may enjoy the beautiful scenery.

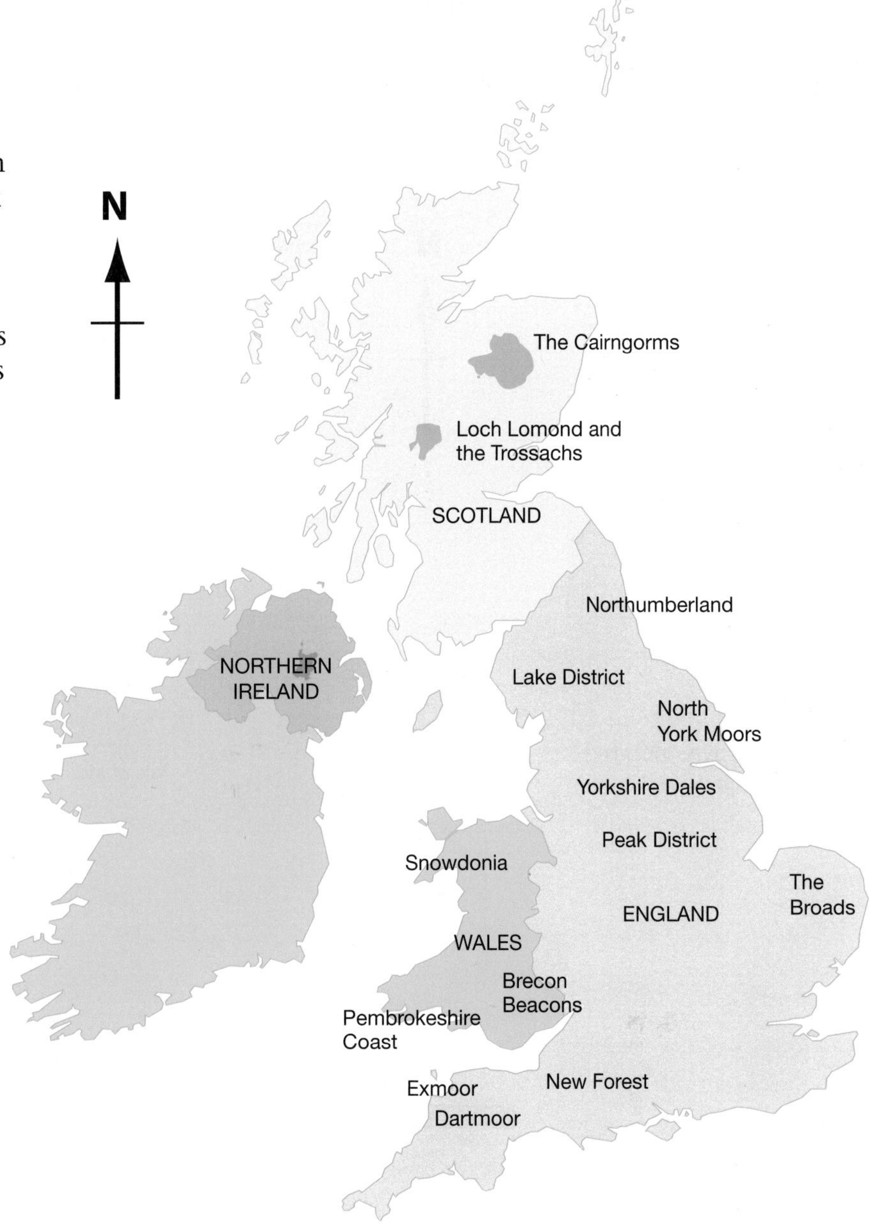

■ *The National Parks of England, Wales and Scotland*

Activity

1. *Research at least one countryside or coastal area and locate it on your map.*
2. *In pairs, produce posters advertising the activities that can be done in these areas. Make them as exciting as possible, including all the information that visitors would need to know.*

Key points

Tourism destinations in the UK include:

- towns and cities
- seaside resorts
- spa towns
- the countryside, including the National Parks.

The UK's islands

Because the United Kingdom is made up of islands, there are also many off-shore islands which are loved by visitors. The sea has always had a special draw for visitors and the fact that islands are only accessible by crossing water makes it more of an adventure!

Examples of islands as tourist destinations include:

- Isles of Scilly: found off the coast of Cornwall and reached by sea or helicopter from Penzance; they are known for their balmy climate and unspoilt scenery.

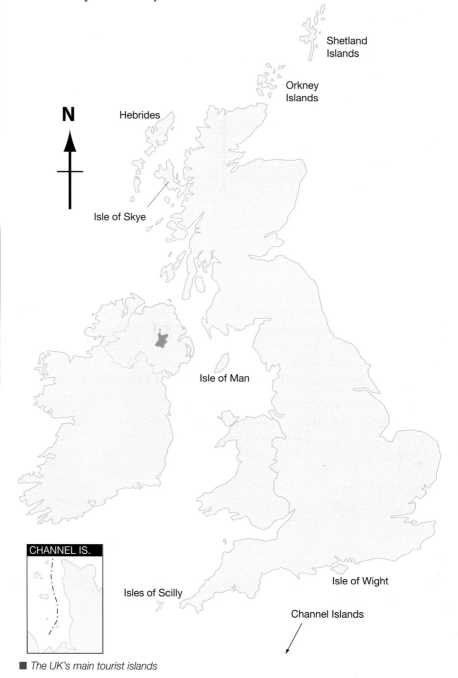

The UK's main tourist islands

- Isle of Skye: this Scottish island is known for its link with Bonnie Prince Charlie (1720–88) and is loved for its wild scenery.
- Isle of Man: this island in the Irish Sea is host to the TT motorbike races. It has an individual atmosphere and is proud of its semi-independence.
- Channel Islands: close to France; they have a mild climate and provide a tax haven; home to TV's *Bergerac*.

In summary

- Tourism in the UK is very important – visitors come from all over the world, as well as different parts of Britain.
- People visit towns and cities for their facilities and shops, buildings and heritage. Spa towns are popular for their architecture and heritage.
- The seaside is popular for traditional 'bucket and spade' holidays as well as entertainment and leisure facilities.
- People visit the countryside for leisure and sporting activities as well as to enjoy the beautiful scenery.

Airports

Every capital city and many major cities in the UK have airports, most of them classed as 'International' airports where visitors can officially enter the country. London alone has five airports – Heathrow, Gatwick, Stansted, Luton and London City. Some airports are positioned so they can serve a whole area, such as Leeds/Bradford or East Midlands.

All airports are allocated three-letter codes which are used internationally. The larger airports have codes which are easily identifiable – smaller ones tend to have less easily recognised codes. Examples include:

- London Heathrow – LHR
- London Gatwick – LGW
- Manchester – MAN
- Belfast – BFS

These codes are used on airline tickets and baggage labels. Next time you go to an airport, look at the codes on your documents.

Activity

Research the following airport codes:

- STN
- EDI
- ABZ

■ *The UK's main airports*

Seaports

Because the UK is a collection of islands, travel by sea is also important. In general:

- ports on the south coast of England have ferry crossings to France, the Channel Islands and Spain
- the west coast of the UK has crossings to Ireland
- the east coast of the UK has crossings to the Netherlands and Scandinavia.

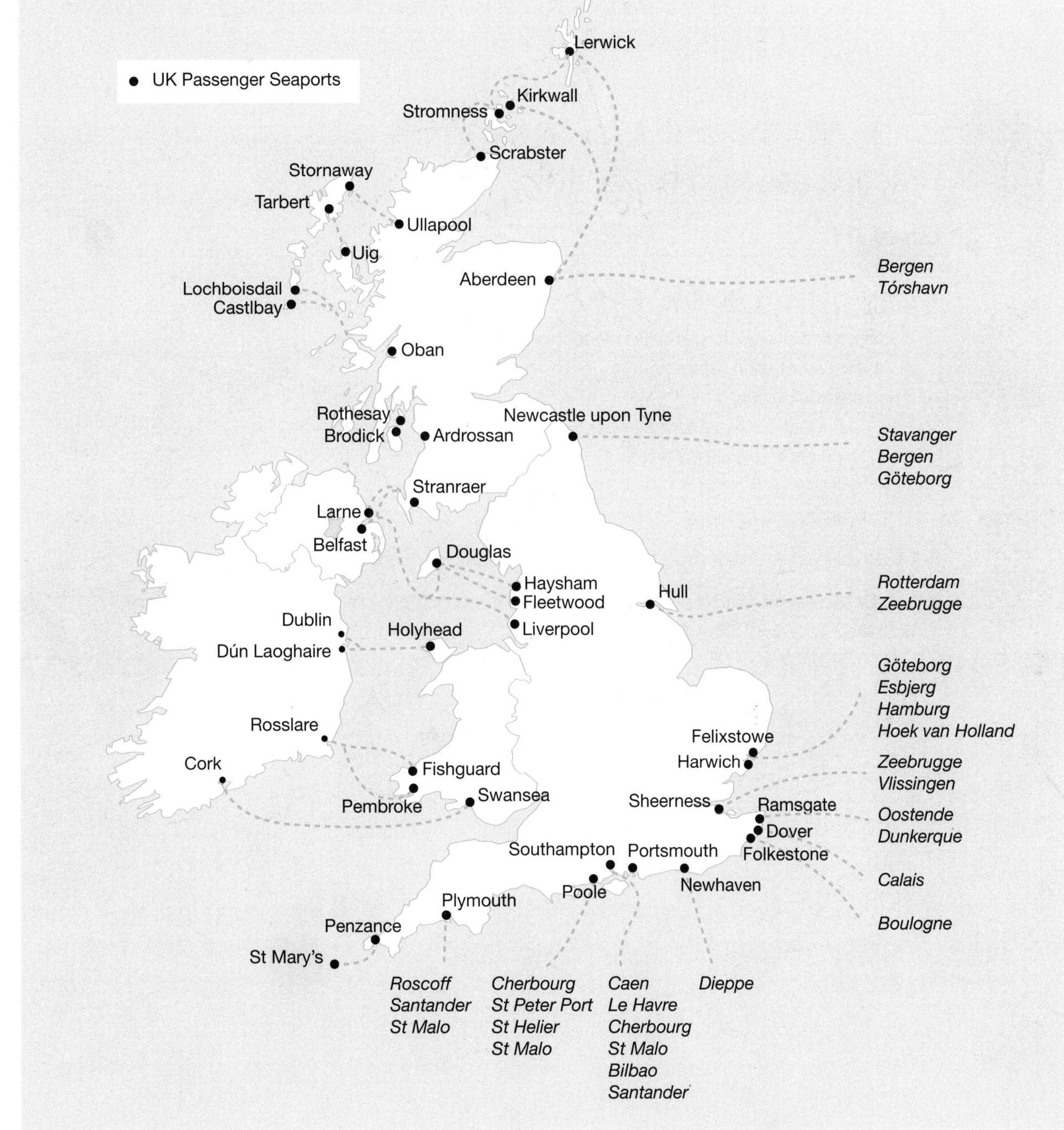

■ *The UK's main seaports and sea routes*

Activity

In groups, draw a poster for one of the sea crossing areas:

- UK to Ireland (Northern and Eire)
- UK to France
- UK to Netherlands and Scandinavia.

You could use a Travel Atlas or ferry timetables and brochures. You could look at Stena Line, SeaFrance, Brittany Ferries or Caledonian McBrayne.

Practice assessment activity

Level P1

1 Draw a large blank map of the UK then locate and mark:

a) the capital cities of England, Scotland, Northern Ireland and Wales
b) at least six of each category:
- seaside resorts
- cultural or historical towns or cities
- countryside or coastal areas
- spa towns
- islands.

2 Locate at least six major airports and mark their three-letter codes.

3 Locate six seaports and draw a passenger route from each one; ensure you include routes to both the Republic of Ireland and Europe.

3.2 Understand the appeal of UK travel and tourism destinations for different types of visitors

This section covers:

- range of destinations and different types of visitor
- visitor attractions
- topography
- facilities
- arts, entertainment and sightseeing
- transport links.

Range of destinations and different types of visitor

Earlier in this unit you have seen a few examples of why visitors from within the UK (domestic visitors) or from other countries (international visitors) travel to different destinations. Remember they could be going to towns or cities, a seaside resort or a countryside area. People will choose to go to different places because they want different things from their trip.

There are different kinds of visitor, and each of them will look for different reasons to choose the UK as their holiday destination.

The reasons for choosing a holiday are as individual as people: one visitor's ideal may be totally wrong for another person. Each one is different – celebrate the differences!

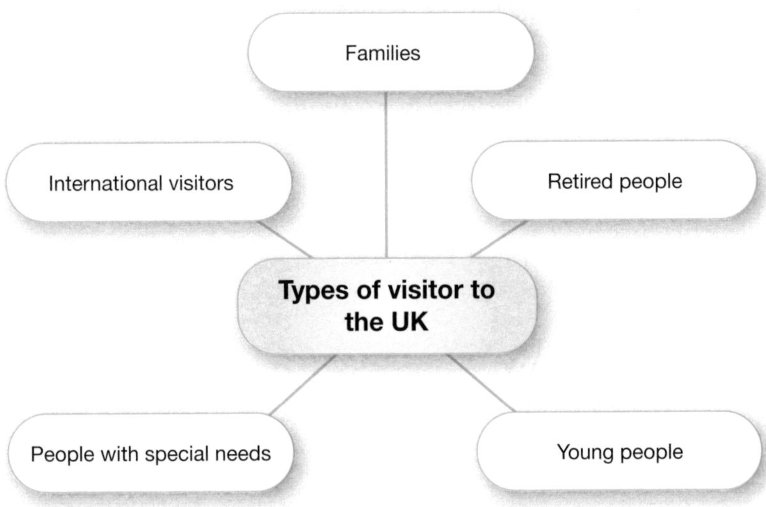

Families

Families will principally need to keep the children happy and occupied while providing relief for adults! Some families will look at destinations which provide activities on-site or within the price, such as Butlins or Haven holidays. Destinations such as Center Parcs provide a safe environment for participating in sporting activities, and an all-year-round swimming zone. If the weather is good, then families might be happy making sandcastles on a safe beach.

Talking point

In groups, take one of the types of visitor. Using brochures, leaflets and guides, design a collage of destinations and attractions suitable for the specific group of visitors you have chosen.

Retired people

Retired people may also be looking for activities with other similar people; ballroom dancing weekends or painting holidays are popular. Sometimes older people may simply want the opportunity to sightsee in peace!

Young people

Young people usually like to have plenty of opportunity to meet others so look for clubs, bars and other places to meet. They may well want to have activities during the day in order to socialise.

People with special needs

The special needs may be physical or otherwise. Visitors may be wheelchair users, or hearing or sight impaired. Reasonable adjustments have to be made in order to accommodate these needs, except where the provision of ramps, etc. would affect a protected building.

Overseas visitors

Overseas visitors may need some help with guiding. The provision of leaflets in foreign languages, multi-language signs or bilingual guides (guides who speak more than one language).

Talking point

Both the National Trust and English Heritage encourage visitors but also aim to preserve land and buildings from destruction. In groups, discuss whether these two aims can co-exist and what can be done to lessen the negative impact of tourism.

Visitor attractions

You have already looked at a number of different reasons why visitors may choose a particular place – one of the main draws is what there is available to do! Visitor attractions can be almost anything people can enjoy looking around or learning more about.

The National Trust and English Heritage

You may think that only older people are interested in historical properties – both the National Trust and English Heritage work hard to encourage visitors of all ages, and provide special activities for children and school parties.

The National Trust

THE NATIONAL TRUST

The National Trust is a huge organisation – it owns more than 700 miles (1,125 kilometres) of coastline including the Giant's Causeway in Antrim, Northern Ireland, and the White Cliffs of Dover in Kent. It has 3.4 million members and owns hundreds of historic houses.

The National Trust's core purpose is 'to look after special places for ever, for everyone'. There are National Trust properties all over England, Wales and Northern Ireland, and there is an equivalent organisation in Scotland (NT Scotland). It is a charity and is therefore dependent on membership fees, entry fees and donations to carry on its work.

1. Look at the National Trust website and find three national properties, one in England, one in Wales and one in Scotland. A link to this website has been made available at www.heinemann.co.uk/hotlinks. Enter the express code 2196P.
2. Again look at the website and search for a property closest to your home. Perhaps you have been there? Discuss with a group why you might want to visit it.
3. What is the aim of the National Trust?
4. How does the National Trust raise funds?

(Logo reprinted with kind permission)

Case studies

English Heritage

ENGLISH HERITAGE

English Heritage is a public body with responsibility for all aspects of protecting and promoting the historic environment. They look after more than 400 historic properties and monuments including Stonehenge, Dover Castle and parts of Hadrian's Wall. They also act as the government's advisor on the historic environment, set standards for conservation and give grants to help other individuals and organisations. They are partly funded by the government and partly through money raised by visitors and other supporters. You can find out more about the work of English Heritage by visiting their website, a link to which has been made available at www.heinemann.co.uk/hotlinks. Enter the express code 2196P.

(Logo reprinted with kind permission)

Activity

What are the theme parks in your local area or the nearest holiday region? Investigate the parks:

- What is the main theme or themes?
- Who are the main customers?

Most theme parks are aimed at older children to teenagers, but many appeal to 'children' who are grandparents!

Theme parks

Theme parks can range from large parks with different themed areas, such as Thorpe Park in Surrey, to parks based around a particular theme, such as Flamingo Land in North Yorkshire. These parks usually have rides and attractions included in the entry price. Some of the rides can be thrilling or frightening, depending on your point of view, and are known as 'white knuckle' rides because of the way riders grip the handlebars!

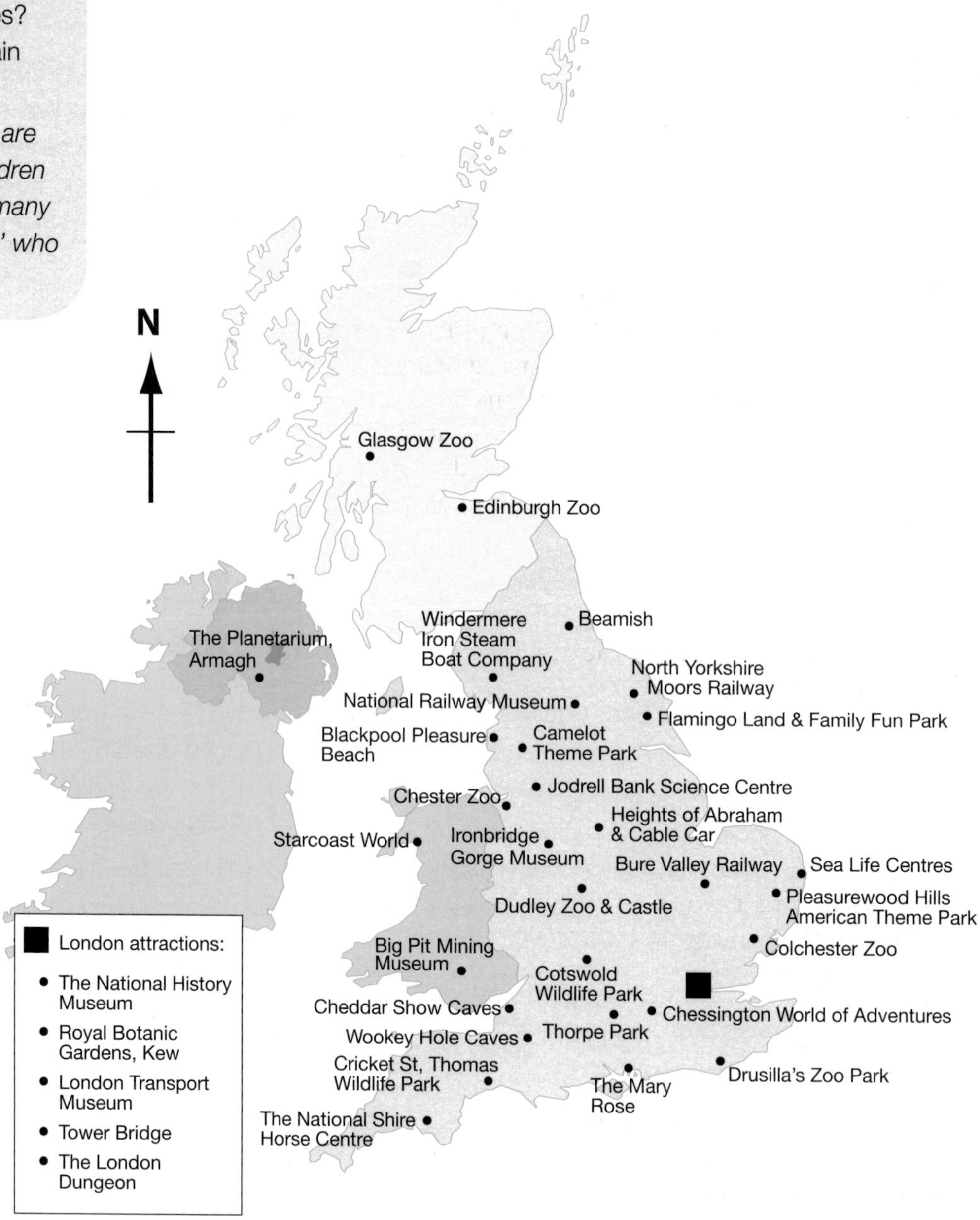

■ *Attractions in the UK*

Museums and heritage sites

Don't think of museums as simply dusty places with things in cupboards! Many modern museums are interactive, using technology to enable special effects such as erupting volcanoes and earthquakes! There are many new museums which have been given Millennium Funding – money provided by the European and UK governments for special projects, to celebrate the millennium; these include Magna near Sheffield, as well as some of the great London museums such as the Science Museum or the Victoria and Albert Museum.

One of Shropshire's top attractions is the Ironbridge Gorge, which is known throughout the world as the birthplace of the Industrial Revolution. Today the area is far from industrial. Although the revolution started here, most of the factories are long gone and the natural beauty of the gorge has been restored. Many visitors are attracted to the Victorian-themed museums operated by the Ironbridge Gorge Museum Trust.

Activity

Using the Star UK website (a link to this website has been made available at www.heinemann.co.uk/hotlinks. Enter the express code 2196P), which provides statistics on tourism in the UK, look at the top museums and the number of visitors they attract. Draw a graph comparing the top ten museums.

Wildlife parks and zoos

There are many attractions which feature animals in the UK, such as Monkeyworld in Dorset or Drusilla's Zoo in East Sussex. Many of these are also concerned about conservation and breeding, as well as just showing the animals off. Some attractions have animals living 'in the wild' in enclosures, such as Longleat Safari Park in Wiltshire. Again, many of these attractions are aimed at families but attract people of all ages, particularly because of their conservation work.

Topography

Not all attractions are man-made in towns and cities! Many places attract visitors because of their natural features, called **topography**. Topography is the shape of the ground's surface such as hills, valleys, plains and slopes.

Mountains and lakes

Some people visit mountainous areas for climbing or skiing. The Grampian Mountains in Scotland are the scene of ski-resorts such as Aviemore in the winter and are popular with mountain climbers in the summer. The Yorkshire Moors are visited because of the opportunity to go fell-walking (hiking in mountainous terrain). Even children can walk up Snowdon in Wales – and could even go up by mountain railway (funicular) if feeling tired!

One of the most visited attractions in the UK are the cruises on Lake Windermere in the Lake District. Not surprisingly this area is known for its lakes – and mountains.

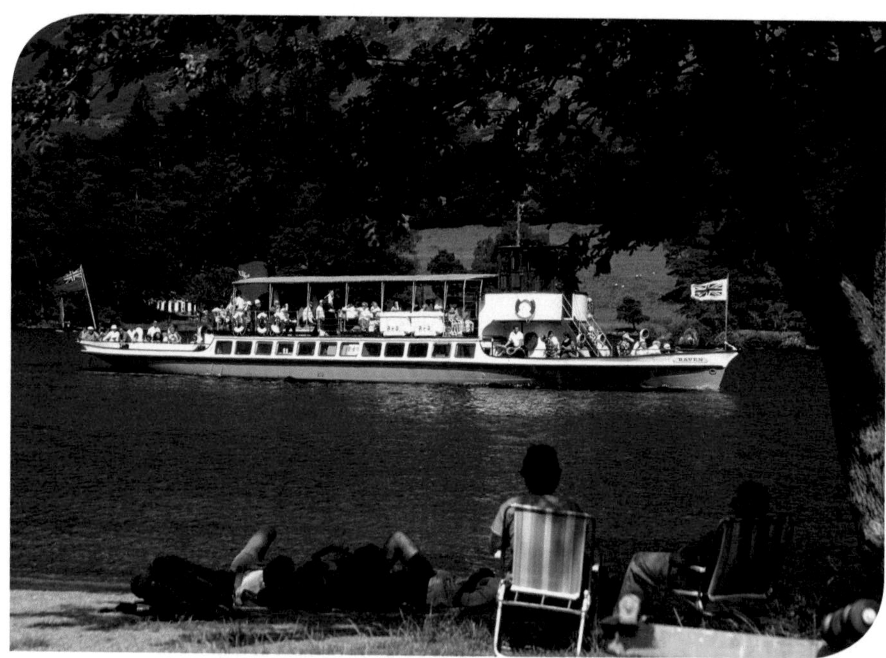

■ *Tourists enjoying the sunshine, both on land and on the water, at Ullswater in the Lake District*

Beaches and rivers

Some areas of the UK are known for their beaches. Blackpool has miles of sand and Holkum beach in Norfolk was used in a film called *The Piano* as an unspoilt area.

Many people like to holiday on rivers as well – boating up the Thames or the Grand Union canal system can be a relaxing holiday. The Norfolk Broads has a whole industry based on the rivers and waterways of East Anglia. Boats of all shapes and sizes can be hired by individuals or large parties.

Talking point

Look at a map of inland waterways and rivers in the UK. In groups, investigate one of the waterways and find out what activities you can do there. Present your findings to the rest of the group.

Activity

Visit the Hoseasons website, a link to which has been made available at www.heinemann.co.uk/hotlinks (enter the express code 2196P), or your local travel agent for a brochure or information on boating holidays in the UK.

1 *Name three areas of the UK where you could take a boating holiday.*
2 *What types of boat could you travel in?*
3 *Why do you think people enjoy waterway holidays?*

Hoseasons

Find a UK boating holiday
Please send me a brochure

Hoseasons
Your freedom – your choice

What are you looking for? Find it How to use the Keyword Search

Boating Holidays in Britain

Hoseasons Boating Holidays in the UK

Information Pages

Win a £1000 holiday Your Email Address Sign me up!
Terms & conditions

Home | Request a brochure | My booking details | About us | Travel Agents | Contact us | Advertise through us

Find a UK boating holiday
Or
Search by brochure code

FREE e-mail update service for the latest news and offers

- Holiday Lodges and Parks in the UK
- Holiday Cottages in the UK
- Holiday Lodges and Parks in Europe
- Villas with pools in Europe
- Boating Holidays In Europe
- Holidays in Ireland

Hoseasons
Your freedom – your choice

Quick Search
Select Holiday Type...
Select a location...
No. in your party...
Apr '06 | 6
No. of nights...
Reset | Search

Romantic Breaks | Special Offers

Explore the beauty of Britain's waterways

From the moment you set off on your boating holiday in your self-drive hire cruiser or traditional narrowboat, onto Britain's vast network of canals, rivers and inland waterways, you're at the helm in more ways than one. That's because you have the freedom to decide where to go, where to stop and what to visit.

Find a UK boating holiday online

Relaxed and unhurried, you have the widest choice of UK holidays and quality boat rentals. You'll have the freedom of long, lazy days cruising through an ever-changing tapestry of unspoilt countryside, abundant wildlife and historic towns and cities in England and Wales. You could be moving slowly through the reeds and flat grazing marshes of the Norfolk Broads, passing riverside cottages and stopping at welcoming inns. Imagine cruising past buttercup-filled meadows on the River Thames. Or navigating up a Scottish Loch, cutting a wake through its dark waters as you head for the friendly shelter of your chosen mooring.

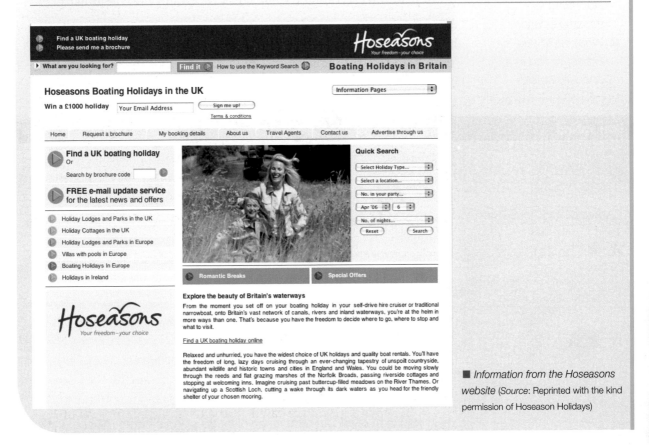

■ *Information from the Hoseasons website* (*Source*: Reprinted with the kind permission of Hoseason Holidays)

Facilities

If you decide you want to visit somewhere in the UK, you are going to need somewhere to stay!

Types of accommodation available

Many tourist destinations provide a variety of accommodation, from bed-and-breakfast places, which might be in a private house, to a large hotel with a variety of bars and restaurants. Many families in particular may want to have the freedom of self-catering and there may be a range of opportunities from converted farmhouses to lighthouses and stables.

- Some people prefer self-catering because of the freedom it allows in terms of meal times – and children particularly may be happier eating familiar food. Self-catering also tends to be cheaper than hotel accommodation initially, although some self-catering is very luxurious.

Don't forget that whatever a customer wants, someone, somewhere usually provides it – at a price!

Over to you

1 *What is the highest star rating for accommodation?*
2 *What could you expect to find in a one-star hotel?*

- Bed and breakfast is often good value for money and particularly suitable for people who are only staying a short time or are touring.
- Hotels usually have many more leisure facilities and encourage guests to use their bars and restaurants. Hotels can range from inexpensive to luxurious accommodation at city or 'country house' hotels.

Rating tourist accommodation

It is very easy to assess the level of quality and service you can expect from hotels and other guest accommodation using the five-star rating system (see below).

Star rating	What it means
☆	Acceptable overall level of quality; adequate provision of furniture, furnishings and fittings. One-star hotels tend to be smaller, privately-owned properties. Accommodation is simple and practical with limited facilities and services.
☆☆	Two-star hotels tend to be small, privately-owned properties, including resort hotels, inns and small commercial hotels. Accommodation offers a good degree of space and convenience. Décor and furnishings may be simple but are well maintained. All bedrooms will have en-suite or private facilities.
☆☆☆	A more formal style of hotel, likely to be larger than one- and two-star hotels, with a greater range of facilities and services. Bedroom accommodation will be spacious and designed for comfort and convenient use, including colour television, telephones, radios and desk/dressing table areas. Public areas will include lounge seating, a restaurant and bar.
☆☆☆☆	More formal service is expected at this level. Accommodation is of a very high standard, offering a wide range of facilities and services. All bedrooms will be designed and furnished for comfort and ease of use, with very good-quality furniture, beds and soft furnishings. All rooms will have en-suite bath and shower facilities. Service will reflect attention to detail and quality. There must be a formal reception and porters' desks with uniformed staff offering a proactive style of service. The restaurant will be open for lunch and dinner seven days per week.
☆☆☆☆☆	Accommodation must be of luxury quality with services to match. There will be spacious bedroom suites and public areas, and a selection of catering options all offering cuisine and service of the highest international quality. An extensive range of facilities will include leisure, retail and conference services. Highly trained and professional staff provide exceptional levels of anticipatory service.

Other facilities

- Camping and caravanning may be available in local fields or in well-organised caravan parks, with a variety of facilities.
- Some areas may have excellent sport and leisure facilities – sailing or bowling, tennis or cycling could all encourage visitors who are looking for something to do at their destination.
- Other people may be content to head for the shops – cities will have a huge selection, whilst there are also out-of-town areas such as the MetroCentre in Gateshead or the Outlet Centre in Swindon.

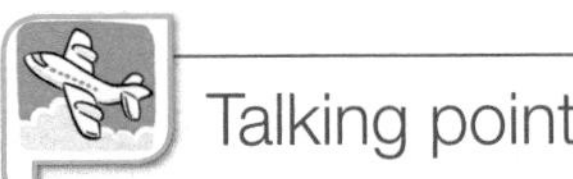

Talking point

In groups, discuss what type of accommodation is available in your area. What services do these offer to guests?

Case studies

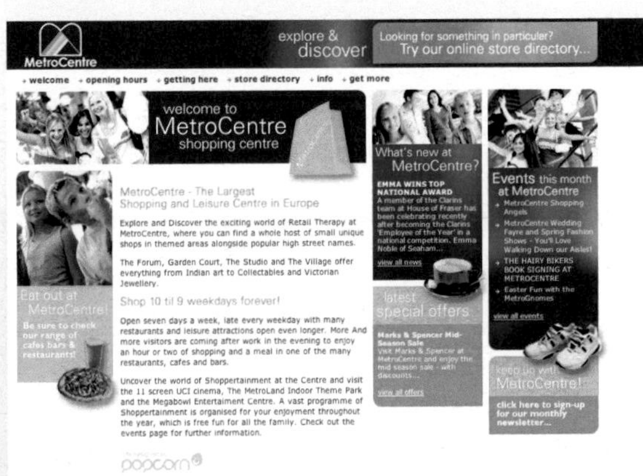

■ *Website for the MetroCentre in Gateshead* (Reprinted with kind permission)

Look at the information about the MetroCentre above and visit their website (a link to this website has been made available at www.heinemann.co.uk/hotlinks. Enter the express code 2196P).

1 Who do you think is MetroCentre's main client group?
2 What facilities are there as well as the shops? How do these encourage a range of clients?

Arts, entertainment and sightseeing

Arts and entertainment

Arts and entertainment can bring in visitors from all over the UK and from many other countries. Think of the Glastonbury music festival (usually noted for its mud!) or the Edinburgh Festival where established acts perform alongside the 'fringe' acts.

London is known worldwide for its theatre district and has world-renowned shows and film premieres. Many UK towns and cities have their own programmes of events, some even have festivals dedicated to art or music or literature, such as the Cheltenham Literature Festival. Glasgow is host to the T-Music Festival each year while other towns may host small niche festivals dedicated to classical music, crafts or literature.

Over to you

Have you visited a large shopping and leisure centre? What did you do there?

Case studies

Liverpool Empire Theatre

The Liverpool Empire Theatre is the largest two-tier theatre in the country and hosts a variety of shows. Located close to the main train station and opposite the impressive St George's Hall, this is one of the city's oldest theatres. A mixed variety of shows include musicals, touring ballet companies and major productions such as *Blood Brothers* and *West Side Story*. It is also the main venue for international and mainstream rock and pop acts. The plush interior is well maintained and a licensed bar is available on the premises. Booking can be made in person, by phone, online or by post.

1 How can you make bookings at the Empire Theatre?

2 Look at a website such as ticketmaster's (a link to this website has been made available at www.heinemann.co.uk/hotlinks. Enter the express code 2196P). What events are happening at the theatre in the next month?

Activity

In pairs, choose a local town or city. Research the theatres, art galleries, exhibitions and local events available. Describe the three top attractions in that location for the next month.

Sightseeing

When you have reached your destination, there are many ways you can get to know it better.

- In many towns and country areas, there are often guided walks led by authorised 'Blue Badge' guides or countryside rangers. These can be very informative and may happen all year round at different times, enabling tourists to see different aspects of an area or location.
- A popular activity is to go on a 'ghost walk' during which visitors are taken on a walk through dark areas of the city as ghostly tales are told (this is often led by someone in a black cloak and a large hat!).
- Another way of seeing a destination is to go on a sightseeing boat trip – many towns and cities next to rivers include such trips, including London, where multilingual commentaries are available.
- Many resorts also have land trains or mini-trains available, often with commentaries, so that tourists can see the sights from the relative comfort of an open-air seat. For example, you can see the grounds of Blenheim Palace in Oxfordshire from its mini railway, and Bournemouth, Weymouth and Swansea are all resorts that operate land trains along the coast.

A land train

In summary

- There are different kinds of visitor, and each of them will have different reasons to choose the UK as their holiday destination.
- Types of visitor to the UK are both domestic and overseas visitors and include families, retired people, young people and people with special needs.
- Popular examples of visitor attractions in the UK are museums and heritage sites, theme parks, wildlife parks and zoos, beaches and National Parks.
- Many tourist destinations provide a variety of accommodation, from bed and breakfast to large hotels and self-catering apartments.
- Other facilities for tourists to the UK include camping and caravanning, sport and leisure facilities, and shopping centres.
- Activities for UK tourists include various forms of arts and entertainment, such as theatre and music festivals, and sightseeing tours.

Transport links

All of the transport systems in the UK (road, rail and sea and airport links) allow visitors to travel easily from one area to another (traffic jams permitting!). There is no use in having wonderful tourist destinations if people can't get there!

Road

Of course, it is important that visitors to the UK are able to get to their destination. Many domestic visitors travel by car, as it is the most convenient, if sometimes frustrating, way to travel. There is a network of motorways throughout the UK, serving many of the main resort areas.

Activity

1. *You need to travel from Birmingham to Penzance. Which roads would you need to travel on?*
2. *You want to travel from Edinburgh to Folkestone – on which roads would you travel?*

■ *UK road network*

Rail

There is also a network of rail routes, often using London and other cities as main hubs. Trains can be a quick and, if booked in advance, a good-value way of travelling.

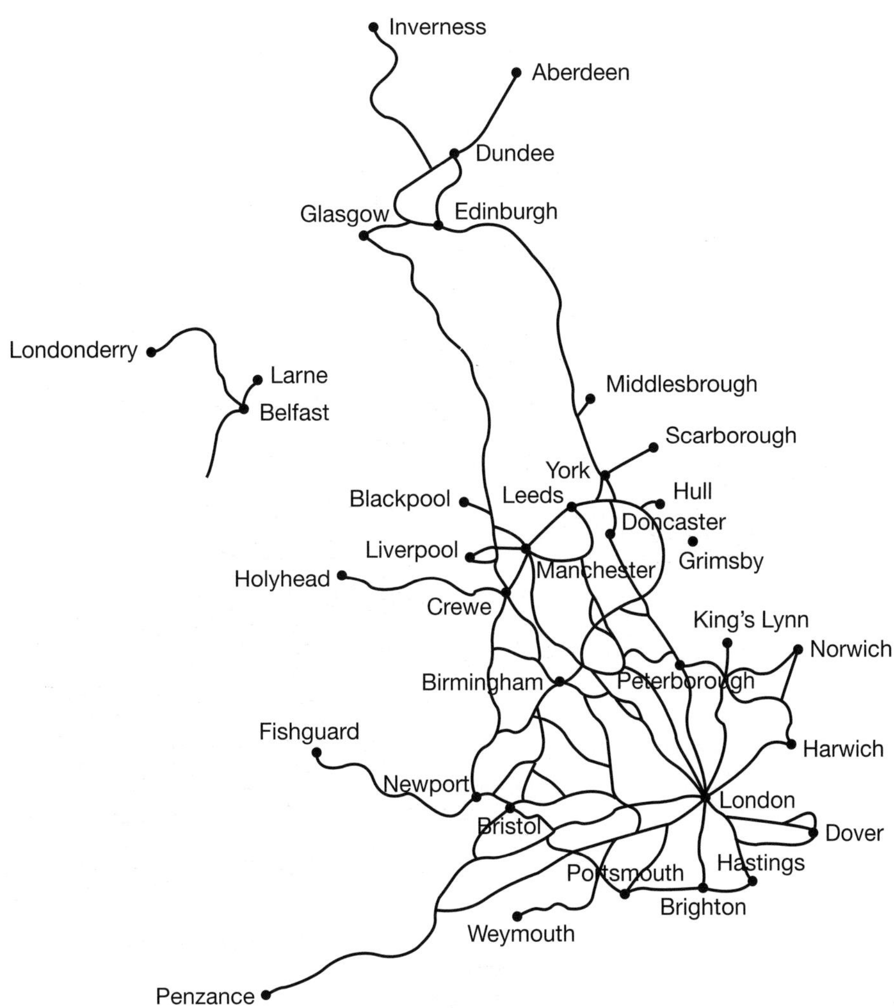

■ *Intercity railway network of the UK*

Sea links

Most of the coastal regions are easily accessible by the rest of Europe and many have special deals advertised abroad. You will see that the motorway system links well with the ports. (For a map of ports and sea links with other countries, see page 103.)

Airport links

Look again at the road and rail maps – you will see that these also link to the airports and major cities. (For a map of airports in the UK, see page 102.)

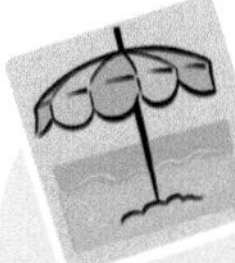

Practice assessment activity

Levels P2/M1/D1

1 Choose three different tourist destinations. These must include a town or city, one seaside resort and one coastal or countryside area (check with your tutor that the chosen destinations are suitable). Describe the appeal of each of these destinations to at least two different types of visitors in terms of:

- attractions
- topography
- customer services
- facilities
- arts and entertainment
- sightseeing
- transport links.

P You may produce a tourist brochure for each destination. (P2) ✓

M **2** For the same three destinations, analyse the appeal of each destination for different types of visitors (families, young people, retired people, inbound tourists and people with special needs). Indicate the extent to which the destinations meet the needs of each visitor type. (M1) ✓✓

D **3** For one of the three destinations you have chosen, recommend ways in which this destination could widen its appeal for different types of visitors. Give reasons for your recommendations. Include as much detail as possible. Write a letter to the tourist committee at the local council giving this information. (D1) ✓✓✓

3.3 Know how to use sources of information to find out destination and travel information

This section covers:

- sources of travel and destination information.

Sources of travel and destination information

Planning journey routes

In order to be able to provide information about the journey route to a UK travel destination, you will need to know how to obtain and read timetables and maps, etc. Maps can be useful – most car drivers will have a set of road maps in the car. You could also use an atlas, particularly a Travel Atlas, which has specific transport maps.

The Internet can be a useful source of information – use search engines, such as Google™, if you are not sure of the website address. The advantage of using the Internet is that the information will be up to

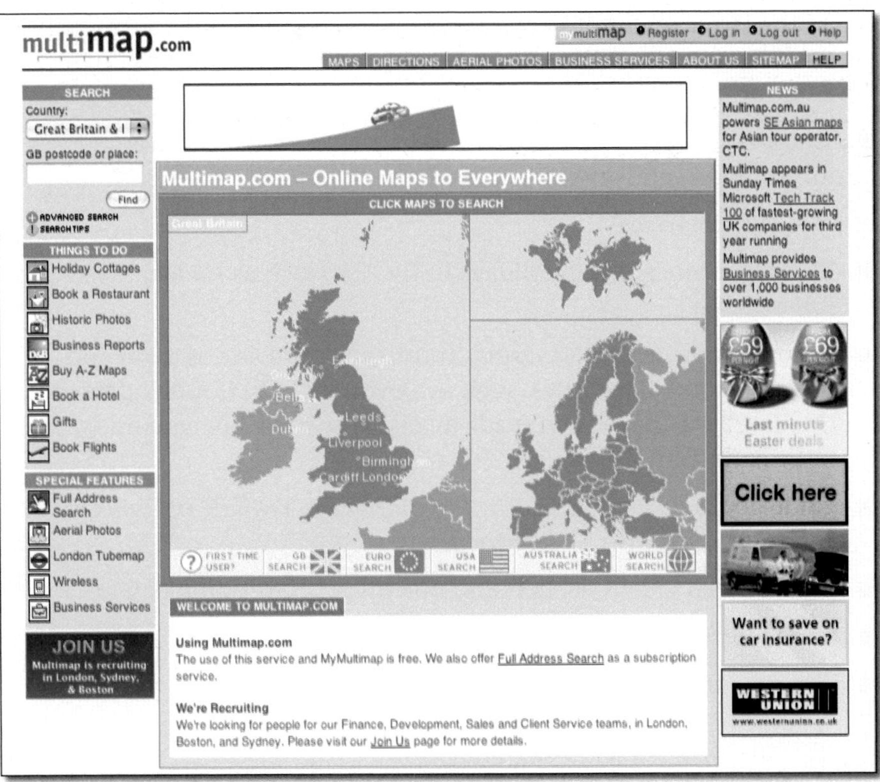

■ *Multimap™ is an Internet site that can help with route planning* (Reprinted with kind permission)

date, although it may sometimes be difficult to obtain. Internet sites such as Streetmap™ or Multimap™ will also help in route planning. Links to these websites have been made available at www.heinemann.co.uk/hotlinks. Enter the express code 2196P.

Activity

Find and use two different sources of information for the following journeys (make sure you make a note of the publication or website address):

- Birmingham to York
- London to Penzance
- Edinburgh to Ayr.

List the distance and route by road, rail and coach for each journey.

Destination information

A great deal of information is available on different UK destinations – after all, they need to market themselves to their visitors! Some sources of information include:

- VisitBritain, the official tourist office for those visiting Britain, funded by the Department of Culture, Media and Sport (a link to this website has been made available at www.heinemann.co.uk/hotlinks by entering the express code 2196P)
- Tourist Information Centres (local ones will probably have information on the whole of the UK)
- holiday brochures
- TV programmes about holidays in the UK (such as *Holiday* and *Wish you were here*)
- regional websites, for example, Tourism South East, or town and borough council websites, such as Devon County Council (links to these websites have been made available at www.heinemann.co.uk/hotlinks by entering the express code 2196P)
- guide books, for example, *The Rough Guide to England* or *Peak District (Ordnance Survey/AA Leisure Guides)*
- promotional videos, leaflets and newspaper travel supplements
- trade journals, for example, *Travel Trade Gazette*
- libraries and other educational resources.

Practice assessment activity

Levels P3/M2

P **1** You have been asked to plan three journeys for a businessman travelling alone and a family of three with a small baby. The journeys are:

- London to Aberdeen by air
- Penzance to Birmingham by rail
- Glasgow to London by coach.

All the journeys are for day time only and during the week. How long will each journey take? Make sure you use at least three different types of information sources and reference them. Keep detailed records of how you found this information. (P3) ✓

M **2** Research the journeys and present your results to your customer. Describe where this information came from and give full details of all aspects of this journey. Provide a detailed schedule of times, dates and costs. (M2) ✓✓

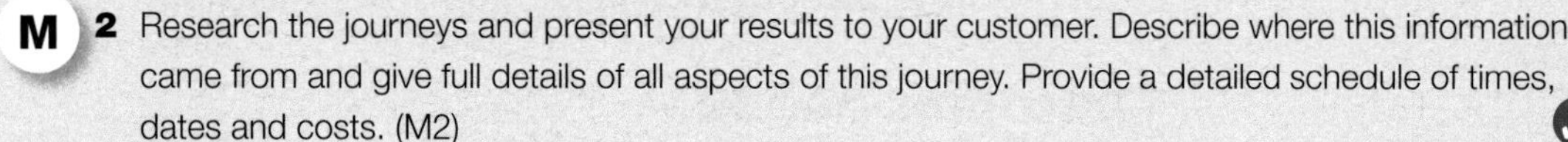

3.4 Plan holidays in the UK to meet specific customer needs

This section covers:

- customer needs
- mode of travel
- accommodation
- things to do.

Now you will be able to bring together all you have learnt so far, to give advice and information based on your own knowledge!

Customer needs

Remember, you have already looked at different kinds of visitors and considered what their needs might be (see the table below and also pages 58–65).

Type of visitor	Possible needs
Families	■ Early suppers ■ Accommodation with cots/high chairs ■ Access to a crèche ■ Activities in the area suitable for children ■ Easy parking
Young people	■ The opportunity to meet others ■ Inexpensive food and drink ■ Entertainment ■ Outdoor activities ■ Cheap travel
Retired people	■ Easy access and transport ■ Appropriate activities ■ Cultural activities ■ Good restaurants and food
Incoming visitors	■ Guides ■ Translations ■ Emergency contact numbers
People with special needs	■ Easy access to facilities ■ Appropriate information sources ■ Appropriate facilities

Talking point

In groups, discuss and produce one side of flip chart paper for each client type. The sheet should include your ideas on what each client group might need.

Duration of holiday

- Some people are 'time poor/cash rich' – this means they may prefer to take a short weekend break in a good hotel instead of, or as well as, a longer holiday.
- Some self-catering or holiday centres will only offer long weekend or mid-week breaks (although they can be joined together!); this may sometimes be with a special theme such as 'The Sixties', 'Chocolate Heaven Weekend' or 'Murder Mystery'.
- Other people will want to take a traditional one- or two-week break, particularly in the summer.

Chocolate Heaven Weekend

Menu

Chocolate and chive curry soup

Fish in a dark chocolate sauce

Beef Wellington in chocolate pastry

Death by chocolate

Coffee and chocolate mints

Type of destination

Don't forget the UK can offer every type of destination, from lively (Blackpool, Brighton, London) to quiet (Cotswolds, Wales, National Parks). There are fashionable venues (London, Edinburgh, particularly during the Festival) as well as the traditional type of seaside town (Scarborough, Hunstanton).

Location

Again, you have looked at a variety of these (see pages 93–110) and you have researched a number of different destinations.

Over to you

Look at some of the information you have gathered on different types of tourist destinations in the UK and remind yourself of the variety.

Mode of travel

People decide on different transport methods for a number of reasons – these could be convenience, price, time taken, reliability or frequency. In general, the points listed in the chart on the following page may apply.

Key points

- Each method of travelling in the UK has different advantages and disadvantages.
- Customers will make their own decisions about how to travel taking into account the convenience, speed, reliability, frequency and cost of each method.

	Convenient	Fast	Reliable	Frequent	Cost
Air travel	No – airports are usually some distance from the destination	Yes, though subject to cancellations and delays	Yes – except for busy periods	Sometimes	Expensive if many people are travelling, except for budget airlines
Rail	Depends if a train station is near the destination	Yes, though subject to cancellations and delays	Usually	Yes	Can be expensive if many people travelling; cheaper if booked in advance
Coach	Extensive network	No – takes longer than car journeys	Yes	At times	Relatively cheap
Self-drive	Very convenient	Can be if door-to-door, but traffic jams can delay	Yes	On demand	Can be good value if several people in the car

Activity

Divide into groups of three or four. Each group should research a suitable holiday for one of the following groups:

- *a family with three children under the age of 10 years*
- *two retired couples who are still fit and active*
- *two teenage boys on their first visit to the UK from Germany.*

For the customer, identify the following details:

- *type of customer*
- *destination chosen, type of destination and location*
- *type of accommodation, price and contact details, reason for accommodation choice*
- *duration of trip*
- *transport information and cost*
- *facilities*
- *entertainments, activities and attractions.*

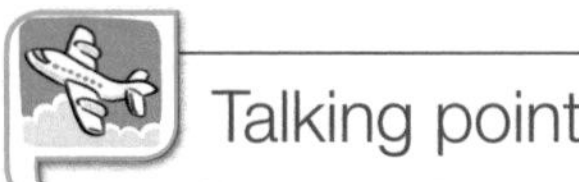

Talking point

In pairs, write down as many types of holiday accommodation as you can. Include as much variety as you can – caravans, motor caravans, cottages, farms, etc. Try to be creative!

Accommodation

Your customers may want anything from self-catering to 5-star hotels. Each person will have their own requirements, perhaps a luxury spa break or a cheap bed and breakfast. Some places may not be suitable for children, whilst others may have limited appeal to an older generation looking for a quiet break.

Things to do

You have looked at the range of entertainments, activities, attractions and facilities available at UK holiday destinations earlier in this unit (see pages 93–115). It is important to be clear about the types of activities and attractions your clients are looking for and to give them a range of options, with clear information about location, price and times of opening.

Key points

When giving customers information about their accommodation, don't forget that they will need to know:

- contact details
- how to reach the accommodation
- what is included in the price.

In summary

- The UK has a huge range of different travel destinations – capital cities, seaside resorts, historical towns, and countryside and coastal areas.
- Airports and seaports are important to both domestic and incoming tourists. Airports have an international 3-letter code allocated to them.
- Each destination appeals to various customers for different reasons.
- Information on these destinations can be found from a whole range of sources, both paper and electronic.
- All this information can be used to plan holidays for different customer types.

Test your knowledge

1. Name the capital cities of each of the UK's countries.
2. Name four types of attractions a city is likely to contain.
3. How do some UK seaside resorts encourage visitors despite the climate?
4. Name four ferry ports in the UK.
5. List London's airports.
6. What are the main aims of the National Trust?
7. Name six National Parks in the UK.
8. Name three of the UK's mountain ranges.
9. List six activities tourists can do in the UK countryside.
10. How are hotels rated?

Practice assessment activity

Levels P4/M3/D2

Read the following customer information.

Customer 1

Mr and Mrs J. McDonald want to go for a weekend in London, so that they can go to the theatre to see a musical. They would like to stay in a mid-range hotel within walking distance of the Theatre District for two nights. Mrs McDonald wants to be able to go shopping as well. The McDonalds live in Bedford, and want a convenient way of getting to London but are concerned about driving in the capital. They want to travel in February as it is Mrs McDonald's birthday, and they have recently retired.

Customer 2

The Hussein family want to spend a week by the sea. They live in Leeds, have a dog and want to have a self-catering house on the Yorkshire coast. They want to travel in the second week in August, on Saturday. They need to be able to travel together, and have a lot of luggage (as well as the dog!).

In case the weather is bad, they want to know what suitable attractions and leisure pursuits are available. They do not have a lot of money to spare and would want good value for money.

Customer 3

Four young men want to have a holiday after completing their A-levels. They want to go for a week, preferably all-inclusive, where they can meet a lot of other young people and have fun. They do not drive and don't have a lot of money to spare. They don't mind where they go in the UK, and live in London.

P **1** Complete the form below for the three customers described above. You will need to research all the information, carefully noting the sources of this information on a separate sheet. (P4) ✓

M **2** Give reasons why you selected the accommodation named, and why the selected method of transport was chosen. Reasons should be given in terms of relative cost, timings, comfort, convenience and frequency. (M3) ✓✓

D **3** Make further recommendations as to how any of the holiday arrangements could be adapted to meet the needs of different types of customer, taking into account different preferences for transport, accommodation, leisure interests and activities. (D2) ✓✓✓

Practice assessment activity continued

Consultant name:	
Customer name:	
Destination suggested:	
Accommodation suggested:	
Cost of accommodation:	
Facilities:	
Location:	**Contact details:**
Form of transport suggested:	
Transport details: Outward departure date/time:	
Arrival time (approximately):	
Return departure date/time:	
Arrival time (approximately):	
Cost of transport:	
Local facilities/attractions:	**Other information:**
Reasons for choosing accommodation:	
Reasons for choosing transport method:	

**On the back of this form, to achieve D2, you will need to add your recommendations for adapting these holidays for different customer needs.*

4 European Holiday Destinations

Introduction

Around half of all UK holidaymakers go out of the UK for their trips. This unit will look at the vast range of destinations in Europe.

- You will look at why different destinations appeal to different types of holidaymaker.
- You will be able to discover why destinations all have different appeal, from specific features to fashion and image.
- You will also be able to use brochures to select and cost holidays, as well as looking at the individual elements of a holiday. This will hopefully be very helpful when arranging your own holidays!
- You will also look at the culture and traditions of different countries, which form some of the reasons why people want to travel – to experience the 'different'.

How you will be assessed

Unit 4 is assessed internally, so the Centre delivering the qualification will assess yrou against the criteria. On completion of this unit learners should be able to:

4.1 know the location of major European holiday destinations and gateways

4.2 understand factors influencing the appeal of European holiday destinations

4.3 cost selected holidays to Europe

4.4 provide information to customers travelling to European holiday destinations.

Assessment grades

The Edexcel Assessment Grid for Unit 4 details the criteria to be met. In general, to gain a Pass (P) you are asked to describe and provide costs or information; to gain a Merit (M) you are asked to explain and work independently; and to gain a Distinction (D) you are also asked to analyse and evaluate.

4.1 Know the location of major European holiday destinations and gateways

This section covers:

- European countries and holiday destinations
- topography of European destinations
- European gateways from the UK.

European countries and holiday destinations

Countries

For the purposes of this Unit, Europe is considered to be all of continental Europe, west of the Urals and including the Republic of Ireland, the Canary Islands, the Azores and Cyprus. 'Europe' is often as far as tourists want to go on short-haul flights (under 4 hours).

Most visitors travel either on 'city breaks' to capital and other major cities, or to resorts around the Mediterranean Sea or mountains. Some countryside areas, particularly in France, are popular for leisure activities such as hiking and boating. The Alps and Pyrenees are centres for skiing in the winter.

■ *Paris, the capital city of France, is the most popular European destination for visitors from the UK*

■ *Spain is a popular package holiday destination for British tourists*

■ *Many tourists from the UK go skiing in the Italian Alps during the ski season*

Activity

On a blank map of Europe locate and name the following countries, and mark on their capital cities:

- Austria
- Belgium
- Czech Republic
- Denmark
- France
- Germany
- Greece
- Hungary
- Italy
- Portugal
- Spain
- The Netherlands.

Even more than the UK, Europe provides great contrasts. The ancient cities of Rome and Florence in Italy, and Athens in Greece, have been part of the cultural education of wealthy people for centuries; they visited these cities as part of the 'Grand Tour' of Europe. The recent fall of the communist regime in the USSR has meant that access to the old eastern European countries has become easier.

The rise of low-cost airlines has made transport much cheaper and the Internet has made it simple to find information and make bookings in other countries. Many people in industrialised countries are working long hours and are 'cash rich, time poor', so a short break to Europe which can be taken over a long weekend is increasingly popular.

Holiday destinations

One of the nearest European cities to the UK (and the most popular) is Paris. It is known as a romantic city and is easily accessed by air, rail (Eurostar) or road. The Eiffel Tower is a world-renowned landmark and the boats on the River Seine provide a popular excursion, but there are lots of other reasons to visit Paris.

Activity

In small groups, draw a spider diagram of your images of a European city. You may like to look at Paris, Amsterdam, Rome or Venice, etc. Just write down the first things which come into your head about the chosen city; for example, Venice might be gondolas and singing gondoliers!

Case studies

Paris

■ *Paris is a popular city break destination*

Paris has long been the favourite destination of UK visitors. In the valley of the Seine, it is a city of boulevards and squares, parks and pavement cafés. Many people go to visit the galleries and museums of Paris, such as the Louvre (home of the famous painting of the *Mona Lisa*), where a huge glass pyramid dominates the entrance. Nineteenth- and twentieth-century art is found in the Musée d'Orsay, home of many Impressionist paintings.

For people who enjoy visiting beautiful churches, there are many, including Notre-Dame (home of the 'hunchback') and the Sacré Coeur, high on the hill of Montmartre overlooking the city. For even better views, you can go to the top of the Eiffel Tower or the Arc de Triomphe.

Paris is a very romantic city and lovers can cruise down the River Seine on the *bateaux mouches* or stroll through the Tuileries gardens.

There are many designer shops such as Chanel and Gucci off the Champs Elysées and smaller individual shops, all with Parisian 'chic'. You can stroll down the Left Bank of the Seine and see the artists' quarter and the flea markets selling pictures and bric-a-brac. This is truly a city for everyone and can now be reached in less than three hours from central London by Eurostar.

1 Why is Paris popular with young couples?
2 Where can people interested in art and culture go in Paris?

Budapest

■ *Panoramic view of the Danube River and the Chain Bridge from Gellért Hill in Budapest*

Budapest is the capital of Hungary, just over a two-hour flight from London. The city is one of those which has emerged from communist rule and is becoming a very popular destination.

The River Danube flows between the old centres of Buda and Pest, which merged in 1873. Buda has a medieval city with palaces and churches on top of Castle Hill, a limestone crag overlooking the river. Pest is much flatter on the river plain, with boulevards, shops and grand buildings.

The city is full of bars and restaurants, art galleries and museums of local Magyar heritage. There are many natural hot water springs where people can swim in indoor or outdoor pools. In the winter, you can skate in the City Park, or in summer travel on the children's railway from Moskvater. For music lovers there is the Liszt Academy and the Autumn Festival in October.

The city has a definite eastern European feel but with modern comfort and facilities.

1 Why is Budapest suitable to visit all year round?

2 What is the difference between the two halves of the city?

Activity

On a blank map of Europe, mark three destinations for each country around the Mediterranean Sea. Keep this map safe as you'll need it for other activities in this unit.

Summer sun destinations

Although short breaks are becoming increasingly popular, more people still spend a one- or two-week holiday on the Mediterranean beaches. Mediterranean sea resorts are found in the Spanish Costas, Balearic Islands, Corsica and many Greek islands.

Many of the big resorts, such as Torremolinos in Spain, were once fishing villages, but now have all the leisure attractions to keep visitors occupied. As well as almost guaranteed sunshine and high temperatures from April to October, food and drink tend to be relatively cheap and there are many facilities such as water parks, golf courses and water sports. There are also bars, restaurants and clubs to ensure an interesting nightlife!

Activity

Add the Canary Islands and Madeira (part of Portugal) in a different colour to the summer sun destinations map.

Case studies

Tenerife

Tenerife is one of the Canary Islands, which although Spanish, with a real flavour of mainland Spain, are situated off the coast of Africa. This means that Tenerife has warm weather and sunshine all year round and is very popular as a winter sun destination. The beaches in the south are soft and sandy, but in a dramatic contrast, the north has dark, volcanic beaches. A major tourist attraction, the dormant volcano, Mount Teide, is in the north of the island.

There are many resorts, such as Playa de Las Americas, which are lively and cosmopolitan and offer a wide choice of bars, discos and nightclubs. The resorts also have a range of shops and boutiques selling international as well as Spanish goods. There are restaurants and cafés which serve a variety of food. The atmosphere is lively and appeals to a wide range of people from young families and teenagers to older travellers. There are also many water sports facilities from water-skiing to scuba diving.

There are also smaller resorts such as La Caleta, which was a picturesque fishing village and still retains much of its character. Here there are small bars and restaurants, without the hustle and bustle of the larger resorts. This would be ideal for families with small children or those looking for a peaceful getaway. Resorts like Puerto de Santiago are in the steep hilly area, perfect for walkers and nature lovers.

1. Using a tour operator's brochure, find a resort on Tenerife which would be suitable for:
   - a family with small children
   - a middle-aged couple looking for peaceful walking and water sports.

Case studies

Valloire

Valloire is situated in the French Alps. It has been a winter ski and summer walking destination for many years, and grew out of a farming community in the lush river valley.

There are year-round ski-lifts to take people to the mountain top. In the winter, a number of lifts mean that people of all abilities can ski down the sides of the valley, and in summer the walkers are accompanied by herds of cows with tinkling cowbells eating the lush grass and flowers.

The village has many bars and restaurants where visitors can relax in the evening – in winter this is known as *après-ski* where *vin chaud* (warmed, mulled wine) soothes the aching muscles. There are also bars and restaurants on the mountains to refresh skiers as they ski down the pre-prepared runs, or *pistes.* There are many shops which cater for skiers, climbers and walkers, where boots, skis and snowboards can be hired in winter and hiking and climbing equipment in summer. There is also a swimming and sports complex, and children's playground. In winter a ski-school operates, with a children's section.

1 Why do you think Valloire is successful as a ski resort? What facilities does it have for skiers?
2 Look at a ski brochure. Find out what the different colours on the *pistes* mean.

Some resorts, such as Puerto Pollensa in Majorca, still retain their original atmosphere, and are much more peaceful. These are suitable for older couples or families.

Winter sun destinations

Much of the Mediterranean is too cool to be a year-round destination, except the Costa del Sol in southern Spain. The islands further south in the Atlantic, nearer to the coast of Africa, stay relatively warm and receive visitors all year. These include the Canary Islands of Tenerife and Gran Canaria, and Madeira.

Mountains and ski areas

Of course, some people don't want to spend their winter holiday in sunshine, but in snow! Skiing can be an exhilarating experience in the sunshine and crystal clear air, and once people have experienced the freedom they are often hooked. Snowboarding is becoming a popular winter sport, particularly among younger people, and the ski resorts also offer their own culture of clothing and music.

The Alps and the Pyrenees have ski resorts which operate between December and March. These can vary from traditional 'chocolate box' destinations such as Seefeld in Austria, to purpose-built skiing towns such as Flaine in France.

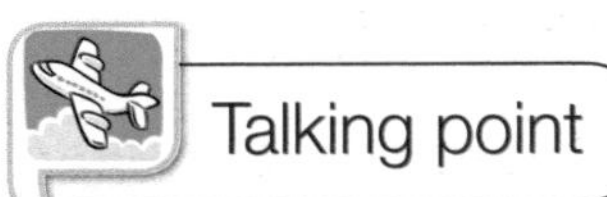

In groups, discuss any summer sun destinations you may have visited. Draw up a list of attractions and facilities found at these resorts and display them on a poster.

- Why have these resorts been so successful?
- Why do so many people prefer to holiday at these resorts rather than in the UK?

Activity

On your map of Europe, add the Alps and the Pyrenees mountain ranges. Mark on five ski resorts in different countries.

Rural destinations

Just as in the UK, there are areas in Europe which are popular for their scenery and countryside. You have already looked at an Alpine resort, Valloire, which encourages summer visitors who come to walk and climb in the mountains. Lakes such as Lake Geneva in Switzerland offer visitors sailing, fishing and other water sports. Rivers such as the Dordogne in France are popular for boating and rafting.

One of the most popular areas for UK visitors is the lakes in northern Italy, such as Lake Garda. Here walking, climbing, fishing, sailing and other outdoor pursuits are very popular – as is sitting on a hotel balcony looking at the beautiful lakes and mountains scenery!

Other popular rural destinations in Europe include the forested areas of France, such as the Alsace region or the Black Forest in Germany. There are also beautiful river valleys which are popular for water pursuits and sightseeing, such as the Dordogne in France as well as the Loire Valley which is lined with *chateaux* (fortified houses or castles).

Cruise areas

Increasingly, there are many younger people going on cruises, which previously had a rather 'stuffy' image. The introduction of easyCruise with its orange livery has opened up the market, providing inexpensive basic cruising with add-ons – rather like the low-cost airlines.

Favourite cruising areas are around the Mediterranean, visiting mainland ports and islands en route. Other cruising areas include the Canary Islands and Madeira as well as the Fjords of Norway and other Scandinavian ports.

There are many activities to keep guests occupied on cruises. After eating many delicious meals in the cruise liner's various restaurants, people can

■ *An easyCruise ship at the French port of Nice, on a European cruise*

■ *Cruise ships offer passengers an all-inclusive holiday*

work the extra calories off in the gym, by swimming or in keep-fit classes. There are also more gentle pursuits such as drawing, local history classes and card games. Evening entertainment is also popular and many cruises have top entertainers and shows. Dances and discos, children's activities and bingo, also help to make cruise liners very popular.

Activity

On your maps, add four cruise destinations in each of:

- the Mediterranean
- Canaries and Madeira
- Scandinavia.

In summary

Popular European tourism destinations include:

- city break destinations
- summer sun
- winter sun
- mountains and ski areas
- rural destinations
- cruise areas.

Key points

In Latin, *Mediterranean* means the 'middle of the earth'.

Topography of European destinations

In order to be able to give helpful information about European destinations, you will need to know about the physical features which have affected the landscape and therefore the kinds of activities.

Seas and oceans

- The Mediterranean Sea is hugely important to visitors. The warm sea laps at the coastline of many countries and islands.

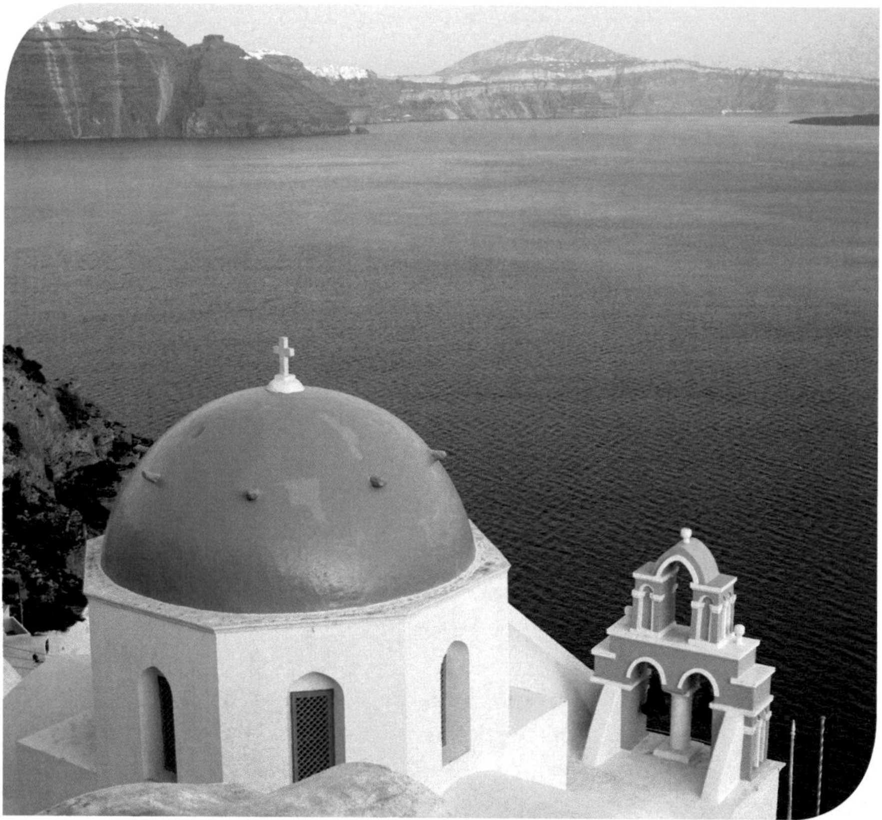

Greece is bordered by the Mediterranean and the Adriatic and Aegean seas, and has relied on the sea in the past for its life-blood

- The Atlantic, on the other hand, is a colder and fast-moving ocean, providing tides and opportunities for surfing.
- The eastern seas, such as the Red Sea, provide opportunities for diving and snorkelling in crystal waters.

Rivers

You should also be aware of the great rivers of Europe, such as the Rhine and the Rhône (both wine-growing areas), and the Danube flowing through the east of Europe. You have already looked at the Loire and the Dordogne in France.

The mountain ranges of Europe are important for summer leisure pursuits and winter sports.

European gateways from the UK

Ferry ports

If you have looked at *Unit 3: UK Travel and Tourism Destinations*, you will be familiar with the ferry routes from the UK (for a map of European ferry routes from the UK, see page 103). Remember, the Channel Tunnel from Folkestone to Sangatte (near Calais) is an important route for UK visitors to reach mainland Europe.

Airports

There are many gateways to Europe's holiday areas, as well as to its capital cities. Again, each airport has an international three-letter code; the most obvious are those which belong to the major cities.

■ *European airports*

Activity

On blank maps, colour in the following:

- mountains – Pyrenees, Alps, Dolomites
- rivers – Danube, Rhône, Rhine, Dordogne, Loire
- seas and oceans – Mediterranean, Adriatic, Aegean, Atlantic.

Activity

Identify the airport and country which these codes refer to:

- PAR
- PMI
- FAO
- AGP
- DUB
- AMS
- IBZ

Over to you

It might be fun next time you are at an airport to identify as many three-letter codes as you can.

Activity

In pairs, choose a European country and research the different kinds of holiday destinations within it. Provide a large map with the major destinations on it and add a key for each different type of destination.

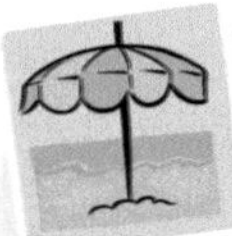

Practice assessment activity

Levels P1/M1/D1

P **1 a)** On blank maps, accurately locate at least six European destinations for *each* of the following type of destination:

- summer sun
- winter sun
- winter sports
- countryside areas
- city break
- cruise areas.

b) Locate at least six European airports used by UK holidaymakers (with their three-letter code).

c) Locate six European passenger ferry ports. (P1)

M **2** Explain the appeal of two different types of European holiday destinations. Choose two different types of European holiday destination, such as a city break and a countryside area. Produce an introduction to a holiday brochure, in booklet form, explaining why people should visit these destinations. Make it as interesting as possible, with pictures and quotations to 'sell' the destination. Remember to look at all the destination has to offer, i.e. natural features, local attractions, facilities, culture, access, climate and image. (M1)

- Choose somewhere you or your family are interested in going to and be really enthusiastic as though you need to persuade the others to go there.
- Always check with your tutor that the destinations you have chosen are suitable and that there is likely to be enough information.

D **3** Analyse how a European destination could increase its appeal to holidaymakers. For one of your chosen destinations, or a different one if you prefer, suggest ways in which it could increase its appeal, giving reasons for your suggestions. You might like to look at providing an all-weather suitable attraction or increase the range of accommodation or guiding. You might like to produce a map or model to illustrate your ideas. (D1)

4.2 Understand factors influencing the appeal of European holiday destinations

This section covers:

- natural features
- local attractions
- facilities
- traditions and cultural aspects
- accessibility from the UK
- climate
- image.

It is sometimes said that each destination has a 'pull' factor – something that draws visitors to that particular place. This 'pull' factor may be one factor or a combination of factors; it depends entirely on what each customer wants from his or her holiday. You are going to look at some of the major reasons visitors choose a particular place.

Natural features

Mountains

The most obvious natural features of Europe are the mountain ranges of the Alps or Pyrenees. Winter sports addicts need slopes and snow and that means mountain slopes. In general, the higher the slope the greater the chance of a good snowfall. Where there are facilities for skiing there will also be the infrastructure for summer sport activities such as climbing and walking.

Lakes

Lakes often are part of a mountain landscape and British visitors have been visiting the Italian and Swiss lakes for centuries for water sports and walking. More water sports, such as rafting, can be pursued in the rivers of mainland Europe, such as the Dordogne. The great rivers of mainland Europe, such as the Rhine, have cruisers from which passengers can watch the beautiful scenery.

Forests and woods

Forests and woods also provide opportunities for activities such as riding and mountain biking, and have been popular 'back to nature' holidays.

Beaches

The beaches of Europe, particularly on the Mediterranean, are renowned for their beauty. They can range from the rocky (for example, Praia da Rocha in Portugal) to fine sand (for example, Skiathos in Greece), and can be tiny fishing hamlets to huge purpose-built resorts.

Local attractions

Most visitors will look for something to do at the destination. They might go because of the beach but will probably expect to visit an attraction while there. Other destinations, such as cities, are visited because of the attractions there. Many resorts will offer coach-trip excursions to local attractions.

Historical sites and museums

Historical sites are extremely important and give visitors a sense of links with the past.

- There are prehistoric caves, many thousands of years old, in the Dordogne area of France (Rocamadour).
- There are architectural and artistic treasures in the Renaissance cities of Italy, such as Florence, as well as Roman remains such as the Coliseum and Forum in Rome.
- Some areas are designated World Heritage Sites, such as the Acropolis in Athens. Sometimes whole towns or cities are protected as World Heritage Sites. Many of these sites have museums.

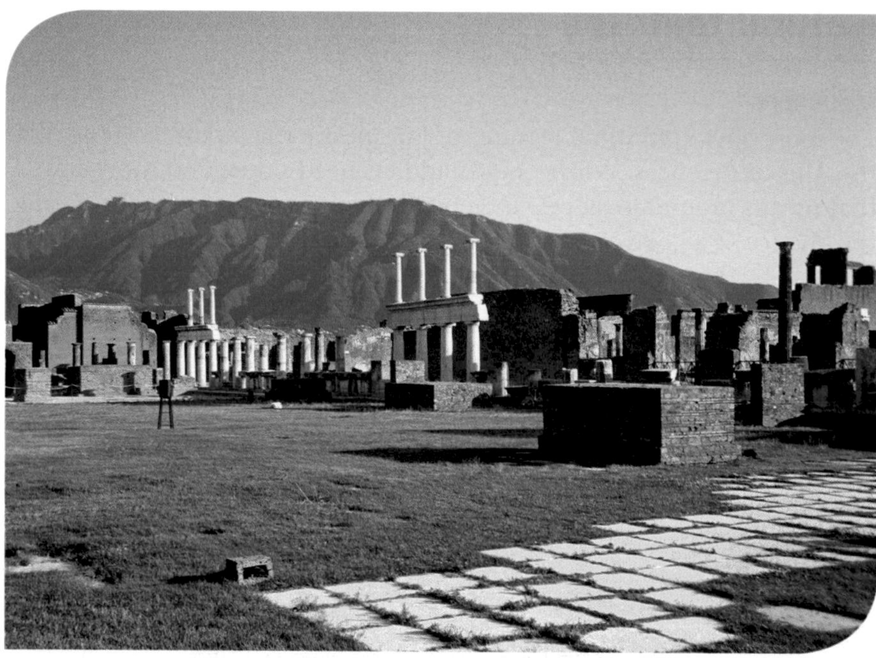

■ *The Forum at Pompeii in southern Italy. These Roman remains are popular with tourists*

■ *The Louvre in Paris is one of the world's greatest museums and art galleries*

Activity

In pairs, find information on World Heritage Sites in a chosen country and make a collage of images.

- The capital cities of Europe are home to museums full of national and international objects and art. These include the Louvre in Paris, the Prado in Madrid and the Uffizi Gallery in Florence.

Theme parks

At the other end of the scale, European theme parks are much enjoyed by 'children' aged from 8 to 80 years! There are many such parks with various themes all over Europe. These are sometimes geared to younger

children such as Efterling in the Netherlands or Disneyland Paris. There are also other theme parks, such as Futuroscope at Poitiers, France, with a science theme or Parc Asterix in France, which is named after the comic strip character.

There are many aqua parks, particularly in southern Europe. In Spain, these include the aqua park at Universal Mediterranea, Port Aventura, and those in the major resorts at Torremolinos and Magaluf. Aqua parks tend to be on a smaller scale than those in Florida, but still provide a cooling way to spend a hot summer's day, particularly for children and young people.

Facilities

Accommodation

You have already looked at the range of accommodation in the previous unit. Accommodation on the mainland of Europe tends to be less expensive than in the UK, and provides an equal variety of ways to spend a night's sleep! In addition, there are state-run hotels (*paradors*) in Spain and Portugal, which are converted castles and monasteries, or *gîtes* in France, which are rural cottages and converted farm buildings available for self-catering hire.

Transport

Local transport is often used by visitors, particularly if they arrive by air. Travelling on local transport can be an exciting part of the holiday – for example, journeying by tram in the Czech Republic when unable to read any signs can prove very interesting! Many European destinations have subsidised local transport, and these can include small railways or funicular (mountain railways) as well as trams and trolleys. Many destinations have land trains, which look like old-fashioned carriages, usually without sides, which take tourists around resorts or towns. There may also be bicycle taxis or horse-drawn carriages, which can be an exciting and alternative means of getting around.

Shopping

This can be a really exciting way to spend your time. Visitors are often entranced by foreign markets with unfamiliar local goods and different colours, and by the smells of local food. Goods can be excellent value for money, such as leather and jewellery in Italy and Spain.

Nightlife

The quality of nightlife can be very important to young people, and can in some cases be the main reason for choosing a resort. Some areas, such as Ayia Napa in Cyprus or Ibiza in Spain, are extremely popular with clubbers and attract DJs and clubs from the UK and United States. Cities such as Prague are popular for hen and stag nights, with relatively cheap clubs and bars. For other people, more sophisticated pursuits such as theatres or concerts plus dinner dancing are sought. The New Year's Eve ball in Vienna is an example of an internationally renowned event.

Sports

Some destinations are chosen because of their links with sport. Fans will travel to important matches, such as the European Cup Final or Winter Olympics, in order to watch the first-class sport. The Commonwealth Games and Olympics attract thousands of tourists.

Others may travel in order to pursue their sport, such as white-water rafting or pot-holing in the Dordogne, or horse riding in the Black Forest. Many people travel to the Mediterranean coasts to play tennis and golf, particularly on the Costa del Sol in Spain and the Algarve in Portugal.

Traditions and cultural aspects

'Culture' in this context means the way people live – their art, music, traditions and beliefs; essentially what makes each area unique.

Many European destinations are now dependent on tourism and so make sure their welcome encourages visitors to return. However, some resorts, particularly in the former communist countries of eastern Europe, have expanded very quickly and some local people find the sudden appearance of plane-loads of (comparatively) wealthy tourists confusing and may resent this change.

Visitors must be careful not to cause offence and to be aware of local customs. In southern Europe, for example, in Spain, Italy and Greece, it is usual for several generations of families to go out together. It is much less acceptable, even now, for young people to be alone together before marriage, and young women are expected to behave appropriately. 'Binge-drinking' is also much less common, as wine is usually drunk with food and children are often given a little with water. Some resorts are no longer willing to clear up after British 'lager-louts' and are making sure that all visitors are aware they may be arrested for drunkenness.

Some southern European countries still have a *siesta* – a short rest or sleep after lunch in the heat of the day. Shops and offices may be closed until the cooler, late afternoon. This practice is gradually changing, but beware – shops may open early in the morning and remain open until late in the evening but close for several hours from midday.

In Islamic countries, Bosnia for example, women are protected by their dress and may be expected to be escorted in public. Consequently, female western visitors may feel uncomfortable in some areas if unaccompanied, particularly if the head and shoulders are uncovered and shorts or short skirts are worn.

In some areas, you should always ask permission to take photographs of local people – otherwise you may cause offence. In the case of military sensitive areas, it could also cause arrest at worst and the film destroyed at best!

Local cuisine

Although hamburgers are sold everywhere, countries still retain their traditional dishes. Many people find buying food from markets and local restaurants a most enjoyable part of a holiday, and are eager to try unusual dishes and ways of eating.

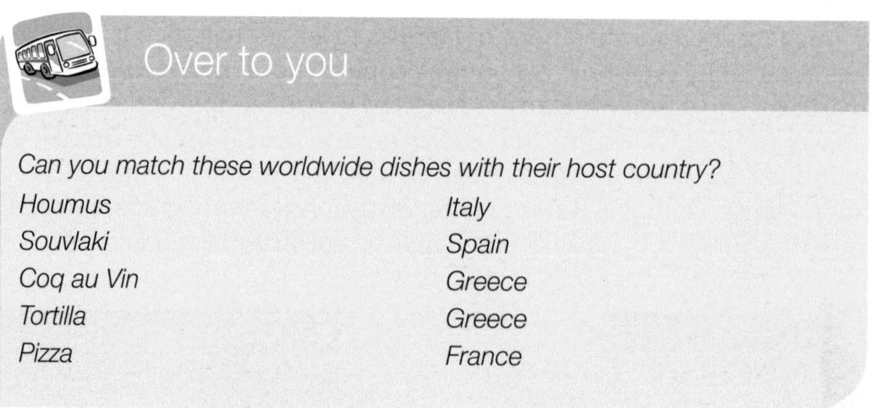

Over to you

Can you match these worldwide dishes with their host country?

Houmus	*Italy*
Souvlaki	*Spain*
Coq au Vin	*Greece*
Tortilla	*Greece*
Pizza	*France*

Unacceptable behavioural practices

You should always make sure you know what is acceptable locally – for example, the thumbs-up OK sign has a different meaning in parts of southern Europe. When in Islamic countries, the right hand is the 'clean' hand and should be used for eating.

Religious practices

Most cities will have a cathedral, mosque, synagogue or other religious building. Tourists may wish to visit holy sites but will need to be flexible because different religions will need to be able to worship in their holy places at various times of the day. Muslims, for example, pray regularly throughout the day.

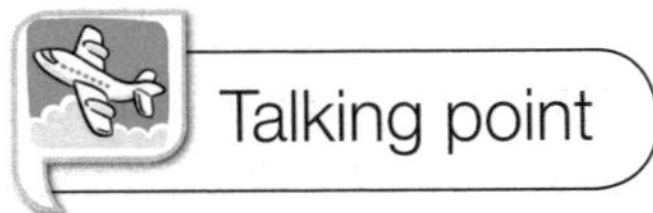

Below are a number of gestures which can be offensive depending on your destination. In your group, can you think of any others?

Gesture	Country	Meaning
Palms thrust forward	Greece UK	Insult Stop
Tugging at earlobe	Spain Greece Malta Portugal	Sponger Warning Sneaky Wonderful
Thumbs up	UK Sardinia	OK Obscene gesture

There may be many local festivals, often linked to religious celebrations. The period around Easter is often a time of religious processions and festivals in southern Europe.

Activity

Using the Internet, find out about ten different festivals and fairs that are held in Europe. Be prepared to plot these places on a blank map.

Accessibility from the UK

Travelling by air

It is important that visitors to Europe can reach their destinations easily. The low-cost airlines, such as easyJet, Ryanair and bmibaby, have greatly increased the number of provincial airports in Europe and decreased the cost of travelling by air.

Activity

Look at the websites for bmibaby, Ryanair and easyJet. Links to these websites have been made available at www.heinemann.co.uk/hotlinks by entering the express code 2196P. Plot the airports these airlines use, both in the UK and Europe, on a blank map.

Of course, many travellers to holiday beach resorts travel by charter aircraft. These aircraft have been chartered or hired for specific holiday destinations and durations by tour operators such as Thomsons.

Package holidays are sold with the transport, accommodation and transfers between arrival airport and accommodation included. This is a convenient and relatively hassle-free way of travelling, particularly as the services of a tour operator representative are often included. However, travellers do sometimes feel that they are 'herded' and may prefer to put together their own independent holiday; it is easier than ever to put together all these elements using the Internet.

Sometimes transfer times are long – particularly for winter sports destinations as there is unlikely to be a large airport in the mountains! Some transfer buses will also go via other hotels and resorts to the final hotel, so transfer can take a long time, even if the distance is short!

Transfer times can be lengthy, especially if there are many stops! For example:

Palma airport

↓

Hotel Sol, Palma

↓

Hotel Toucan, Magaluf

↓

Hotel Sol Vista, Magaluf

↓

Hotel Los Gigantes, Magaluf

↓

Hotel Prinipe, Magaluf

Rail links

In Europe, there is an extensive subsidised rail network of fast and efficient trains. It is possible to link easily with the Eurostar from London to Paris, and to travel to many European destinations including Belgium, Italy, Germany and the south of France.

Roads

Roads in Europe tend to be relatively uncrowded (apart from the Peripherique round Paris!) and can be a pleasant way to travel.

Climate

People travel to different places for a number of reasons. One of these is to experience different climatic conditions. Climate is a measure of atmospheric conditions, such as temperature, sunshine and rainfall, that are based on yearly or monthly averages over a period of not less than 30 days. These figures are usually displayed in holiday brochures, holiday guides and atlases. Major destinations tend to be warmer climates with long hours of average daily sunshine, although popular ski resorts rely on an abundance of snow.

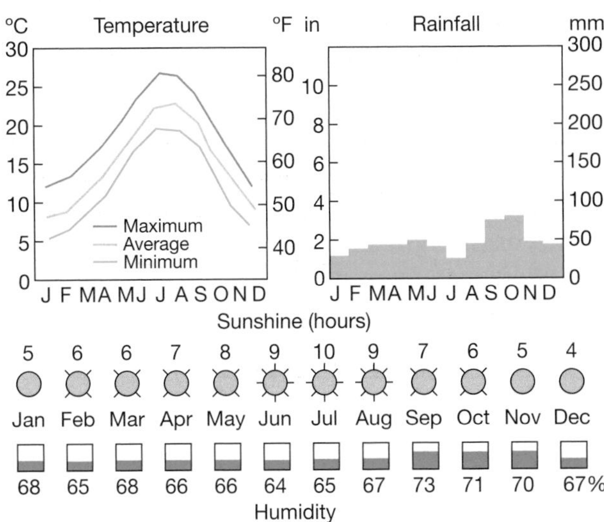

■ *The climate of Barcelona, Spain*

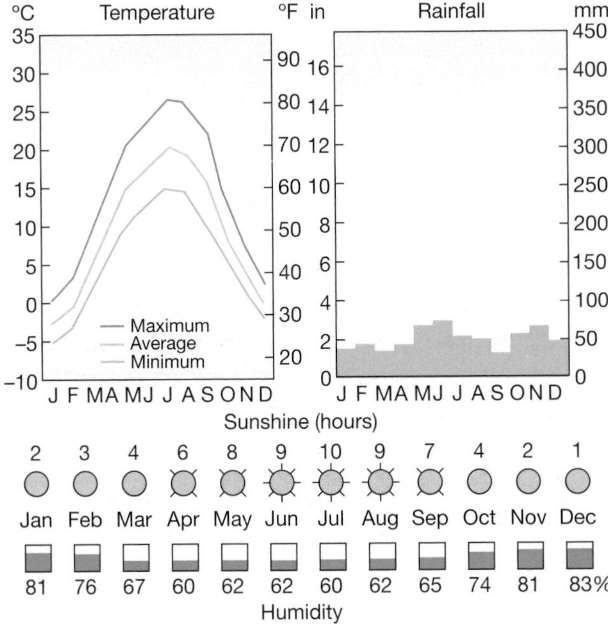

■ *The climate of Budapest, Hungary*

Snow

The amount of snow is governed by the height of the mountains and the aspect – whether the slopes are south-facing (facing the sun). There is sometimes concern that the Alps and Pyrenees won't have enough snow during the winter sports season. The higher the resort, the more likely it is to have reliable snow – and will be correspondingly more expensive!

Daylight

The tilt of the Earth means that daylight and darkness at the Equator are roughly equal all year round; as you move further away from the Equator, the proportion of day/night varies, so that the north of Norway, for example, may have only a few hours of light in the winter but in the summer it can be light for about 21 hours. This will make a difference to some visitors, who may want to see the Aurora Borealis (Northern Lights), a natural cosmic light show in the dark skies. Visitors from the northern hemisphere may fly south during the winter (like migrating birds!) to get more daylight and sunshine.

Key points

It is important for you to know something about the seasonal climatic conditions of popular European tourist destinations when advising customers on their holiday choices.

Seasonal conditions and effects on travellers

Winds are very important to climate. Winds that pass over oceans pick up moisture, which will fall as rain when a land mass is reached. Winds are not always beneficial – some such as the Sirocco, which blows from the deserts of north Africa to Italy and the Mediterranean, are hot, dry and dust-laden, and can make you choke!

In summary

A destination's climate depends on many factors:

- its distance from the Equator (the further north or south you go from the Equator, the greater the temperature variation)
- its distance from the oceans (the further away, the more extreme the temperature and the less rainfall)
- its height (the higher the destination above sea level, the cooler it will be)
- whether the destination is in a prevailing wind area (temperatures will be moderated).

Remember: not every visitor wants hot sunshine.

While seasons can be predicted, there may be natural disasters such as earthquakes, droughts and floods, which can happen at any time. There is always a risk to travel and visitors will need to be aware of these forces of nature.

Information on climate, average rainfall and temperatures is easily available from tour operators' brochures, the *World Travel Guide* and

Internet sources. Passengers ought to be aware of the bitterly cold eastern European winters, the blazing hot Mediterranean summers and how these variations might affect what they want to do.

Image

'Image' is a constantly changing perception. What is in fashion today (Prague, Ayia Napa) may not be in fashion in the future. Resorts like Benidorm have had to adapt after their peak in the 1970s.

There are many other aspects of 'image':

- The tourism gains made by Paris after the publishing of Dan Brown's *The Da Vinci Code* (2003) were then spoilt when there was a series of riots in 2005.
- The bombing of the Madrid railway in 2004 also affected people's perception of Spain being a relatively safe destination. Spain has also had some bad publicity over the Basque Separatist activities in the north of the country.

Visitors should be encouraged to be aware of their personal safety and to follow any Foreign Office guidelines. Nobody is ever guaranteed safety but taking sensible precautions reduces the risk.

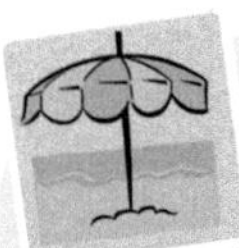

Practice assessment activity

Levels P2/M1/D1

P **1** Describe those factors which affect the appeal of European holiday destinations. Include relevant examples from different countries in your description. (P2)

M **2** Research two different types of European destination (check with your tutor that they are appropriate) in two different countries. Produce a leaflet for each destination, which would encourage visitors to choose this for a holiday. For each, explain how the various factors contribute to the specific appeal. (M1)

D **3** For a specific destination (different from those chosen for M1), assess how a European destination could expand its appeal, for example, by expanding the tourist season or by improving facilities to appeal to different client groups. (D1)

Tip – choose destinations which you would like to visit or have visited – this should make you sound enthusiastic!

4.3 Cost selected holidays to Europe

This section covers:

- standard package holidays
- using brochures
- costing a standard package holiday
- costing independent arrangements
- types of customer.

Standard package holidays

Package holidays may be referred to as package tours, ITs or inclusive holidays. Package holidays are made up from at least two of the following elements:

- transportation (flight, rail, car, ship) from the UK to the destination and return
- accommodation at a hotel or other place to stay
- *plus* one other service; this could be either transfer from the foreign port or airport to the hotel and return, or car hire or similar.

The main advantage of buying a package tour is one of convenience. The client pays one total price and knows that from the time he or she checks in for the holiday to the time he or she returns, the arrangements are made on his or her behalf. Previously the agent would have put together a package but today numerous brochures exist featuring holidays. Brochures are produced by the tour operator, who is a wholesaler of the travel business, just as the travel agent is the retailer. Tour operators buy in bulk and the travel agent sells individual package holidays.

The majority of tour operators belong to ABTA, the Association of British Travel Agents (see also Unit 1, page 14). ABTA is principally a trading organisation which operates for and on behalf of its members – the tour operators and travel agents. It also acts as a mediator for clients. The organisation offers certain guarantees, especially financial guarantees, which operate to protect clients' money and their holidays should any of its members go out of business. ABTA tour operators and travel agents are bonded, i.e. they pay a levy according to their business turnover which acts to protect their clients should their business fail.

Hotels

Tour operators often have their own hotels which are used only by them but often you will find that the same hotel is used by two or more operators. Holiday Inn and Sol Iberotel are examples of hotel groups that have a corporate image and are built and run along similar lines. This means that although each hotel is different, the standard of service, rooms and other facilities will be the same. Small hotels are often family-run with a friendly atmosphere, and can be found in many brochures.

Operators' holiday brochures will always try to show the hotel and resort in its best light, so you must always read the description carefully.

Grading systems

There is no universally accepted method of grading hotels. Some countries like Spain have an official grading ranging from 1–5 stars, but others countries have none at all. For ease of comparison, some tour operators have devised their own grading systems, for example, Thomson uses a 1T, 2T, 3T, etc. grading system, and Airtours uses an AA, AAA, etc. grading system.

Meal and accommodation plans

B & B	Bed and Breakfast.
HB	Half board (bed, breakfast and one other meal, usually taken in the evening).
FB	Full board (bed, breakfast, lunch and evening meal).
A la carte	Open menu offering a range of starters, main courses, etc.; usually only available at 4- and 5-star hotels.
Table d'hôte	Literally means 'table of the host'; set menu offered by the hotel; may be an 'either/or' choice.

When dealing with city breaks for short stays, you will find that some of the smaller hotels have no dining rooms. Breakfast is therefore served in bedrooms and the client has to go to a nearby restaurant with vouchers from the tour operator.

Facilities and amenities

Some of the amenities provided by hotels for holidaymakers are listed below.

Bars	Poolside bar	Gymnasium
Snack bar	Barbeque	Videos
Coffee shop	Children's menu	Games rooms
Children's club	Cots, high chairs	Lift
Baby patrol	Sea sports	Hairdresser
Swimming pool	Tennis courts	TV rooms
Live dancing	Hotel shops	Air-conditioning

Types of rooms

Twin-bedded room	Nearly all holiday prices are based on two people sharing a twin-bedded room.
Single room	Nearly always carries a supplement.
Three/four-bedded room	A true 3-bedded room is larger than a twin but beware – a 'twin + 1' is often a twin room with a third bed added. Four-bedded rooms are often called 'family rooms' (uncommon in city breaks).
Private bath/shower	Modern hotels are well equipped with private facilities but older hotels in Britain, France and Italy often do not have a private bath or shower.
Sea view/balcony	Sometimes the basic price includes a sea view (sv) or partial sea view known as 'side-sea view' (ssv). Balconies (bal) often go with a sea view – usually the client will have to pay extra for this.

Key points

Remember, there are many types of package holiday:

- summer sun (often Mediterranean resorts)
- winter sun (usually Canaries, southern Spain)
- winter sports (usually the Alps)
- city breaks
- camping and mobile homes
- self-drive
- cruises.

Using brochures

The brochure is the principal selling aid between the tour operator, the client and the travel agent. At present, some 20 brochures are produced for every holiday sold.

- Brochures dealing with beach holidays are normally divided into summer sun and winter sun: summer sun deals with April to November and winter Sun deals with November to April, although there may be an overlap.
- The winter sport brochure deals with a season from mid-December to the end of April.

Booking conditions

All tour operators have booking conditions – a contract which the customer agrees to when signing the booking form.

Activity

In groups, find one copy of each of the above brochures and keep them safe so that the group can use them for research.

Activity

Look at the booking conditions – usually near the back of the brochure. Answer the following questions:

1. *How many adults must a child be sharing with to qualify for a free child place?*
2. *What is included in the holiday price?*
3. *What is the fee if a passenger's name is changed?*
4. *What is the cancellation fee if the customer cancels two weeks before departure?*

Costing a standard package holiday

Hotels

It is very useful if you can work out whether you can afford a particular holiday! There is a set formula for costing a package holiday, which will apply, with variations, to most brochures.

Prices are usually given *per person* over 18 years, based on sharing a twin room.

1 The first stage is to take the basic price and multiply by the number of people. For example:
   - **Basic cost £245 x 2 adults = £490**
2 Next, take the child price; usually the first child pays a different price. For example:
   - **First child £140 x 1 = £140**
   - **Second child £200 x 1 = £200**
3 Next, look at the flights – is the cost from the departure airport included or is there a supplement? For example:
   - **Flight supplement £10 x 4 = £40**
4 Then there may be a board supplement. For example, the basic price might include Bed and Breakfast and the passenger wants Full Board:
   - **Board supplement £6 x 7 nights x 4 passengers = £168**
5 Finally, there may be a room supplement (for sea view or mountain view):
   - **Room supplement £4 x 7 nights x 4 passengers = £112.**

If you then add all these up, you will find the total cost for the hotel.

- Have you checked child ages? Discounts?
- Have you checked all supplements? Child insurance?
- Have you charged under occupancy if required?

Over to you

Below, you will find a template which you can use as a guide. It can also be adapted for independent arrangements. Don't forget you may also need to add insurance or car hire, etc. as required.

Costings	Price per person (£)	Multiply by no. of people	Multiply by no. of nights	Cost
Basic cost adult				
First child				
Second child				
Flight supplement				
Board/room supplement				
Under occupancy supplement				
Insurance adult				
Insurance child				
			Total:	

Apartment holidays

Apartments are costed in exactly the same way as hotels – the only extra thing to remember is that if the apartment will take more customers than want to use it, there will be an extra cost per person. This is called the under occupancy supplement (see above). The extra price will be charged for each adult who is travelling. Note that children do not count as 'people' when looking at the number in the apartment – but neither do they pay a supplement. For example, 2 adults and 2 children in an apartment for 4 people, 2 adults ONLY count, therefore under occupancy = £4 x 2 adults x 7 nights = £56.

Winter sports holidays are the same, except the passengers will probably need equipment and lift passes, which again are charged per person – see the ski template below.

SKI COSTINGS	Price per person (£)	Multiply by no. of people	Multiply by no. of days/weeks	Cost
Basic cost adult				
Basic cost child				
Flight supplement				
Under occupancy supplement				
SKI EQUIPMENT – *Either* A or B (*not both*)				
A:				
Learn to ski pack				
Lift pass (if extra)				
B:				
Ski hire				
Boot hire				
Lift pass				
Ski school				
Children's equipment				
Children's club/ Nanny				
Insurance adult				
Insurance child				
			Total:	

Activity

In pairs, each of you choose a holiday you would like to go on and cost it for two people sharing a room, travelling from Manchester for two weeks in July.

When you are sure you have the final answer, ask your partner to assess the cost and check his or her answer with yours. Make sure you both use the template!

Costing independent arrangements

Many people are now confident to book flights and accommodation separately.

Flights

There could be several different ways of getting to the destination airport.

- Budget airlines, for example, Ryanair. These may be the cheapest option and can be easily checked on the Internet. However, beware! There may well be taxes on top of the fare and these can be more than the fare itself!
- Seat only, for example, Thomsonfly. These could be seats on charter flights sold without the accommodation. They may be relatively cheap but are often limited to durations of one or two weeks.
- Scheduled airlines, for example, Iberia. These are usually the most expensive but are the most flexible and may often be changed or cancelled without a fee.

Accommodation

There are many kinds of accommodation, and you must be very careful about what is included in the price. Individual hotels can easily be found on the Internet. There are also many organisations which represent groups of hotels, for example, ActiveHotels.

Ferries

Some ferries have complicated fare structures depending on the length of the car and how long you stay. Others just charge a flat rate for the car and include all passengers. When looking at ferries, you should use the template to make sure you have included everything.

Extras

Remember, you need to add on any of the extras you have looked at with package holidays, such as insurance. Many insurance companies will do special deals for two-week holidays. You may also need to add car hire – there are many international car hire companies, such as Hertz or Avis – as well as car parking at airports, for example, Pink Elephant parking.

Activity

Research the price of a flight from London Gatwick to Malaga for two weeks in August. Check all three methods (budget, seat only and scheduled); keep a note of the websites or brochures you have looked at. Produce your findings in a table and give the advantages and disadvantages of each.

Activity

Research a hotel in Torremolinos, Spain, to link in with the flights you have found. You want a twin room. Find two alternatives. Make sure you note down what sites you have looked at.

Country:	MALAGA (ON AIRPORT)	**Drivers age:**	36
PU location:	MALAGA AIRPORT	**DO location:**	MALAGA AIRPORT
PU date/time:	01/07/2006 - 09:00	**DO date/time:**	08/07/2006 - 09:00

Car(click car name to view info ...)	**Cat.**	**Cost**
NISSAN MICRA 3DR (or similar)	ECMR	£108.00
RENAULT CLIO 4DR A/C (or similar)	EDMR	£123.00
FORD FOCUS 5DR A/C (or similar)	CDMR	£148.00
! R FORD FOCUS 5DR A/C ESTATE (or similar)	CWMR	£166.00
! R FORD FOCUS 5DR AUTO A/C (or similar)	CDAR	£227.00
! R FORD MONDEO 4DR A/C (or similar)	IDMR	£267.00
! R FORD GALAXY 7 STR A/C (or similar)	FVMR	£385.00

■ *Worldwide Cars™ car hire tariffs* (*Source*: Reprinted with the kind permission of Worldwide Cars. Prices correct at time of going to print – prices subject to change on a regular basis)

Don't forget that on an independent holiday there won't be any coaches to take passengers from the airport to the hotel – they will have to rely on taxis or public transport. Although you probably won't be able to pre-book this, a good guide book will give approximate prices!

So, you can see that it is more complicated if you want to put all the elements together independently, but you can get exactly what you want from your holiday and it may be cheaper!

Types of customer

As you have already seen in *Unit 3: UK Travel and Tourism Destinations,* types of customers include:

- families
- young people
- retired people
- people with specific needs.

4.4 Provide information to customers travelling to European holiday destinations

This section covers:

- travel information
- general information
- sources of information.

Travel information

As part of the 'service' to different customer groups, you will need to be able to advise customers on travel documents. For example, some air tickets are handwritten but more often are machine-printed. They will clearly show the departure and arrival airports and flight numbers.

Travel times

All departure times are shown as local time. You must be aware that if passengers fly across time zones, they will need to adjust their watch to the local time or they will be confused. The body takes a bit longer to adjust! Most European countries are only one or two hours ahead of the UK.

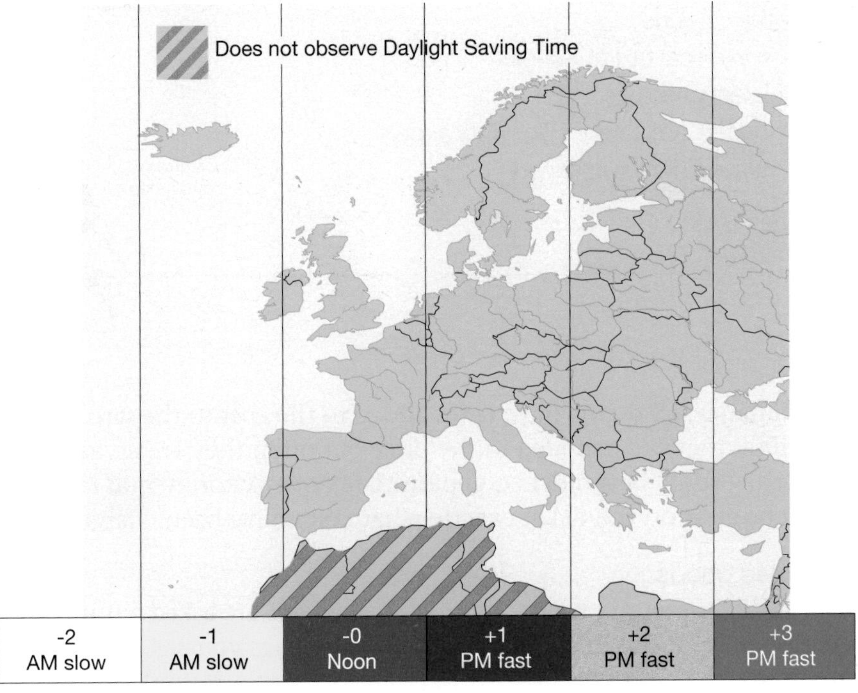

■ *Map of European time zones*

Passengers should be aware of the time variation as this may make the length of the journey difficult to calculate. For example:

- Depart London 0900 local time
- Arrive Paris 1100 local time
- Paris is one hour ahead of London, therefore arrival is an hour after departure.

On the return:

- Depart Paris 1300
- Arrive London 1300 local time
- This is because the flight left at 1200 London time but 1300 local time.

Check-in times

Check-in for most scheduled flights is usually an hour before departure; however, many charter and low-cost flights ask for two hours check-in time. The itinerary produced for the customer should be very clear.

Itinerary for Mr McWhirter

Monday 14 June
0800: latest check-in
0900: depart Edinburgh airport
1130: arrive Amsterdam Schiphol airport
Transfer by local taxi to the Hotel Van Gogh, Amsterdam

Thursday 17 June
Transfer by local taxi to Schiphol airport
1500: latest check-in
1600: depart Amsterdam Schiphol airport
1630: arrive Edinburgh airport

All times are local

Taxes

Unfortunately, all flights have taxes added to the cost to the fare. Sometimes they are included in the price but often they are an added extra. They could be a fuel tax, departure tax or environmental tax. It should be clear on the ticket exactly what taxes have been charged.

Restricted goods

Since in-flight security is very tight, all passengers are asked a number of security questions such as 'Did you pack these bags yourself?' It is important that passengers know they cannot carry certain items on board an aircraft. These include acids, poisons, lighter fuel, fireworks, gas containers, thinners, mercury barometers, wet cell batteries and compressed gas.

Activity

Research the baggage allowance on European routes for the following airlines:

- British Airways
- easyJet
- a charter flight used by a tour operator.

Baggage allowance

This varies from airline to airline and route to route. For economy flights on scheduled airlines, the baggage allowance is usually 20 kg (44 lbs) per person plus carry-on luggage such as a handbag and coat. Infants under 2 years do not have an allowance but certain things, such as pushchairs, are usually carried free. Twenty kg is actually quite heavy to lift but if you have heavy winter clothes, it may be easy to reach it!

Insurance

It is advisable that all visitors have travel insurance against a variety of potential disasters. The policy should cover everything from having to cancel the holiday due to sickness, to loss of baggage. If the passenger travels frequently, it is sometimes more economic to buy a yearly travel policy.

Some travel tickets carry cancellation and amendment fees, particularly on cheaper fares. Package holidays also charge cancellation and amendment fees – usually, the closer to departure, the more the cancellation charge will be; within six weeks it is usually 100 per cent of the charge. You can see it is well worth taking out insurance!

The insurance policy will also cover passengers against having to pay hospital and medicine bills. In EU countries it is possible to have medical treatment for free if you have a European Health Insurance Card. This has the advantage of not having to pay the bills first and claiming back later. The card is available from main branches of the Post Office.

General information

Over to you

Find out what the local language is in the following areas:

- Corsica
- Cyprus
- Switzerland (there are four!)
- Austria
- Sardinia
- Tenerife.

Practise saying 'hello' in each of these languages.

You will need to be able to give information on many aspects of the foreign country.

Language

Although many people in Europe speak English in the main cities or resorts, there are many situations where a smattering of the local language is useful. Most travel guides provide a useful glossary on common words and phrases, such as *please, thank you, hello* and *goodbye.*

Currency

You will also need to be able to give information on local currency. Of course, many countries that are in the European Monetary Union use the Euro. However, countries (like the UK) who are in the European Union but not within the Monetary Union, still use their own currency.

Personal safety

You have looked at the need to be sensible about personal safety, as in any country. Valuables and spare cash should be left in hotel safes and

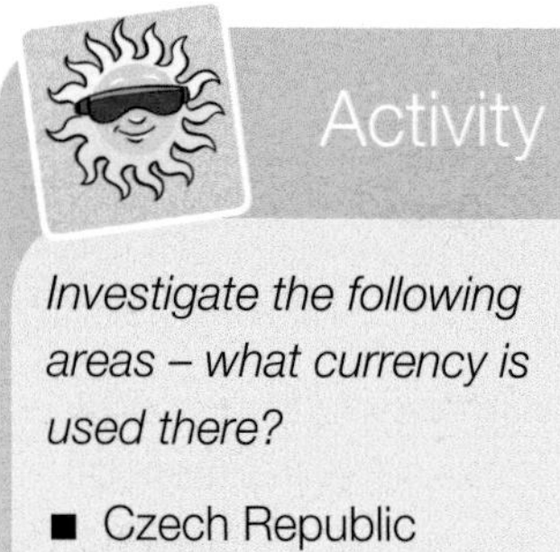

Investigate the following areas – what currency is used there?

- Czech Republic
- Madeira
- Norway
- Andorra.

not carried around. Care should be taken with passports and credit cards – special body purses can be bought. Sensible precautions should ensure problems are minimised, but extra care should be taken in areas where there are many tourists, such as the Eiffel Tower in Paris.

■ *Take care of your belongings and don't attract attention to yourself*

Local traditions

Make sure visitors are aware of any local customs. Many countries do not like beachwear worn anywhere other than the beach – and many countries definitely prefer some clothing on the beach as well!

Sources of information

As for *Unit 3: UK Travel and Tourism Destinations*, make sure you note down the full details of the publication or website, and the date.

- Atlases (especially specific travel atlases, for example, Columbia Press)
- Websites; for example, Tourist Information Offices, map-based sites
- Gazetteers
- Brochures – tour operators produce thousands every year
- Guide books, for example, *Rough Guides*, *Lonely Planet* travel guides
- Textbooks – many travel and tourism textbooks are available
- Trade journals, for example, *Travel Trade Gazette*
- *World Travel Guide*
- Leaflets/fliers.

Practice assessment activity

Levels P3/P4/M2/M3/D2

P **1 a)** For the following customers, find a suitable holiday and details of the estimated costs. (P3) 

M **b)** You will need to prove that you have looked at a variety of sources independently. You should evaluate each of your sources and ask a witness to state that you did this on your own. (M3) 

> Mr and Mrs Choo want to travel on a package holiday to Majorca to celebrate their golden wedding anniversary. They want to fly from Edinburgh airport for two weeks on a Saturday in June or July. They want to stay in a four-star hotel in a relatively quiet area in the north or northeast of the island, and would like to have full board and, if possible, a sea view. They want to take out insurance and park their car at Edinburgh. They ask that you suggest a hotel and set the costs out clearly. They don't mind paying a bit more, as it is a special occasion.

> Students, Miss S. Patel and Miss J. Jones, want to go on an independent holiday to Paris for three nights in May. They don't know whether to go by Eurostar or air, and want a three-star hotel which is fairly central, as they want to go sightseeing. The passengers would like a comparison of costs by Eurostar rail and air travel, plus a choice of hotels and costs. They also want to know how much it would cost to travel from the airport in Paris to the centre of the city by public transport.

> Mr P. Dhal wants to travel with his family, Mrs J. Dhal, Janie (6 years) and Tariq (8 years) on a camping package holiday to Brittany, France. They want to travel by car, on a suitable overnight crossing and stay in a campsite near the coast. The children want a pool and other play facilities. They want a pre-erected tent for one week in August. They ask that you suggest a suitable holiday and cost it for a fairly tight budget.

M **2** Justify (give reasons) why you have chosen the selection of holidays above and how they meet the specific needs of the customers in terms of destination, accommodation, cost and travel. You must make sure you include as much detail as possible concerning the destination. (M2)

D **3** Evaluate to what extent the European holidays you have suggested meet the needs of the customers in each given scenario, and why these particular suggestions were made instead of other options. (D2) 

> Remember to keep records of all your research in the form of a bibliography and specific websites!

P **4** For each of the customers above, produce a fact file covering the itinerary, travel time, restricted items, cultural aspects, time differences, local traditions, and health and safety issues (including insurance). The itinerary should be visually attractive, including pictures of the destination if possible. (P4) 

Test your knowledge

1. Name the capital cities of France, Spain, the Netherlands, Portugal and Denmark.
2. Name the two biggest mountain ranges in Europe.
3. Name the European cities where the following attractions are located: Prado Museum; Palace of Versailles; Mannekin Pis; Little Mermaid.
4. Name the European countries in which the following rivers can be found: Dordogne; Rhine; Danube; Seine.
5. What is a *siesta*?
6. Why should women be careful about how they dress in Muslim countries?
7. What is the difference between a low-cost airline and a charter airline?
8. Name three European ferry ports.
9. What is a European Health Insurance Card?
10. Name three paper-based sources of information on European countries.

5 Exploring Marketing in Travel and Tourism

Introduction

Marketing is an essential activity for a modern, successful travel and tourism organisation to compete in this highly competitive world. This unit is designed to help you explore the principles of marketing and how organisations use them to communicate, so as to attract and retain customers. You will also explore how different organisations develop different products and services to meet the needs of different target markets and how the organisations segment these different target groups.

To complete this unit you will need to develop your market research skills; this could also help you to achieve Key Skills Application of Number. You will learn how to design, carry out and evaluate market research material. You will need to understand how market research is needed to develop new products and services.

The last part of this unit will pull together all the skills you have developed as you progress through the unit. You will be using your creative talents to develop a piece of promotional material for a suitable travel and tourism organisation, in order to promote a product or service for a specific target market.

How you will be assessed

Unit 5 is assessed internally so the Centre delivering the qualification will assess you against the criteria. On completion of this unit you should:

5.1 understand the principles of marketing in the travel and tourism industry
5.2 understand how travel and tourism organisations provide a range of products and services to meet the needs of different types of customers
5.3 be able to design and use market research to meet specific objectives
5.4 be able to produce promotional methods suitable for use in travel and tourism.

Assessment grades

The Edexcel Assessment Grid for Unit 5 details the criteria to be met. In general, to gain a Pass (P) you are asked to describe and design and produce your own material; to gain a Merit (M) you are also asked to explain and analyse; and to gain a Distinction (D) you are also asked to evaluate and draw conclusions.

5.1 Understand the principles of marketing in the travel and tourism industry

This section covers:

- principles of marketing
- marketing objectives.

Principles of marketing

Definition of marketing

Marketing is a complex management tool, which the *Concise Oxford Dictionary* defines as:

> 'The action or business of promoting and selling products and services.'

Marketing is totally focused on the customers' needs and could be easily described as providing:

- the right product
- at the right price
- at the right place
- with the right promotion
- at the right time.

As you can see, these are all directed at the customers' needs and wants. You will investigate each of these points in further depth later in this unit.

The marketing mix

The **marketing mix** is sometime known as the **4Ps** (see diagram below).

■ *The marketing mix*

Key points

The marketing mix is the mix of the 4Ps:

- product
- place
- price
- promotion.

The marketing mix makes up the full package that you are selling to the customer. If any one of these parts is not well developed, this can lead to a product being unsuccessful. After all, there is no point having the most suitable holiday in the world to offer a customer at the lowest price and which the customer only needs to pop around the corner to buy if the customer does not know about it!

Product

This is the product or service that you are providing for the customer. This includes all services. The product in travel can change from customer to customer depending on individual requirements. A different hotel or grading of airline seats will give the customer a different experience and, in turn, a different product.

It is important for an organisation to understand its product, not only its features and details but also how the product is different from competitors' products. This is the product's **unique selling point** (USP) – what makes your product different from everyone else's. Your USP could be something as simple as offering the warmest of welcomes or easier booking facilities.

Key points

A brand is the name, image or logo which an organisation associates with a product.

It is important to remember that a product that is currently satisfying the customers' needs will need to be altered, adapted or even replaced as customers' needs change.

Companies spend a great deal of time and money developing an image and reputation for a particular product. This is known as the **brand**.

■ *The Thomson logo or brand* (Reprinted with kind permission)

Activity

1. *Do a quick survey among 20 people in your class to find out the following answers:*
   What is your favourite soft drink?
   What did you have for breakfast today?
   What type of car do you have or does your household have?
2. *Put your results on a tally chart.*
3. *From your results, work out how many answers are brands and how many are types of products, for example, Ford is a brand but a 4 × 4 or estate car is the product.*

(This activity will give you an opportunity to practise Key Skills Application of Number N2.1.)

Place

Place is about the distribution point of your product. This is easy to confuse with the holiday destination. Try to think of 'place' as the location where the customer goes to buy the product or service. For example, you would not pop over to the Caribbean to buy your summer holiday; you would be likely to book it either through a local travel agent or the Internet. So, the place with regards to the marketing mix is where the product is *sold*.

■ *The 'place' where you buy your product could be the travel agency in your local high street*

Activity

1. *Make a list of local visitor attractions. A trip to your local Tourist Information Centre will help with your research here.*
2. *In your class, pick one attraction each and find out where you can purchase tickets to the attraction.*
3. *Share your answers with your class.*

Talking point

Did you know that you can pay up to 89 per cent more to go on holiday during school holidays? What do you think of the travel and tourism industry's use of variable pricing in this way?

Price

This refers to the price that is charged for the product, and includes discounts. Travel is a very price sensitive market place, with budget airlines competing on the price of flights and some package holidays being sold almost solely on the price. Price is particularly relevant to last-minute deals and bucket shops.

- The lowest price you can charge for a product is the **cost price** – this is the price it cost to produce the product or service.
- The highest price you can charge is dictated by what the customer is willing to pay.

Promotion

Promotion is any activity that is designed to put across a positive image of the organisation or individual. In other words, any interaction with the public or media could be counted as a form of promotion. In fact, word of mouth (where people recommend a company) is one of the most influential forms of promotion. (There is more information on promotional methods and techniques later in this unit; see pages 199–210.)

Target marketing

Not every product is going to appeal to everyone. If there was only one summer holiday that suited every customer, then travel agents would only have to stock one summer holiday to sell! However, every customer is slightly different with different needs and expectations. For example, the holiday requirements of a group of four 18-year-old lads wanting their first holiday away from home without their parents will be different from a couple who have just retired and want a once-in-a-lifetime experience.

Target marketing is about creating products that are aimed (or targeted) at different groups of people. These groups are called **market segments**.

Market segmentation

A market segment is a group of customers with similar needs. Imagine the travel market is like an orange and that the different groups are its segments. The more specific you make each segment, then the smaller the segment becomes. For example, if the market segment was package family holidays, this is a large segment, but if you break it down further into package family holidays to Spain, the segment becomes smaller although it is still a large segment of the current market.

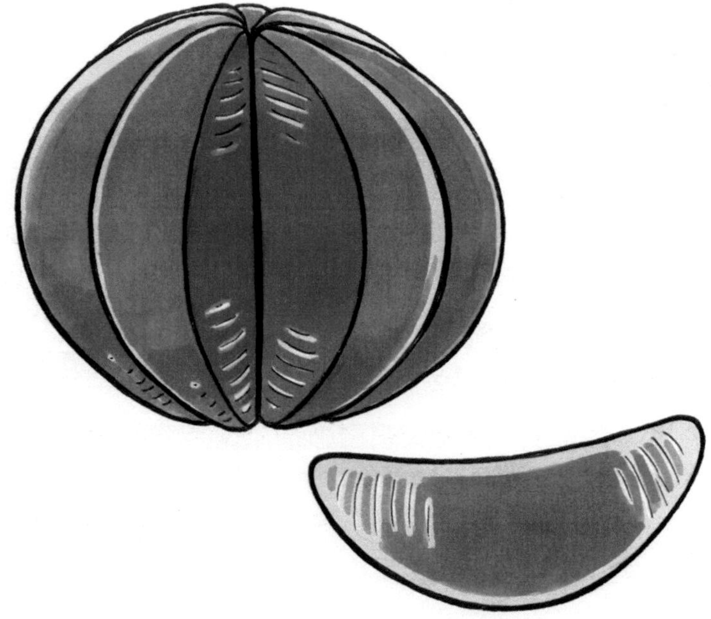

■ *Imagine the travel market like an orange – each segment represents a different group of customers*

The travel industry segments the market in many ways. The first segmentation is the split between business and leisure travel. Many travel agents and tour operators tend to specialise in one area or the other, for example, Going Places concentrates on leisure travel and American Express and Hogg Robinson concentrate on business travel.

By grouping together a set of customers with similar needs – a market segment – you can develop a product or products for the group's needs.

Types of customers

Customers are individuals, with their own individual needs and wants. However, to produce a travel and tourism product for each individual would make holidays too expensive for the average person. To make the cost of a holiday affordable, travel and tourism organisations produce products that will appeal to large groups of people.

Grouping customers is done in many different ways; however, the main aim is to group customers with similar needs and wants so that the organisation produces a product that addresses the group's needs. This group would be called a market segment. Below are the different ways that are used to segment a market.

Talking point

1 Make a list of all the requirements that you would have if you were going on a seven-day 'summer sun' holiday to Spain with three of your friends.
2 Compare your list with others in your group and make two lists – one of similarities and one of differences.
3 Is this a good method of segmentation?

Demographical

Demographics are about what a person is – it tends to view a person as you would describe an object. Methods of segmentation can include age, gender, size and ethnic group. (Some of these methods that are used will be discussed in Section 5.2.)

Geographical

This is concerned with segmenting a market on where the market lives or works. There are regional and national variations on how you would sell a product or service to a customer group. There can also be regional variations with regards to needs and expectations.

English Nature is one organisation whose visitor attractions are local and regional by nature. The organisation segments England into regions and you will find National Nature Reserves in every region. Their website allows you to find a wild place you can visit by searching on a place name or postcode.

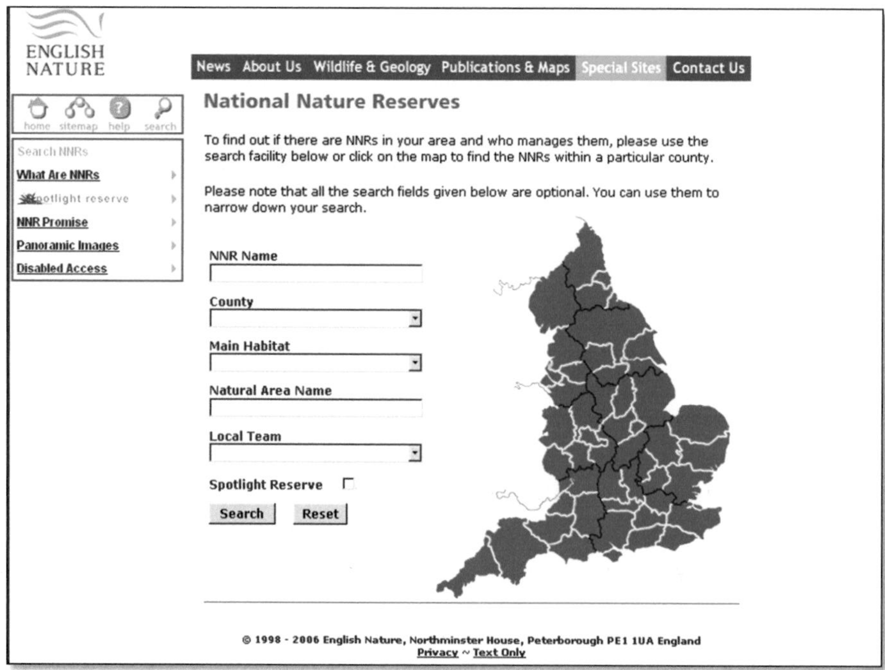

■ *English Nature's visitor attractions are local and regional by nature* (Reprinted with kind permission)

Over to you

Consider the different needs and expectations which the following two groups would have when travelling to London for a three-day trip:

- a group of elderly American tourists on a package trip titled 'Historical Britain'
- a group of twelve 20–30-year-old women going on a 'hen' weekend.

Socio-economic

This is a slightly more complex form of segmentation. You might think that you could segment a market on how much money a person earns or by social class; however, each of these categories individually has proven to be a little simplistic. Socio-economic factors are therefore taken into account according to the type of employment (employment status) and income, and these groups include most of the population. (For a more detailed consideration of socio-economic factors, see Section 5.2, page 186.)

Behaviour

These methods of segmentation are concerned with how a person or family lives. The methods are complex to assess and it can therefore be expensive to collect the data and analyse the results. However, they do take into consideration the way people live and to a greater extent what their expectations and needs are.

Case studies

A trip across the Pond to you!

You have just received the letter below.

Texas Tourism School
4011 93rd Street
Texas, USA

Hi,

My name is Sue-Ellen and I am a student at the Texas Tourism School. My class and I are planning to travel to the UK this summer for our European study visit. We are planning to come to your area and I am hoping that you can help us by describing what there is to do round your way.

I would like to know at whom each place is aimed so that I can make sure that the right people go to the right place.

Thanking you all for your help.

Sue-Ellen Jackdoor

Can you help Sue-Ellen and her classmates? Make a list of visitor attractions in your local area and try to work out the target market for each one.

Marketing objectives

Marketing objectives are developed from an organisation's mission statement (see *Unit 2: Exploring Customer Service in Travel and Tourism*). The mission statement is the specific area that an organisation wishes to address and what it wants to achieve in those areas. For example, part of Peregrine Adventure's mission statement is:

> 'Peregrine operates tourism that fosters understanding, appreciation and conservation of the cultures and environments we visit. We operate in a socially and environmentally responsible manner.' (You can find out more information about Peregrine by visiting their website which has been made available at www.heinemann.co.uk/hotlinks by entering the express code 2196P.)

Aims

To achieve its mission statement, the organisation develops a number of **aims**. These are the organisation's major goals to achieve the overall mission (the mission statement).

Some of the types of marketing aims that an organisation could have are listed below.

Create awareness of the product or organisation. It is important for consumers to be aware of your product and services so that when they are deciding to choose a holiday, for example, they will associate your organisation with that purchase.

Increase market share. Market share is important for organisations as a larger market share represents a larger number of sales and in turn larger profits.

Increase profit. Most travel and tourism organisations require profits to pay shareholders and owners.

Challenge competitors. If a competitor opens close to your location or undertakes advertising it is likely that the organisation is trying to attract customers that you have or are trying to attract. This may lead you to increase you own promotional activities to retain and attract customers.

Introduce new products. Customers need to be aware of new products on the market. Promotion is one method of communicating these new products to a large number of customers.

Product development. For the same reason that new products need to be communicated, so do product developments. This can be especially so if you are expecting current users to upgrade.

Improve image of product or organisation. From time to time an organisation or product may get a bad or negative image. Products need to have images reviewed from time to time and updated to meet current consumers' needs and tastes.

Target new customers. Marketing activities can help you to focus on the customers that your product appeals to and help you communicate your product to them.

Retain existing customers. Your current customers' needs and expectations develop over time and these changing needs have to be catered for. For example, many long-haul airlines have started to provide better sleeping conditions in business-class cabins as they have identified a desire among business travellers for better sleeping arrangements.

Branding. The branding is the name, logo or image that is associated with your product. The brand is the image that the consumer identifies with. For example, the brands of clothes that you choose to wear reflect the way you choose to be identified.

Activity

Choose an organisation in the travel and tourism industry. Come up with a specific objective for each of the marketing aims in the list beside this activity.

Objectives

Aims are fine but they are still general and do not highlight the steps to achieve the organisation's goals. The steps to achieve an aim are called **objectives**. Without objectives nobody will understand what the goal is.

SMART objectives

All objectives have to be SMART:

■ *SMART objectives*

Specific: the objective has to be stated in such a way that everyone who is involved in the objective understands what he or she is trying to achieve. For example, the objective 'To make the airline better' is not specific and does not tell people how to improve the airline.

Measurable: you have to be able to measure your level of success against the objective. The objective 'To have more happy customers' is not particularly measurable and it is very difficult to measure how well you achieve the objective. However, the objective 'To reduce customer complaints by 10 per cent' is easy to measure your performance against.

Achievable: there is no point in setting an objective that is not achievable as you will always fail to achieve it. The effects of this are that staff can become demotivated and uninterested in trying to achieve other objectives.

Realistic: although it is possible to sell every seat on an airplane or to have a fully occupied hotel, in most cases it is not realistic to expect to achieve this on every occasion. Goals have to be realistic for very much the same reasons, as they have to be achievable.

Timed: all objectives must have a time frame. Without a time frame there is no point at which you can stop and evaluate whether you have achieved an objective.

Here's an example of a SMART objective:

> 'Within/by the end of the next three months we will increase the amount of holiday insurance cover that we sell by 10 per cent.'

- It is specific in that everyone in the organisation knows what the aim is.
- It is measurable as the organisation can look at the financial records and see what percentage increase has been achieved.
- The current situation within the organisation has to be understood to ensure the objective is achievable or realistic. However, an increase of 10 per cent is not an unusual amount, but will depend on current sales levels.
- The time frame has been set so that at the end of the three-month period, it will be possible to compare the organisation's achieved results with the objective to see if it has been achieved, and how and why it has been achieved or not.

Over to you

Which of the following objectives are SMART objectives?

a) *Increase sales over the next three months.*

b) *Reduce customer complaints by 10 per cent.*

c) *Increase average spending by 10 per cent by the end of the year.*

d) *Rewrite the objectives that were not SMART as SMART objectives.*

In summary

- Marketing involves promoting or selling a product or service.
- Each product or service has a unique marketing mix: Product, Place, Price, Promotion (the 4Ps).
- Products are usually developed for a group of customers with similar needs. This is called a market segment.
- Objectives are targets for organisations to work towards. Objectives must be SMART (Specific, Measurable, Achievable, Realistic and Timed).

Practice assessment activity

Levels P1/M1

For this practice assessment, you need to look at one travel and tourism organisation. This might be:

- a real organisation, to which your tutor has organised a visit
- a real working environment, like a college travel centre
- case studies on an organisation.

P **1** Describe the principles of marketing used by travel and tourism organisations to meet marketing objectives. (P1) ✓

You need to include the following principles:

a) definition of marketing
b) marketing mix
c) target marketing
d) market segmentation
e) marketing objectives.

(Note: these are the principles in general used throughout the industry.)

M **2** Explain how the principles of marketing are used by a travel and tourism organisation to meet its marketing objectives. (M1) ✓✓

For the principles that you described in task 1, you now need to explain how the organisation you have chosen to look at uses the principles.

5.2 Understand how travel and tourism organisations provide a range of products and services to meet the needs of different types of customers

This section covers:

- travel and tourism products
- services
- types of customer.

Travel and tourism products

Travel and tourism is a huge industry with a wide range of different products. Unlike in some industries, travel and tourism products tend to be services and experiences rather than tangible (physical) goods. For example, if you are going to buy a car, you could look at the car, give it a test drive and make a decision about whether you are going to buy it. In this way, the car is a tangible product. However, if you are going to buy a holiday or a plane ticket, you cannot try it first before making the purchasing decision.

Families enjoying a package holiday

Package holidays

A package holiday is a holiday that has at least three different services put together. Two of these will be transport to and from the destination and accommodation while on holiday. The third part is usually made up of either transfer from the airport to the hotel or excursions.

A package holiday could be as simple as a weekend coach trip around the Cotswolds or as complicated as a two-week fly-drive holiday across the United States.

Package holidays are created by tour operators. This is done in advance and then information about the package holiday is sent to travel agencies. When the customer goes into a travel agency the agent has a number of different packages that can be sold to the customer. It is similar to buying a computer package with everything you need, rather than buying each part and assembling your own computer. The advantage to the customer is that he or she only needs to buy one product for the holiday rather than having to organise each component, or part, separately.

Activity

Using a holiday brochure (you can get one from any travel agent), pick a package holiday you would like to go on. Make a list of all the components of the holiday.

Attractions

Attractions draw people to a particular area. There is a huge range of different attractions from natural attractions such as the seaside or beautiful scenery to man-made attractions like a theme park or a heritage site. Britain's main attraction to foreign visitors is the country's history and heritage.

Talking point

Using either the Internet or a visit to your local tourist information office, find out what your local attractions are. Discuss in your group what you think the target markets for each of these attractions is.

Accommodation

This is where you stay on holiday. The range of different types of accommodation is wide, depending on your needs and how much you wish to spend. A tourist could stay in a suite in a five-star London hotel and spend hundreds of pounds a night; alternatively, youth hostel or bed-and-breakfast accommodation can cost under £20 a night. The type of accommodation is dictated by where you are travelling to, your budget and your needs.

Activity

Research the range of accommodation that is provided in your local area. You could do this on the Internet, using hotel and accommodation guides or by visiting a Tourist Information Centre.

Make a list of all the different types of accommodation.

Why do you think there is such a wide range of accommodation offered?

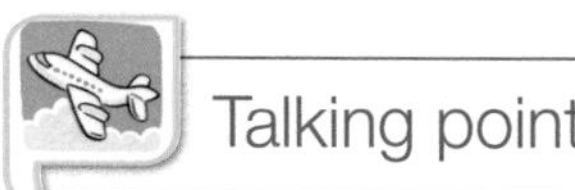

Talking point

In a small group, make a list of all the different types of transport you can think of for air, land and sea. Then compare your list with the rest of the class and see how many different forms of transport you have found.

Transport

There are three main ways to get to your destination:

- by air
- by land
- by sea.

The type of transport used to go on holiday depends on the needs of the individual. Some people want to get to the destination as quickly as possible; others view the travelling as a part of the holiday. This is particularly so with walking and cycling tours where the travelling *is* the holiday.

Tourist destinations

A tourist destination is a place where tourists go on holiday. This might be a historical town or city like Chester in the UK or Rome in Italy, or it could be a resort like Blackpool or an island such as Ibiza in Spain or Corfu in Greece.

Insurance

When a customer is on holiday there is the possibility of something going wrong. This could be an accident to the individual, the loss of the holidaymaker's belongings or a natural disaster. Holiday insurance is vital to give the customer the peace of mind and financial cover in case of an accident.

A holiday insurance package is designed to cover a particular type of holiday. You have to make sure that the type of cover a holidaymaker takes is correct for the activities on that specific holiday.

Services

As described in the introduction to this section, travel and tourism products are a combination of a physical product and a number of services. The services are no less or more important than the product. The level of service will contribute as much to the overall holiday experience as the location of the holiday.

Customer services

Most travel and tourism holidays have a number of customer services that are designed to meet the needs of the customers, for example, room service. Hotels offer room service so that guests can have their meals in the hotel room. This service is particularly popular with businesswomen who are staying in a hotel on their own, as it means that they do not have to sit alone in the hotel restaurant. (See also *Unit 2: Exploring Customer Service in Travel and Tourism*.)

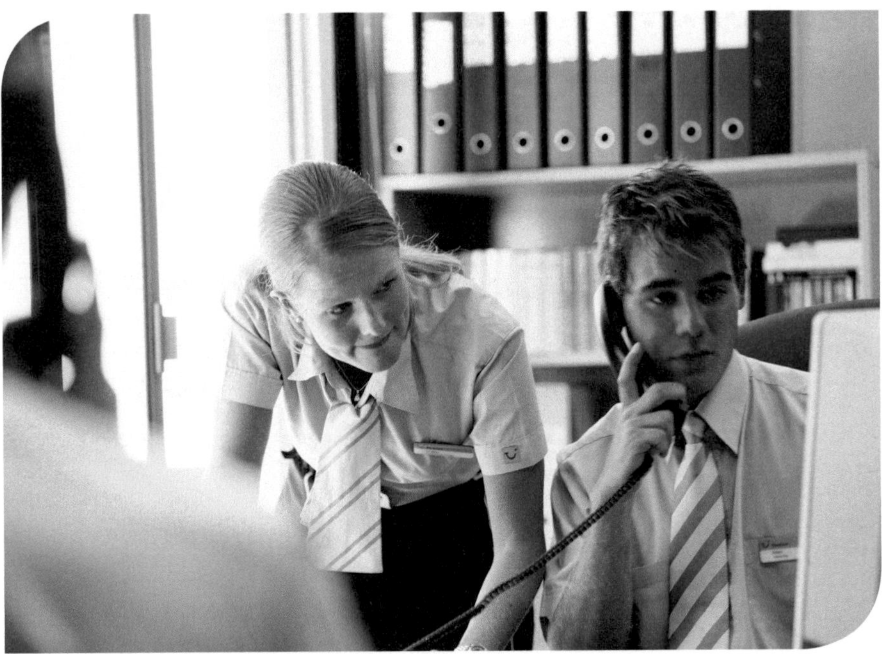

■ *Providing customer service information in a travel agency*

Additional services

Many travel and tourism organisations will also offer additional services for customers. These additional services are designed to make the experience more personalised for the customer, for example:

- Pre-allocated seating is offered by a number of train operating companies on their longer journeys so that customers do not have to worry about overcrowding.
- Most airports have VIP (very important people) lounges. This is so that first-class and VIP passengers have a private lounge in which to wait for their flights.

Services to meet specific needs

Not all customers have the same needs, so travel and tourism organisations have developed specific services to meet the needs of these individuals. Examples of this include:

- To meet special dietary needs, flights to and from Israel offer a kosher menu option for Orthodox (Hasidic) Jews.
- Kids clubs are designed to provide entertainment for children on holiday, so that the parents can have some time for themselves knowing that their children are safe and being entertained.

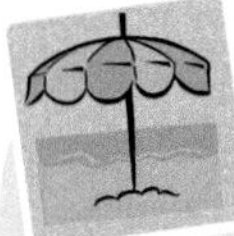

Practice assessment activity

P ***Level P2*** 

Describe how the products and services of one travel and tourism organisation are provided to meet the needs of different types of customers.

For this assessment activity, you will need to consider the following types of products and services:

- the product might include package holidays, accommodation, tourist attractions, transport or insurance
- the services should include customer services, additional services and services to meet special needs.

For each product and service you should identify:

- the target market
- the needs they are designed for.

Types of customers

As discussed in Section 5.1, the whole of the travel and tourism market is segmented into different groups so that products can be provided to meet these different groups' needs.

Demographics

Demographics are about the physical you – for example, your age and your gender. You will now look at the main demographic methods that are used in the travel and tourism industry.

Specific age groups

Another way of segmenting the market is by age. This is used in package holidays, with companies producing packages for different age groups. Saga Holidays, for example, specialises in holidays for the over-50s, whereas Club 18–30 produces a completely different type of holiday targeted at 18 to 30-year-olds. This segmentation works well for these products but age is a very broad way of segmenting a market. After all, not all 18 to 30-year-olds are the same or have similar needs.

■ *Holiday products are often targeted to specific age groups*

Ethnic groups

Although this might seem a good way to segment a market, it creates some issues. People of the same ethnic group do not necessarily share the same needs and wants. However, there are organisations that segment their market on ethnic grounds, for example, MasterSun organises holidays for Christian groups. There are also some cultural-based holidays which have more appeal to one ethnic group than another; for example, tours around 'Bollywood' locations in the UK have brought over 200,000 Indian tourists to the UK.

Single-sex groups

Some people prefer to go on holiday with people of their own sex. This may have nothing to do with sexual preference but because they feel more comfortable and relaxed in a single-sex environment. American Round Up is a company that provides hiking and horse-riding holidays and runs women-only trips.

Geographics

Another method used to segment the market is the customer's geographical location (where he or she is from). This is used by independent travel agencies which may put together holidays, tour and travel arrangements focused on the needs of the local population. For example, a family in Preston would not see the appeal of Blackpool (16 miles away) the same as a family from Glasgow: the Preston family will see Blackpool as a day trip whereas the Glaswegian family might

Over to you

How far would you travel to go to the following types of visitor attractions/events?

- Stately home
- Theme park
- Aquarium
- Museum
- Art gallery
- Carnival

consider Blackpool as a holiday destination. These two perceptions would affect the way in which the two families would use Blackpool as a resort. The uses of products and services can also vary depending on the geographical location of the customer.

Socio-economic groups

This method involves segmenting society on grounds of employment status and income. (*Socio-economic* means that relating to social and economic factors.) The chart below lists the Office for National Statistics' socio-economic classifications.

Office for National Statistics' socio-economic classifications

1 Higher managerial and professional occupations

1.1 Large employers and higher managerial occupations

1.2 Higher professional occupations

2 Lower managerial and professional occupations

3 Intermediate occupations

4 Small employers and own account workers

5 Lower supervisory and technical occupations

6 Semi-routine occupations

7 Routine occupations

8 Never worked and long-term unemployed

Note: For complete coverage, the three categories (i) Students, (ii) Occupations not stated or inadequately described, and (iii) Not classifiable for other reasons are added as 'Not classified'.

(*Source*: Office for National Statistics. Crown copyright material is reproduced with the permission of the Controller of the HMSO and the Queen's Printer for Scotland)

Although the groups are graded 1–8, this does not mean that group 1 is better than group 8, just that they have a different employment. However, it is reasonable to say that groups 1 and 2 could have similar needs and wants.

Behaviour

Behaviour refers to how people live and their lifestyle and circumstances.

Lifestyle and family circumstances

Segmenting by lifestyle and family circumstances looks into how you live. This is because your needs will change as you go through the stages of the family life cycle (see below). At each stage of the life cycle a person's income and responsibilities change, and each change is significant because it will affect the individual's needs when he or she buys a product.

Stage	Comments
Bachelor	Young and single with limited or no family responsibility
Newly married	Young and married with no children
Full nest 1	Family with youngest child under school age
Full nest 2	Family with youngest child of school age
Full nest 3	Children are still at home but are now working
Empty nest 1	One partner working and children have left home
Empty nest 2	Both partners are now retired
Solitary survivor 1	One partner deceased; the other is still working
Solitary survivor 2	One partner deceased; the other is retired

■ *The family life cycle*

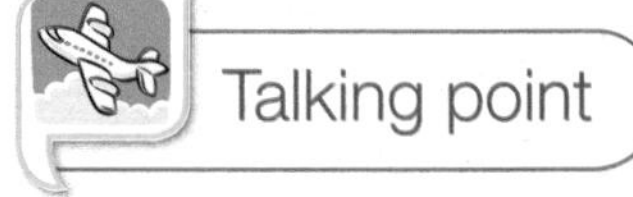

In a small group, discuss what you think will be the changes in income and responsibilities at different stages of the life cycle.

Lifestyle segmentation is slightly more complicated than segmenting by employment and income or age. Most organisations set their own segments and names for lifestyle segmentation. One example is the Baked Bean family: this family has a low household income and usually more than one child. Although it is a low spending-power segment, it is also a large segment and therefore has products targeted at it, for example, holiday camps and package holidays. The segment is very price sensitive but also has child provision needs such as 'kids clubs'.

Special interests

This is a major growth area in travel and tourism. People are becoming better educated about holiday destinations and therefore more people are deciding to have holidays that cater for a particular interest. This could be to follow a sports team or a particular activity, or to develop or gain a new skill. There are, for example, a number of hotels and bed-and-breakfast places throughout the UK that specialise in accommodation for bikers, with secure parking for their motorbikes, drying rooms and easy access to main routes.

The market is segmented in order to provide a product to a group that has similar needs.

School and other organised groups

This is a specific market segment. Although schools are cost-sensitive groups, they tend to have a large number of customers so it is possible to produce a product tailored to their needs. Other groups could include clubs and organisations. Kuoni (the tour operator) has a department that specialises in producing tailor-made trips for these groups, which includes organising sports tours.

A school trip to the dinosaur museum

Religious groups

There are a large number of organisations that provide holidays and travel arrangements for different faith groups, whether it is a pilgrimage, a retreat to contemplate on a person's faith, or simply a holiday that has provisions for a particular faith. For example, Mastersun provides family package holidays that also have provision for practising Christians.

Case studies

Ian's balloon rides

Ian has been running his balloon-ride company for about four years. He has now decided to open a second centre in your area which will specialise in running local balloon rides (weather permitting).

Until now, Ian's business has been targeted at the 'holidaymakers market' in his local town, but he would like to find out what other markets he could target. Ian has asked you to help him research the best target markets for his business in your area, so that he can develop products for these markets.

Conduct a survey to find out about the people that would use Ian's services. You might like to focus on:

- the age of the people
- whether they would use the service
- their reasons for using Ian's service
- the price they would pay for the service.

In summary

- Methods of segmenting a market include: social economic groups, age, religious groups, ethnic groups, single-gender groups, location, gender, lifestyle and family circumstances.
- Whichever method of segmentation the organisation uses, its aim is to identify a group of individuals that have similar needs and expectations of a product, so that it can produce a product that addresses those needs.
- The needs and expectations of customers will change over time, so organisations will review their products regularly, especially if they use customer feedback to develop their products.

Practice assessment activity

Level P2

Describe how the product and services of one travel and tourism organisation meets the needs of different types of customers.

For this task you need to select one travel and tourism organisation. This may be an organisation that you have visited, had a guest speaker from, or from which you have got a study pack. Your description should include a broad type of customers that the organisation provides for.

5.3 Design and use market research to meet specific objectives

This section covers:

- market research objectives
- types of market research.

The more you know about a customer's needs and wants, the more likely your product or service will suit the customer's needs.

Market research involves finding out information about your market. This could be about:

- what a particular group's needs are
- changes in a group's needs
- the market's perception of a product (what customers think about the product).

Market research objectives

You learnt above that marketing is focused on the customer and his or her needs, so one of the main functions of research is to find out what those needs are. Market research can also be used for the reasons listed below.

Identification of customers

To be able to develop a product or service for customers, you firstly need to identify the different type of customers that are in the market. This is so that you can group customers together in market segments and develop products to suit this market segment.

Identification of customer needs

Customers will have their own requirements and needs from the product and services. Market research can be used to identify what these needs and requirements are so that the product can be tailored to the needs of that specific market segment.

Product development

Customers' needs and expectations will change over time for a number of reasons including previous experience, education, trends and fashions. Therefore there is a need to continually develop a product to meet these changing customers' needs. Market research is used to identify what these changing needs are and the results are used to develop the product or service.

To measure customer satisfaction

It is vital in the competitive world of travel and tourism to gauge the level of customer satisfaction. In *Unit 2: Exploring Customer Service in Travel and Tourism* you looked into the effects of low customer satisfaction on a business's success. Market research is used to investigate satisfaction levels and how to develop products and services to increase customer satisfaction.

To gauge means to measure.

To target new and existing products to customers

Market research is used to help target customers with products. The research is used to not only develop products to suit the needs of these customers but also to identify the best way of communicating with these customers. This could be done by using an existing customer database but also by running competitions and surveys to get customer contact information.

Unless an organisation knows what the customer's wants or needs are, how can it develop products and services to address those needs? Without research an organisation will not know what customers desire and can only guess at what the customer wants. The more information an organisation has about its market, the better it will be able to segment the market and develop products, etc.

Types of market research

There are two main types of research:

- desk, or secondary, research
- field, or primary, research.

Secondary (desk) research

This is research that has already been done for another reason (so it is the second use of the information). It is sometimes known as desk research, as this is where the research takes place.

Information can go out of date.

Secondary research could be information that an organisation has collected such as sales figures or customer comment forms, or it could be information from outside the organisation, for example, from the government or a specialist research organisation.

Benefits of secondary research

The main benefit of secondary research is the speed with which an organisation can gather the results. Secondary research is usually relatively cheap to obtain compared with the costs of employing people or commissioning a research organisation to carry out primary research and analyse the information.

Primary (field) research

This research is being done for the first time and is purposely designed to meet an organisation's needs. There are four main methods of conducting primary research:

- questionnaires
- observation
- focus groups
- surveys.

Questionnaires

Questionnaires are commonly used in customer service to obtain customer feedback. The important thing to remember when designing a questionnaire is that it should be objective and not cause bias.

Quantitative data is data that can be used statistically to make charts and graphs showing trends.

Questionnaires may be designed to obtain information that is factual and which can be turned into numbers or statistics. For example, 20 people were asked to give a yes or no answer to the following question: 'Was your flight on time?' Fourteen people answered yes, six answered no.

You might want an answer that gives a range of opinion. For example, the answer to a question such as 'On a scale of 1–10, how did you rate the service (10 being good, 1 being bad)?' This type of data is called **quantitative data**. It is useful for identifying trends but does not go into the customer's personal opinions or feelings in depth.

Advantages of questionnaires

- Questionnaires are a good method of obtaining customer feedback.
- The data is easy to manipulate and is used to work out trends.
- They are relatively cheap to use, after the initial time invested in developing the questionnaire and the printing cost.
- Customers can see that the organisation is interested in their opinion.

Disadvantages of questionnaires

- Questionnaires tend to give polarised viewpoints. In other words, people tend only to fill in questionnaires if they either had a very good or bad experience.
- Unless the questionnaire and data are rigorously collected and acted on, it tends to become less useful.
- Data collected can be only quantitative. It often does not give details of customers' feelings or how customers would like to see the product or service developed or improved.

AVIS Customer Opinion Survey

Please indicate your level of satisfaction with each of the areas below by placing an 'X' in the appropriate box.

1. YOUR OVERALL OPINION

	completely satisfied	very satisfied	fairly satisfied	somewhat dissatisfied	very dissatisfied
a. *Overall*, how satisfied were you with this Avis rental?....................................	☐	☐	☐	☐	☐
	definitely will	**probably will**	**possibly will**	**probably will not**	**definitely will not**
b. Based on this rental experience, how likely are you to recommend Avis to a friend?....................................	☐	☐	☐	☐	☐

2. RENTING YOUR VEHICLE

Thinking about the people you dealt with when you rented your Avis vehicle, how satisfied were you with each of the following aspects:	completely satisfied	very satisfied	fairly satisfied	somewhat dissatisfied	very dissatisfied	not applicable
a. Waiting time at the counter before being served?....................................	☐	☐	☐	☐	☐	☐
b. Courtesy?....................................	☐	☐	☐	☐	☐	☐
c. Helpfulness?....................................	☐	☐	☐	☐	☐	☐
d. Knowledge?....................................	☐	☐	☐	☐	☐	☐
e. Speed of processing your rental?....................................	☐	☐	☐	☐	☐	☐
f. Explanation of the charges and conditions?....................................	☐	☐	☐	☐	☐	☐

3. THE VEHICLE

Thinking about the vehicle itself, how satisfied were you with:	completely satisfied	very satisfied	fairly satisfied	somewhat dissatisfied	very dissatisfied
a. Interior and exterior cleanliness?....................................	☐	☐	☐	☐	☐
b. The extent that the car rented matched your preference at reservation?........	☐	☐	☐	☐	☐
c. Make and model of the vehicle?....................................	☐	☐	☐	☐	☐

4. RETURNING YOUR VEHICLE

When you returned your vehicle, how satisfied were you with:	completely satisfied	very satisfied	fairly satisfied	somewhat dissatisfied	very dissatisfied	not applicable
a. Accessibility and signage of the vehicle parking?....................................	☐	☐	☐	☐	☐	☐
b. Waiting time before being served?....................................	☐	☐	☐	☐	☐	☐
c. The greeting you received, and the helpfulness of the staff?..........................	☐	☐	☐	☐	☐	☐
d. Their knowledge and speed?....................................	☐	☐	☐	☐	☐	☐
e. The final charges being easily understood, and as expected?.......................	☐	☐	☐	☐	☐	☐

5. YOUR RENTAL OVERALL

Thinking about this rental experience:	Business		Leisure		Replacement Vehicle	
a. What was the **main** reason for this rental?....................................	☐		☐		☐	
	completely satisfied	**very satisfied**	**fairly satisfied**	**somewhat dissatisfied**	**very dissatisfied**	**not applicable**
b. How satisfied were you that Avis provided value for money?.........................	☐	☐	☐	☐	☐	☐
c. If you queried anything about this rental, how satisfied were you with the response you received from Avis and its staff?....................................	☐	☐	☐	☐	☐	☐
	definitely will	**probably will**	**possibly will**	**probably will not**	**definitely will not**	**not applicable**
d. How likely are you to rent from Avis again?....................................	☐	☐	☐	☐	☐	☐

■ *The car rental company Avis uses a questionnaire to obtain feedback from its customers.* (*Source*: Reprinted with permission of Avis Europe Plc)

Case studies

Moses is planning to start up a new independent travel agency in your town called *Home from Home Travel*. He is planning to organise holidays in which the family pet is invited. However, he is concerned that there may not be the demand for his specialist services in your local area.

- Produce a questionnaire which Moses could use to assess if there is demand for his services in your town.

Observation

This method of research involves observing customers. It is good for monitoring how customers use a facility and how they interact with a product. For example, the managers of an international airport might observe the ways passengers move around the check-in area. They might wish to understand how space is used in order to decide the best places to put facilities, in order to speed up customer flow around the area.

Advantages of observation

The main advantage is that you are not interacting with the customers; you are watching how they behave naturally rather than asking what they think. People's behaviour can differ a lot from what they think their behaviour is.

Disadvantages of observation

You are only monitoring the customer's behaviour. You do not have any insight into why this behaviour is happening.

Qualitative data is data that gives people's opinions and feelings.

Focus groups

A focus group involves bringing together a small group of product users. It can be used to test products or give detailed opinions and information about feelings. This is known as **qualitative data**. It cannot be used to show trends but shows consumers' perception of products and their feelings about different products.

Tour operators may use focus groups when considering developing new package holidays, especially if the product is targeted at a particular type of customer.

Advantages of focus groups

- Focus groups offer a detailed insight into what the customer feels about the product and service.
- This is the only method of primary research that really gives an understanding of the customer perception of the product/service.

Disadvantage of focus groups

- As the data is qualitative, the focus group has to be small enough to allow you to manage all the data. However, a small sample group might lead to a misleading or non-representative sample (the people in the focus group do not truly reflect the market).
- Focus groups can be quite expensive in time and money to run and organise.

Surveys

A survey is a targeted way of collecting data. To find out general trends or the average opinion, an organisation could ask everyone in the market their view. However, this would be too expensive and time consuming, so to save time and money, a sample is chosen that represents the market to be questioned.

Sometimes on your local high street, you may see researchers stopping people to ask them questions. You might notice that they do not stop everyone but select people to ask. This is because they are only looking for a particular type of person for the sample.

Surveys can be carried out in three different ways:

- telephone survey
- postal survey
- person-to-person survey.

Telephone survey

As the name suggests, this is a survey that is conducted on the telephone. Although this can be carried out in-house (using the organisation's own staff), there are many companies that specialise in this type of research.

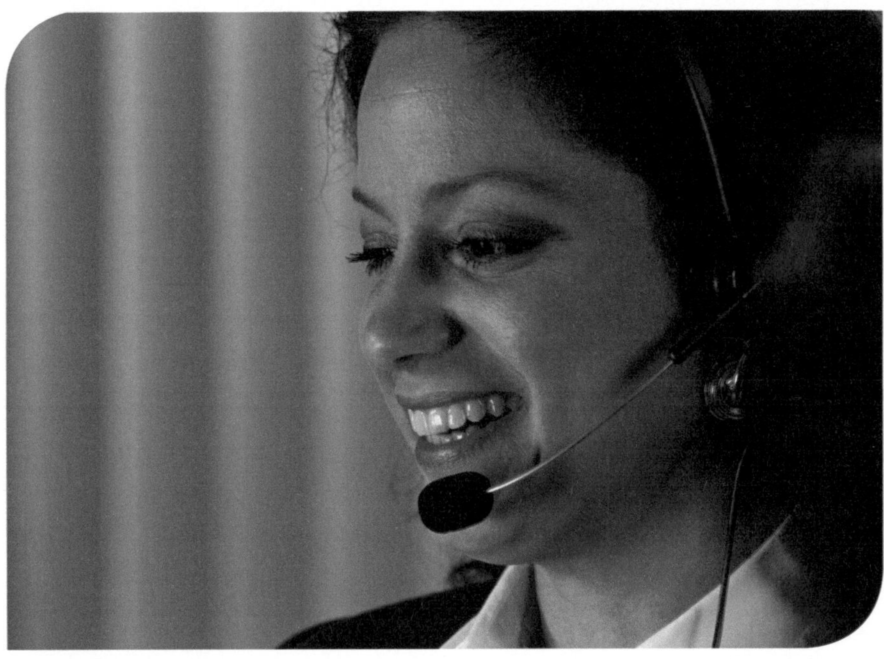

Conducting a telephone survey

Advantages of a telephone survey

- Data can be obtained quickly, especially as it can be entered straight into a database while the questions are being answered.
- For primary research, this is relatively inexpensive as the number of interviews conducted by one member of staff can be quite high.
- As you are speaking to the customer you can ask supplementary questions if you do not understand the customer's response.

Disadvantages of a telephone survey

- The survey can have a low response rate, especially if you are cold calling (calling a person that has had no previous contact with your organisation).
- As you are speaking to customers in person, they may tone down their reply so as not to cause offence. Although this is pleasant, it will not give you the customers' true feelings, which can affect the validity of your research.

Postal survey

This is a survey that is conducted by post. It has quite a low response rate. A number of companies offer entry into a prize draw or discounts off products so as to increase the response rate. The travel agency Thomas Cook sends a postal survey to every customer on their return from holiday to judge customer satisfaction and also to help the company develop its products to suit customers' needs.

Advantages of a postal survey

- Customers have time to consider their response so the data will be less likely to be tainted by emotion.
- It is cheap to run as limited staff time is used.
- Customers are more likely to be honest than in a one-to-one situation.

Disadvantages of a postal survey

- It is time-consuming as it takes a long time for letters to be delivered and replies to be returned.
- It has a low response rate.
- Supplementary questions cannot be asked.
- There might be problems understanding customer responses or even their handwriting.

Person-to-person survey

This is a survey that you carry out in person. You might see this sort of market researcher in your high street.

Advantages of a person-to-person survey

- This type of survey has a higher response rate compared to the other methods of research, as it is harder to refuse a person face to face rather than over the telephone when you can just hang up.
- Supplementary questions can be asked if answers are not understood.
- The researcher can choose whom they survey. This is particularly important if you are trying to target a market segment. For example, there is little point asking a 50-year-old man about package holidays for the under-30s.

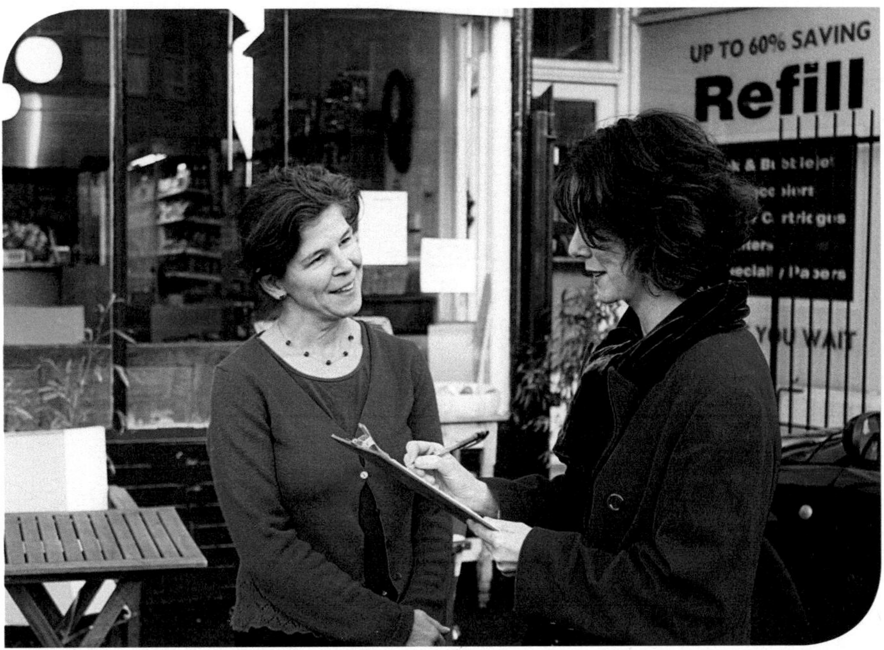

■ *A market researcher conducting a survey in the street*

Disadvantages of a person-to-person survey

- It is a very expensive method of researching as the organisation has to pay for researchers to collect the information.
- People will not consider their answers as much as with a postal survey, possibly just telling the researcher what they think he or she wants to hear in order to get away as quickly as possible.

In summary

- Market research supplies managers with information to help them make more informed decisions.
- There are two types of market research: primary (new research) and secondary (information that has previously been collected).
- Methods of primary research include: questionnaires, surveys, observation, focus groups.

Practice assessment activity

Levels P3/M2/D1

P **1** Design and use a piece of market research material which is suitable for use in a travel and tourism context to meet specific objectives. (P3) The context could be a work situation or simulation, or a project such as planning a study visit. You need to:

a) State what the marketing research objectives are. These could include:

- customer demographics
- current needs
- opportunities for further product development.

b) Include your research material.

c) Present your findings in the form of a graph, chart or diagram.

M **2** Explain the appropriateness of the market research for the selected travel or tourism organisation. (M2) Your answer could include:

- the advantages and disadvantages of the selected research method
- a conclusion based on your success.

D **3** Draw conclusions from the results of the market research and suggest changes to be made. (D1) You need to suggest changes based on your results as to how improvements could be made to existing products and services. Suggestions should be appropriate to the context.

5.4 Produce promotional material suitable for use in travel and tourism

This section covers:

- promotional materials
- evaluating the success of promotional material suitable for use in travel and tourism.

Promotional methods vary as much as companies do, from the common to the bizarre. This section looks at the most commonly used techniques and media.

Promotion is an important part of the product delivery system. After all, if customers do not know what an organisation is offering, how can they purchase its goods and services?

Promotional techniques

Advertising materials

Advertising is any promotion that you pay a third party for in order to promote your product through their medium.

Promotional design is discussed later in this section (see pages 206–8). First, you will look at the advantages and disadvantages of each of the main media.

■ *VisitWales have a successful advertising campaign*

Television advertisements

These are advertisements that an organisation pays for to appear on television. They are commonly known as commercials.

Advantages of TV advertisements

- Television is a passive medium as it is not interactive – you do not have to make any effort to watch a television commercial whereas most other media requires some effort on your part. This means that people take notice of television adverts even when they are not taking any notice of the television.
- A TV advertisement does not only have images but also sound, so the advertisement can be stimulating and changing.
- Most commercial television channels in the UK are either regionalised or tend to specialise in a particular area of interest. This means that the organisation can target selected interest groups by advertising on a particular channel. For example, Leger Holidays advertises battlefield tours on the History Channel.

Disadvantages of TV advertisements

- The main disadvantage is the cost of not only showing the advertisement but also producing the advertisement in the first place. Only large local and national travel and tourism organisations can afford to advertise in this way.
- Television is a passive medium – the customer does not have any information except what they can remember from the advertisement (compared to a newspaper advertisement that they can keep referring to).
- Only a minimum amount of information can be put across in each commercial.
- Although TV advertising is very good at getting customers to be aware of a product, it is not very good at converting that awareness to sales.
- For a TV advertisement to be memorable, it has to be repeated many times, so increasing the cost.
- Many people switch off/change channels to avoid TV adverts. To avoid this, programme sponsorship is becoming a more popular way of advertising products.

Radio commercials

Like television, this is another mass-market form of advertising. The obvious difference is there are no pictures on radio, so the whole of the message needs to be put across in sound.

Advantages of radio commercials

- Radio is the most popular entertainment medium with the average person listening to more hours of radio a day than hours watching television.
- Radio commercials are cheaper to produce and also to air than TV advertisements.
- Radio stations tend to be more regionalised so that small- or medium-size organisations can afford to promote on this medium to their own local market.

Disadvantages of radio commercials

- Although there are special interest radio stations, they tend not to be as subject specific as television stations but to reflect musical taste. However, musical taste can be linked with socio-economic groups, with groups 1 and 2 more likely to listen to classical music than groups 7 or 8, for example.
- As with television there is no hard copy of the information. This means that the message has to be very clear or the advertisement has to be repeated regularly.

Billboards (advertising hoardings)

These are the posters that you might see around any town or city. They tend to be set beside main roads so that they have a high number of people passing them each day. The average person will look at a billboard for between 5 and 13 seconds, which means that the message has to be very clear.

Advantages of billboards

- They are relatively cheap, compared to TV or radio commercials.
- Advertisements can be targeted at a particular area, e.g. a travel agency could have a billboard giving information about the location of its local branch in that town and different information in a different town.

Disadvantages of billboards

- Due to the huge amount of advertising and street furniture on the streets in the UK, advertising hoardings can be lost in the clutter.
- As there is no movement in most hoardings, this means that it can be quite difficult to attract people's attention.
- The message has to be simple, as people tend not to spend very long looking at a hoarding.

Newspaper adverts

Newspapers, both local and national, run advertising throughout their pages. Local papers, especially local free papers that are delivered to every house in an area, have a high readership and this can be an effective method of promotion for a small business.

Activity

Get hold of a copy of a Sunday newspaper travel section and have a look at the advertisements for holidays. Pick out the ones that grab your attention and cut them out. Stick the advertisements in the middle of a sheet of paper and around the outside try to explain why they grabbed your attention.

National newspapers tend to target different types of readerships. Weekend papers are especially popular for advertising travel products; some weekend papers contain special travel sections.

Advantages of newspaper advertising

- Compared with other advertising media, this is a relatively cheap form of advertising.
- Customers have a hard copy of the advertisement which they can refer to, unlike television, radio or billboards.
- Effectiveness of a newspaper's adverts can be assessed more accurately.

Disadvantages of newspaper advertising

- As this is a popular and effective method of advertising that is used extensively by travel and tourism organisations, individual advertisements may easily be 'lost' among all the others.
- Due to the popularity of advertising holidays in newspapers, customers can easily compare offers.

Window and in-store displays

A display is any collection of material put together to promote a particular product or service.

Brochures and leaflets

Brochures and leaflets are two of the most popular methods of promotion in travel and tourism.

■ *A brochure display in a travel agents*

Leaflets are used by most tourist attractions as an essential way to communicate information about the attraction. Unlike a leaflet, that tends to be a sheet or two of paper, a brochure is a booklet. The main users of brochures are tour operators and travel agents. Brochures are a very good way for a tour operator to display its products and for travel agents to sell them.

Sponsorship

In the past, you have probably been asked to sponsor someone or to get involved in a sponsorship event. An organisation may sponsor a cause or event to gain as much media exposure as possible for itself or its product and to give the organisation a better social image. It is important that the event or person sponsored enhances the organisation's product image and does not offend current customers.

For example, TUI is one of the 'Big 4' travel agents and, as such, is a mass-market product. By sponsoring Tottenham Hotspur Football Club, a premiership football team, TUI is able to get its sponsorship message across to a mass market.

Case studies

Blue Sea Sealife Centre

The Blue Sea Sealife Centre was opened in 1985 on the seafront in Coaston. The number of visitors has been falling for the last four seasons despite the centre's best efforts to keep the displays up to date with the latest technology and create interesting environments for the sea creatures to live in.

Tahiba, the centre's manager, is a friend of your tutor and has asked for your help to come up with a plan to increase the numbers of visitors.

The centre knows that most of the customers live within an hour's drive from the centre and tend to be families with children or school parties.

- Using your knowledge of promotional techniques, decide on two methods of promotion that you could use to target each of the two main user groups. You need to consider the costs involved as the centre has limited funds for promotion.

Special offers and incentives

Air miles

Air miles is a loyalty scheme which started in 1990. Registered members of the air mile scheme receive air miles when making purchases with a wide range of retail outlets, including Shell, Tesco and Southern Electric. The air miles can be traded in for part- or full-payment for travel products from a large range of travel and tourism providers.

Special offers

A special offer is when an organisation offers a particular product or service for a short period of time. This could be a reduction in the cost or some extra component to the product. Travel agents often offer discounts of free child places if you book your holiday early. Hotels often offer special weekend breaks in the quieter time of the year to improve room sales.

Incentives

Incentive schemes are used to encourage customers to repeat purchase a product. Many hotel groups and airlines offer customer loyalty schemes, which give customers free or discounted use of a product as a reward for their loyalty. For example, British Airways rewards customers through its frequent flyer programme called the British Airways Executive Club; the benefits include priority check-in, seat upgrades and bonus air miles.

Competitions

Competitions are another method used to promote a product. They help increase product awareness and give the organisation a way to communicate to potential customers.

Videos/DVDs

These are increasingly being used as a method of promotion. A number of holiday resorts offer potential customers free videos. Although they can be expensive to produce, a video or DVD gives a more detailed description of the resort than a brochure can.

Direct mailshots and text messaging

Most organisations keep a database of current and previous customers and enquiries. This can be used to send information about products to those customers. For example, a theatre preparing to put on a particular drama can use its database to send out information to customers who have expressed an interest in that type of play in the past.

Direct mail is most effective if it is addressed and directed to a person by name rather than to 'Dear customer'. As the computer is used to generate the mailshot, it is the design of the letter that is most important so that each customer feels it is a personal invitation rather than just another circular.

Text messaging

With the massive increase in the last 20 years in the use of mobile phones and the introduction of third generation mobile phones (G3), messaging has become an increasingly used method of communication. Organisations have started using text messaging as a method of communicating products and services to potential and existing customers.

Advantages of text messaging

- Text messages can be targeted at a specific person.

- It is a relatively cheap method of communication to a large number of customers.
- With G3 phones, texting can include pictures, sound and links to websites.

Disadvantages of text messaging

- Text messages can be easily deleted or ignored.
- Technology is currently changing and a single text message may not be in a format that can be received by the customer's phone.

Press releases

A press release is when an organisation provides the press (newspapers, TV news etc.) with information about itself or its products. A press release is usually written in the form of a newspaper story. It must contain a release date (date after which it can be used) and a contact name and details in case journalists require more details.

Activity

Write a press release for your local newspaper promoting your course. You might like to focus on an event or trip that you have been involved in.

Advantages of press releases

- Most people will read a newspaper story and are more likely to believe it than an advertisement.
- It is a cheap method of promotion as the only cost is the time to write the article.

Disadvantages of press releases

- Newspapers have no obligation to use the story.
- The story can be changed or edited by the newspaper.

Evaluating the success of promotional materials

Planning promotional activities

Promotional activities need to be planned. The travel and tourism industry is a very competitive market place with a large number of organisations offering similar products and services. If you do not plan your promotion well, your message risks coming across as confused and its effectiveness will be reduced.

Purpose of promotion and marketing objectives

There are many different reasons why an organisation may decide to run a promotional campaign. Some of the most common reasons are:

- to increase repeat sales
- to increase product awareness among customers
- to encourage new customers to use products
- to inform the market of a new product or changes to products

- because competitors are advertising and the organisation needs to defend its market share
- to counter rumours about the organisation or product.

Before beginning a promotional campaign you will first need to set your objectives.

Identifying the target market

Once you have identified your marketing objectives, you will need to identify your target market. It is important that you know who your customers are before you communicate with them, to ensure that the methods and media you choose will be appropriate.

Choice of promotional methods

The method of promotion you choose will depend on the target market. The trick is to adapt your promotion to target your intended market. If you were trying to promote weekend breaks, for example, advertising on the London Underground where thousands of commuters pass every day would be an effective method.

Designing effective promotional material

On average, you see over 1,200 advertising messages a day! How then do you get people to take notice of yours? The AIDA approach is used as a method of designing advertising so that people will take notice and remember it:

- **A**ttention
- **I**nterest
- **D**esire
- **A**ction.

A is for Attention

Unless you can attract people's attention, there is little likelihood of your advertising campaign being successful. Different methods are used to attract people's attention; these include:

- colour
- fonts and print style
- pictures and drawings
- humour.

I is for Interest

After you have attracted someone's attention you need to keep the person interested in your product or service. This is the second part of the AIDA approach. The most common way that a customer's interest is gained is by slowly developing his or her interest in a product rather than bombarding the person with facts. Fun can be used as a way of

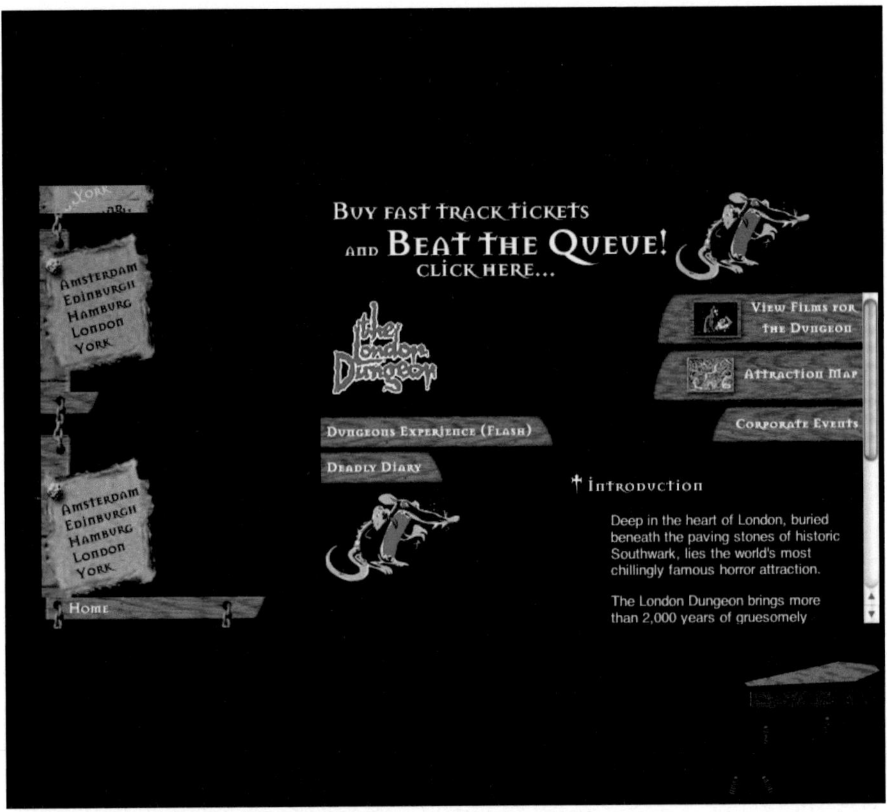

■ *The London Dungeon website* (Reprinted with kind permission)

keeping people interested. Adverts with a simple ongoing storyline encourage people to watch them just to see what happens next.

D is for Desire

After a promotion has created attention and interest, you will need to create desire in the customer to visit or purchase the attraction or product. The three main ways that desire is created in travel and tourism are:

- by making the customer feel that he or she is already there
- by personalising the information so that the customer feels that he or she is the person for whom the product or service was created
- through showing the customer the benefits of the product.

A is for Action

When you have persuaded a customer to buy a product or service you need him or her to take action to buy the product. The following information is often given to encourage a customer to take this action:

- freephone number
- telephone number
- location map
- website

- email address
- address
- fax number.

Activity

Find one travel and tourism poster, leaflet and holiday brochure. Analyse each and identify how they try to complete each of the four steps of AIDA. Compare you answer with others in your group.

It is important to remember who the promotional material is targeted at!

Timing

Timing is crucial for a marketing campaign to be effective. You need to consider not only how long the campaign will last but also the intensity of the promotion. If you are running a short campaign, promotion is likely to be intense. However, in a longer campaign the amount of promotion going on at any one time is likely to be less, otherwise the message can become stale.

The other consideration is *when* to run a campaign. If you are promoting a holiday, you will need to run the promotion when customers are most likely to be deciding on their holiday choice. For summer holidays this tends to be just after Christmas and New Year as customers' thoughts often turn towards summer holidays at this time.

Budget

The amount of money available to spend on a promotion campaign will affect what methods of promotion you can employ. A small business is unlikely to be able to afford a nationwide television campaign whereas a large multiple travel agency will. If you have a limited budget, you might have to be more inventive about your promotion and also more targeted. Remember that effective promotion increases business, which in turn increases profit. For small businesses the use of press releases, word of mouth and public relations will be both cheap and effective.

Evaluation

After a promotional campaign has run its course, it needs to be evaluated.

Purpose of evaluating

The purpose of evaluation is twofold:

- to measure the level of the promotion's success.
- to evaluate the effectiveness of each promotional method used.

Methods of evaluating

It is very important to consider evaluation while you are designing a campaign. Although it can be relatively easy to identify how effective a campaign is compared to its overall goal, it is harder to evaluate the effectiveness of each type of promotion that you have used. This is because you may not be involved in just one form of promotion at any one time but might be using a number of different channels. An effective method of evaluating each type of promotion is to build in some way of identifying how the customer has heard of your product or service. This might be by giving a small discount if a code is quoted (the code being different for each form of promotion). The other main method of evaluation is to use market research.

Appeal to target audience

It is vital to remember that whatever method of marketing communication you choose, it must appeal to the target market. For example, text messaging may not be a good method for communicating to an older market segment compared to a younger one, as older people are less likely to use text messaging. Your communication also has to be in a place where the target market will see it and where it will help to reinforce the image that you have for your products or services.

Activity

You have been asked by a member of a local history group to help them design a promotional campaign to promote a town history tour to raise money for the local hospital. They plan to run the tours every evening in June and July except Sunday, from 5 to 7pm. They do not have a big budget so they want to make sure that their promotion is effective. They want to know:

- what promotional method they should use
- when is the best time to promote
- how much they should charge.

In summary

- Methods of promotion include: advertising, displays, brochures and leaflets, sponsorship, special offers, incentives, competitions, DVDs/videos, direct mail, press releases, shows and events.
- The six stages of a promotional campaign are:
  1) Identify objectives of the campaign
  2) Identify the target market of the campaign
  3) Choose promotional methods and media
  4) Produce promotional material
  5) Run and monitor the campaign
  6) Evaluate the effectiveness of the campaign.
- When planning a promotional campaign, consider: target market, objective of campaign, timing of campaign, budget, evaluation methods.

Practice assessment activity

Levels P4/P5/M3/D2

P **1** Describe promotional techniques used by travel and tourism organisations to promote their products and services. (P4)

Your description must include reference to all of the following promotional methods and material:

- advertising (including TV, radio, magazines, specialist and trade)
- window and in-store displays
- printed material (brochures, leaflets, flyers)
- sponsorship
- special offers and incentives
- videos
- direct mailshots and text messaging
- press releases
- events.

Your should use examples to support your description.

P **2** For a selected travel and tourism organisation produce a piece of promotional material suitable for use in context. (P5) You need to include the context that the promotional material is produced for including the target market the promotion is aimed at and objectives of the promotion.

M **3** Analyse the effectiveness of the piece of promotional material you produced for task 2 and explain its appropriateness to the needs of the target market. (M3) You need to explain both the appropriateness of the design and the content.

D **4** Evaluate the effectiveness of promotional material in meeting the needs of the target market and suggest improvements. (D2)

For this task you need to get the opinion of the target audience on the promotional material you produced for task 2. This can be via witness statements, questionnaires or a write-up of oral reports. You might want to give the target audience a current piece of promotion to compare with your promotional material.

From this evaluation, make suggestions as to how you would improve your piece of promotional material and why.

Test your knowledge

1. What are the 4Ps of the marketing mix?
2. What is a unique selling point (USP)?
3. What is a brand?
4. What is meant by the term 'target market'?
5. Why are markets segmented?
6. What are SMART objectives?
7. Why is it necessary to set objectives?
8. Identify three different travel and tourism products.
9. List four different ways in which a market can be segmented.
10. From your answer to question 9, explain how you would use each method of segmentation and why you would use it.
11. What are the drawbacks of each method identified in question 9?
12. Give three reasons for carrying out market research.
13. Name the two different types of data that you can collect.
14. What are the two main types of market research?
15. What are the three methods of primary research used in the travel and tourism industry?
16. Give three types of survey that you could carry out.
17. Identify five promotional methods.
18. Give three reasons for carrying out a promotional campaign.
19. What does the term 'advertising medium' mean?
20. What does AIDA stand for?
21. Explain the term 'target audience'.
22. Why is it important to evaluate the success of a promotional campaign?

6 Business Skills for Travel and Tourism

Introduction

Working in travel and tourism involves dealing with people in order to get jobs done. Workplaces therefore have a number of systems and procedures to help things run smoothly for all involved.

Most organisations need to make a profit and every sale means that money exchange takes place. In this unit you will look at the different payment methods and the problems that might arise when using them. You will also look at systems in place for the administration of the sales process. This includes completing documentation and any problems that might occur.

Health and safety is very important in the travel and tourism environment as some activities can be potentially very dangerous. Staff working in a travel and tourism organisation must be aware of the health and safety risks and how they can be eliminated.

Personal skills and qualities are also needed to work effectively in the travel and tourism industry; this unit will help you to identify and describe the skills and qualities needed. One of these skills is team working. You will also investigate how teams operate in different organisations.

How you will be assessed

Unit 6 is assessed internally so the Centre delivering the qualification will assess you against the criteria. On completion of this unit you should:

6.1 understand how financial and administrative procedures are used in travel and tourism

6.2 know how health, safety and security is maintained in travel and tourism organisations

6.3 know the personal skills and qualities needed to work in travel and tourism organisations

6.4 understand how teams operate in travel and tourism organisations.

Assessment grades

The Edexcel Assessment Grid for Unit 6 details the criteria to be met. In general, to gain a Pass (P) you are asked to describe and to complete documentation; to gain a Merit (M) you are also asked to compare and analyse; and to gain a Distinction (D) you are also asked to evaluate and recommend improvements.

6.1 Understand how financial and administrative procedures are used in travel and tourism organisations

This section covers:

- administrative procedures
- financial procedures.

Administrative procedures

A travel and tourism organisation may have thousands of customers a year. To make sure that every customer receives and pays for what he or she wants, the organisation needs to have well designed and structured administrative procedures. For the first half of this section you will be looking at the procedure used for processing the sales of products and services; for the second half you will be looking at the financial procedures used.

The sales process

An organisation may have thousands of sales taking place at any time. For this reason the organisation requires a system or procedure to follow so that all sales are recorded properly and the customer receives what he or she requires. This system is called the sales process.

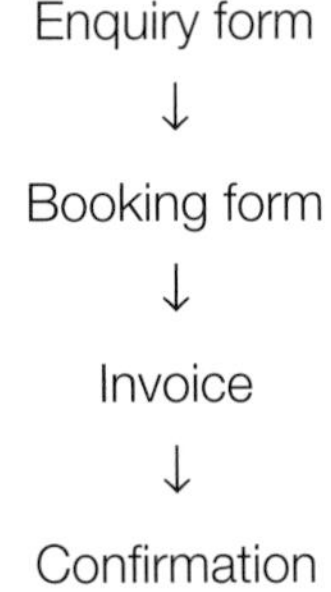

- Other paperwork required
- Customer file
- Letters dealing with discrepancies and inaccuracies

Customer enquiries

It is important for the organisation to record every enquiry so that it can be followed up, to try to convert the enquiry into a sale. For this reason the organisation needs to record some customer details. This can be done either on a standardised form or on a computer database.

Activity

Design a standardised customer enquiry form for a travel agency. Consider what information you will need to help you follow up the enquiry. Compare your form with others in your group.

Bookings and reservations

BOOKING FORM

Clients' Name	Clients' Address
Home Telephone Number	Day time Telephone Number
Email Address	Mobile Telephone Number
Date of Travel to to to	Number of Adults .... Number of Children ....
Tour Operator Booking Code	Location
Preferred departure Airport	Car Hire Required Yes / No
Travel Insurance required Yes / No	Traveller Cheques required Yes/No Amount £........
Special Requirements	Payment Method Visa/ Mastercard ( ) Debit Card ( ) Cheque ( ) Cash ( )

A booking form

When a customer books a product or service, this information also needs to be recorded. You will need to record not only the customer's personal information but also the details of the product that the customer has booked (for example, the product details, cost and any special requirements, etc.). You should also inform the customer of the organisation's cancellation policy and record any deposit that has been paid. A copy of this information needs to be given to the customer so that he or she knows what has been paid for and to give the customer peace of mind.

Activity

Design a standardised booking form for a tour operator. Consider what information you will need to help you follow up the enquiry. Compare your form with others in your group.

Key points

A credit sale is a sale where the customer will be paying for the goods at a later date. This is common with business-to-business transactions.

Invoicing

Invoices are sent out with every item which is purchased on credit. This is so the customer has a statement of how much he or she has already paid for the product and the outstanding balance which is due to be paid. It is not uncommon to pay for your holiday in a number of steps or increments. An invoice should include all the details of the product or services that are being purchased as well as a statement of the account to date and amounts received, etc.

Confirmation

A confirmation needs to be sent to verify any information or payments that have been received. This confirmation serves two purposes:

- it informs the customer that payments have been received
- it provides a record of incoming monies for the customer's file (this record will give the dates of payment).

Activity

You have just received a letter from a customer complaining that she has been billed £400 too much for a summer holiday that she has booked with your travel agency. You check your records and realise that the customer was billed incorrectly.

- Write a letter of apology to the customer explaining that you will be correcting the error and will reissue the bill to her.

Over to you

You are working for a tour operator, selling 'summer sun' family holidays directly to the customer from a call centre in your town. Make a list of all the details you think you might want to keep in a customer file.

Customer files

Each customer should have a personal file. This used to be a physical paper file but with the use of technology, most organisations today keep their customer files as database entries.

It is important to keep the customer file up to date with all the information that you have about that customer's current and past needs. As you have seen in *Unit 5: Exploring Marketing in Travel and Tourism*, this information has great use when it comes to the promotion of future products and services.

Letters

Most organisations will have a number of standard letters that are designed to deal with discrepancies. The benefit of using a standardised letter is that all the staff within the organisation who deal with these discrepancies will know what the standardised letter says. This saves time and confusion when dealing with the customer after he or she has received the letter. Common examples of discrepancies are listed below.

Incorrect name on the booking form

This can lead to problems when tickets are issued for flights and possible difficulties when booking into the hotel or accommodation.

Incorrect product details on confirmation

This could lead to the customer receiving the wrong product. You have to remember that holiday products can be very complex with a large number of variables, for example, the type of room, departure airport, length of stay, etc.

Activity

Choose a local travel and tourism organisation. Write a standard letter which could be used when a customer has been over-charged for a booking made with your organisation.

Incorrect price on invoice

This would lead to the customer either under-paying or over-paying for the product.

- Under-charging for a product could lead to you having to write a letter asking for extra funds.
- Over-charging would mean that you have to refund monies to the customer.

Incorrect address on the customer file

This issue could lead to major problems especially if tickets and itineraries are sent out to the wrong address. However, since many different methods of communication are used today, it would be possible to telephone or email the client to get the correct address details.

Financial procedures

For most products and services a customer needs to pay for the product or service. There are a number of different methods of payment, which are described below.

Manual methods of payment

Cash

Cash transactions are a secure form of transaction. However, there are risks involved in having large amounts of cash on a company's premises, and this generally leads to the expense of installing a safe or strongroom on-site. There is also the issue of fake currency, although notes can be checked with the use of ultraviolet detection systems or detection pens.

■ *A cheque and cheque guarantee card*

Cheques

A cheque is a promissory note (it promises to pay the bearer or recipient a certain sum of money) that either an individual or an organisation writes. A cheque cannot be transferred but can be paid into a bank account like cash. Cheques from individuals should always be accompanied by a cheque guarantee card. Banks can be contacted during working hours to validate cheques of higher amounts.

Postal orders

A postal order is similar to a cheque but unlike a cheque it is purchased from a post office and is valued for the face amount. Postal orders are mainly used for small amounts to be sent through the post. There is a cost involved in the purchasing of a postal order.

■ *A postal order*

Traveller's cheques

A traveller's cheque is a promissory note (it promises to pay the bearer or recipient a certain sum of money) which is used to gain foreign currency. The traveller's cheque will have a face value in the currency it is bought in. For example, if you were going to the United States your traveller's cheque would be in US dollars. These cheques are not legal tender in the country but can be exchanged for local currency at a bank.

Banker's draft

A banker's draft is similar to a cheque but is written and guaranteed by the bank, the amount being on the face of the draft. They tend to be used for large amounts of money when for security reasons you do not want to carry the amount in cash.

Key points

Manual methods of payment are:

- cash
- cheques
- postal orders
- traveller's cheques
- banker's drafts.

Computerised payment systems

The growth of the Internet and increased access to credit and debit cards mean that computerised payment systems account for the largest amount of transactions. Below are some of the different methods that you might come across.

PDQ 'swipe' machines

Today, 95 per cent of electronic purchases are made by credit card. A PDQ 'swipe' machine is used to record credit and debit card transactions. It is connected directly to the financial provider through a telephone line.

■ *A PDQ 'swipe' machine records credit and debit card transactions*

Payment service provider (PSP)

This is an Internet version of a PDQ machine. It collects payments on the Internet from orders on a website. A PSP might take payments in several currencies.

Electronic methods of payment are:

- PDQ (credit and debit cards)
- payment service provider (PSP)
- payment bureaux
- BACS.

Payment bureaux

There are also companies that run PSPs as a service for organisations to use – these are called payment bureaux and are similar to a bureau de change at an airport.

Banks Automated Clearing System (BACS)

BACS is used for business-to-business transactions and is a popular system for companies that make a large number of transactions each day. It involves the electronic wiring of payment from one bank account to another.

Benefits of each method of payment to the organisation

Cash

Benefits for the customer

The main benefit of using cash for transactions is that there is no processing time to confirm payment from the customer. This means that as far as the transaction is concerned, the amount is paid. (For most other payment methods there is a delay as the monies clear from the customer's account to the organisation's account.)

Benefits for the organisation

As soon as cash is paid into the organisation's account the monies are credited to the account with no delay. However, there can be problems when you have a significant number of cash transactions and this leads to an organisation having large amounts of cash on the premises. In this situation there is the risk of armed robbery and therefore the need for sophisticated security systems, which involve additional costs.

Cheques

The benefit of cheques for both the organisation and the customer is that they are a relatively secure method of transferring money. This is because a cheque only has value to the person or organisation that it is made out to (the bearer). The disadvantage of this method of payment is that there is a 3–5 working-day clearing time on cheques; in other words, if you pay a cheque into the bank on Thursday it will not clear until the next Wednesday.

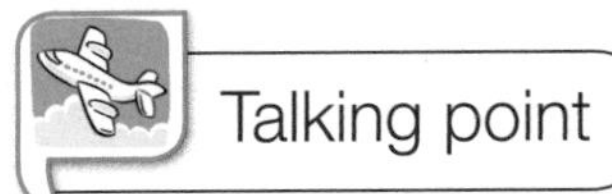

You have just started a small travel and tourism business. Which methods of payment would you choose to use and which would you not? Discuss your answers as a class.

Postal orders

These tend to be only used to send funds through the postal system. The advantage is that if a postal order is lost in the mail and you have the order number you can redeem the postal order and get your money back. Postal orders can be changed to cash at any major post office.

Traveller's cheques

When customers travel abroad to a foreign country where they do not own a bank account, there is the risk of loss or theft of money if they carry large amounts of cash for the holiday. This is particularly so in countries with high crime rates. Traveller's cheques can only be redeemed for money with identification and the signature of the person who originally signed the traveller's cheque when it was purchased. Lost or stolen traveller's cheques can be replaced if a record of the cheque numbers has been kept.

Banker's draft

The benefit of a banker's draft is that it is a guaranteed payment, like a personal cheque from the bank. The organisation benefits as this is a guaranteed method of payment.

PDQ swipe machines

These are used to take payment from credit and debit cards. The benefit for both the customer and the organisation is that the transaction is electronic and Pretty Damn Quick. The machine automatically checks that the funds are available and transfers the money from the credit card or bank account (with a debit card) directly into the organisation's account. The introduction of 'chip and pin' technology has increased security for this method of transaction.

PSP and payment bureaux

With the increase in the use of the Internet to purchase holidays, the use and importance of PSP (payment service providers) and payment bureaux is also increasing. These methods of payment are specifically designed for the Internet. They are a 'middleman' in the transaction.

Activity

Using the information on manual and electronic methods of payment given above, produce a chart describing the advantages and disadvantages of each method.

The benefit of these methods on the Internet for organisations is that they can sell their products in a number of different countries without having issues when it comes to payment in different currencies. This is because the PSP or payment bureaux will pay the organisation in their preferred currency. For example, a UK tour operator could sell a holiday to a US family on the Internet; through the PSP or payment bureaux, the US customer would pay in US dollars and the UK tour operator would receive the money in pounds sterling.

The benefit of PSP and payment bureaux for organisations is that they give organisations a wider market in which to sell their products and services.

BACS

BACS is generally not used to pay for products and services. However, businesses will use BACS to pay their staff. This method of payment means that wages can be paid directly into staff bank accounts, reducing

Case studies

Castle Cars Taxi Company

Simon Foster has run his taxi company for the past 20 years in the town of Oldcastle. He started the company as a single-person operation and has developed it so that he now runs up to six cars on a busy evening. Most of his business during the week comes from corporate customers who have accounts with Castle Cars.

In the evening most customers pay in cash as Castle Cars does not have other payment facilities. Simon is keen to look into different methods of payment to help him run his business more efficiently. He is particularly concerned to reduce the amount of cash sales as he feels that his drivers are at risk from attack if they are carrying a lot of money on them. He is also interested in any payment methods that can help speed up his customers' transactions, as he finds receiving cheques through the post and banking them very time-consuming.

- What advice would you give Simon on the different methods of payment that he could utilise in his business? Write a report outlining each method and its advantages/disadvantages.

the need to either pay by cash, with all the associated security issues, or cheque, which can be a time-consuming process (the cheque needs to be written, banked and accounted for).

Payment procedures in travel and tourism

Most holiday products are not paid for in full but in a staged process. The stages are as follows:

- deposit
- balance
- balance date
- full payment.

Deposit

This is the initial payment towards a product, for example, to book a holiday. Deposits may or may not be refundable depending on the organisation and the terms and conditions attached to the contract.

Balance

This is the outstanding amount that the customer must pay to buy the product or services.

Balance date

The customer might make a number of payments towards the product. These would be spread out on different dates on which the payments must be received by.

Full payment

Before the product or service is taken, full payment needs to be received. This would be the last payment if the customer was paying by instalments.

Paying for holiday products in a staged process helps to spread the cost of the holiday over a number of months, thereby making payment easier for the customer. This in turn increases the number of people that can afford to go on holiday, which increases business for the travel agency.

Conducting a transaction

When you are conducting a transaction you need to take a systematic and logical approach. This means that there are a number of steps that you need to go through to make sure that you complete the transaction correctly.

Step one – Check payment method

You need to find out which method of payment a customer wants to use and if the organisation you are working for accepts that method of payment.

Step two – Issue a receipt

A receipt needs to be issued and a record made of the payment.

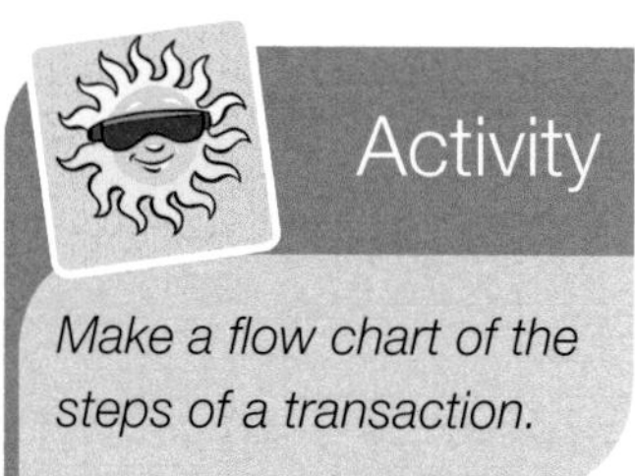

Activity

Make a flow chart of the steps of a transaction.

Step three – Complete appropriate financial documentation

Records need to be updated: the customer file needs to show that a payment has been made and the customer account needs to be updated to reflect this.

Step four – Deal with discrepancies and inaccuracies

Sometimes you will find that there are discrepancies and inaccuracies in the payment methods. The two most common are:

- a credit or debit card is declined
- a cheque is returned from the bank.

Credit or debit card refused

Electronic payment cards will be refused if the credit limit is exceeded or there is no fund in the account of a debit card. The PDQ machine will tell you if a card has been refused on the spot. If a customer's card is refused you should ask the customer for an alternative payment method. In some cases the PDQ machine might ask you to phone a number when a card is refused. You can be asked to retain a customer's card or destroy a customer debit or credit card but this is unusual. It is worth remembering that the credit or debit card does not belong to the customer but belongs to the credit/debit card company that issued it.

Returned cheque

If a cheque has been returned from the bank the situation is slightly different, as the customer is not likely to be on your premises. You need to contact the customer to inform him or her that the cheque has been declined and that you require payment by some other method. This should be done in writing even if you have telephoned the client, so that you have a written copy for the customer's file.

In summary

- Sales process paperwork is made up of: enquiry form, booking form, invoice, confirmation, customer file and any letters. Letters deal with discrepancies.
- Methods of payments include: manual (cash, cheques, postal orders, traveller's cheques and banker's drafts) and automatic/computerised (PDQ swipe machines, payment service providers (PSP), payment bureaux and BACS.
- The typical payment procedure in travel and tourism is: deposit, balance, balance payment, full payment.
- When conducting a transaction: check the payment method, issue a receipt, complete appropriate financial information and deal with discrepancies and inaccuracies.

Practice assessment activity

Levels P1/P2/M1

For your assessment your tutor might organise a guest speaker, a visit or a travel and tourism organisation to look at a specific procedure. To practise, try the general procedure below.

P **1** Describe the administrative systems used in processing the sale of travel and tourism products and services. (P1) You should include the following: enquiry form, booking form, invoice, confirmation, customer file, letters (including letters dealing with discrepancies and inaccuracies). You can use examples from travel and tourism organisations to support your answer. ✓

P **2** Complete administrative and financial documentation for the sale of a travel and tourism product or service. (P2) ✓

You are working as a receptionist for a large resort hotel called 'The Grand Hotel' in Seamouth, a south coast tourist town. You have received the following email enquiry from a travel agent whom you have a taken a number of bookings from previously, called Express Travel, in Tricester.

From: CustomerServices@Express.co.uk
To: Reception@GrandSeamouth.co.uk

Ref: **Enquiry for 3rd June 1 nights 1 twin B&B**

Hi,

Do you have availability and rates for the following booking?

MR L Jones

For 1 Twin room

Arriving for 1 night from 3rd of June

Departing 4th of June

Rate B&B only

Mr Jones will require a cot in the twin room.

If you could get back to me ASAP I would be very grateful.

Tony Sucliff
Tsucliff@Express.co.uk
Express Travel, Mill Road, Tricester, Oxfordshire TR25 4RD
Telephone: 02453 456234

Practice assessment activity continued

a) Complete the following enquiry form for Mr Jones.

<table>
<tr><th colspan="4">Enquiry Form
Number 2341</th></tr>
<tr><td>**Customer name:**</td><td colspan="3"></td></tr>
<tr><td>**Organisation/ Agent:**</td><td colspan="3"></td></tr>
<tr><td>**Address:**</td><td colspan="3"></td></tr>
<tr><td>**Telephone number:**</td><td colspan="3"></td></tr>
<tr><td>**Email (optional):**</td><td colspan="3"></td></tr>
<tr><td>**Arrival date:**</td><td></td><td>**Departure date:**</td><td></td></tr>
<tr><td>**Rooms required:**</td><td>( ) Single
( ) Double
( ) Twin
( ) Suite</td><td>**Rate required:**</td><td>( ) Bed and Breakfast
( ) Half Board
( ) Full Board</td></tr>
<tr><td>**Special arrangement:**</td><td colspan="3"></td></tr>
<tr><td>**Taken by:**</td><td></td><td>**Date:**</td><td></td></tr>
<tr><td>**Signature**</td><td></td><td>**Time:**</td><td></td></tr>
<tr><td>**Rate offered:**</td><td colspan="3"></td></tr>
</table>

Practice assessment activity continued

b) You check your reservation diary and find that you have availability for Mr Jones. You need to complete the booking form to email to Tony at Express Travel so that he can confirm the booking with Mr Jones. Complete as much information as possible for Tony to confirm. The rate that you can offer Tony is £50 for the room.

Grand Hotel *Sea Front, Seamouth, Dorset SE12 477* *Tel:01234 579087 Fax: 01234 579088* *Email: Reception@grandseamouth.co.uk*			
Customer name:			
Organisation/ Agent:			
Address:			
Telephone number:			
Facsimile:			
Accommodation required:			
Number of nights:		**Arrival date:**	
Rate required:	( ) Bed and Breakfast ( ) Half Board ( ) Full Board	**Departure date:**	
Rooms required:	( ) Single ( ) Double ( ) Twin ( ) Suite	**Rate pnpp:**	Single: Double: Twin: Suite:
Special arrangement:			
Payment method:	Credit card type: Visa / Amex / MasterCard / Debit card		
Card number:		**Issue date:**	
Issue number:		**Expiry date:**	
Invoice (by prior arrangement only)			

Practice assessment activity continued

c) Complete the confirmation fax to return to Tony. Tony has told you that Mr Jones' address is 7 Market Wynd, Tricester, Oxfordshire TR25 6TF. Express Travel is to be invoiced.

facsimile transmittal

Grand Hotel

Sea Front, Seamouth, Dorset SE12 477
Tel:01234 579087 Fax: 01234 579088
Email: Reception@grandseamouth.co.uk

To:	Fax:
From:	Date:
Re:	Pages:
cc:	

☐ Urgent ☐ For Review ☐ Please Comment ☐ Please Reply ☐ Please Recycle

Notes:

Practice assessment activity continued

d) Prepare the invoice to be sent to Tony at Express Travel with a copy to put in Mr Jones' customer file. Express Travel has a 30-day credit agreement with you and a 10 per cent commission payment, which you will discount off the invoice.

INVOICE

Grand Hotel

Sea Front, Seamouth, Dorset SE12 477
Tel:01234 579087 Fax: 01234 579088
Email: Reception@grandseamouth.co.uk

Date:	Date of stay:
Invoice to:	**Client's name:**

Room type	Number of rooms	Occupancy	Rate (PNPP)	Number of nights	Total	Net
			Total			
			Commission			
			Subtotal			
			Invoice amount			

Practice assessment activity continued

e) You receive a cheque from Express Travel on 30 June with a compliments slip. Complete the receipt below to send back to them.

RECEIPT OF PAYMENT

Grand Hotel

Sea Front, Seamouth, Dorset SE12 477
Tel:01234 579087 Fax: 01234 579088
Email: Reception@grandseamouth.co.uk

Payment received from:			
Name:			
Address:			
Telephone number:		**Facsimile:**	
Email:		**Postcode:**	
Account name:			
Payment method:		**Date of payment:**	
Opening balance of account:		**Payment received:**	
Closing balance:			
Signed:			
Print name:			

M **3** Fully and accurately complete appropriate administrative and financial documentation for dealing with the sale of a travel and tourism product or service where discrepancies and inaccuracies in procedures are identified. (M1)

When you receive the fax back from Tony confirming Mr Jones' booking you see that the date of the booking has changed from 3 June to the 13 June and the room is for two people and not just one.

a) How would you check that this information is correct?

b) Complete the documentation again accounting for this discrepancy.

6.2 Know how health, safety and security is maintained in travel and tourism organisations

This section covers:

- health and safety
- health and safety awareness
- security.

Health and safety

Health and safety is vital in any business. In travel and tourism there are a number of potential health and safety issues, whether they arise at a theme park, on a cruise ship or on holiday.

The Health and Safety at Work Act 1974 is the law that governs health and safety. This Act states that taking steps to ensure the health and safety of people in the workplace, whether staff or customers, is the duty of everyone. Therefore, if you identify any issues or working practices that you feel are not safe, it is your responsibility to report these to the appropriate person.

Health and safety awareness

Risks

Risk is the likelihood of something happening with the potential to cause harm. Some activities are more risky than others – for example, potholing and scuba diving are considered more risky than lying on a beach because there is a greater chance of physical injury. You would therefore say that potholing and scuba diving are more of a health and safety issue, although lying on a beach also carries its own risks (for example, of sunburn).

Hazards

Hazards are situations that increase the likelihood of an accident or harm occurring. For example, failing to wear sunscreen whilst sunbathing increases the likelihood of sunburn; storing furniture on a fire escape increases the chance of people not being able to escape or suffering injury during a fire.

Risk assessment

To ensure the safety of all people, it is necessary to carry out a full risk assessment of the working or leisure environment or the leisure activity. For example, a risk assessment might be carried out on:

- fire escapes in a travel agents
- an excursion to the zoo
- the use of a swimming pool.

Risk assessment is completed on a standard form. The aim of a risk assessment is to record all the possible risks that are likely to be involved in the use of a particular environment or the running of a particular activity. These risks will then be assessed for:

A risk assessment must be carried out *before* an activity.

- the likelihood of the risk happening
- the likely seriousness of an accident
- the prevention methods in place to avoid the risk happening
- the likely number of people getting hurt for each risk.

High-risk activities

Some activities that you may do are high risk. This means that there is a likelihood of either yourself or someone else getting injured, possibly seriously. If you still decide to run a high-risk activity, you need to inform those involved. You might also need to make sure that special precautions are taken before the event. For example, at motorbike races ambulances are available on-site in case an accident happens. In some cases you will decide that the trip or event should not take place due to the risk involved.

Scuba diving is a high-risk activity and people must be properly trained before attempting it

Risk assessment form

Each assessment must take into account and record any specific hazards arising from the activity or a particular site, before the assessment is complete.

Activity/workplace assessed:			**Assessment date:**			
Manager:			**Assessor:**			
HAZARD (potential for harm)	**Will affect**	**PRECAUTIONS/ CONTROLS in place to reduce risk**	**RISK (with controls)**			**Additional controls needed (details overleaf)**
			L	**S**	**R**	

■ *A risk assessment form* (*Source*: Guildford College of Further and Higher Education)

In the above form, the three columns (L, S, R) are for assessing the level or degree of risk:

- the first (L) is for an assessment of the Likelihood of the hazard taking place
- the second (S) records the Severity of the hazard
- the third (R) records the Risk level.

The table below explains the different assessments for L, S and R.

(L) LIKELIHOOD	**(S) SEVERITY OF HAZARD**	**(R) RISK LEVEL is product of Likelihood and Severity (L × S)**
Hazard exists very infrequently; limited numbers exposed	Could cause minor injury only	Low priority risk score 1 or 2
Likely to occur; hazard exists intermittently or occurs occasionally	Could cause major injury/ three days or more absence	Moderate risk score 3 or 4
Likely to occur soon; permanent hazard or occurs daily/repeatedly; many people may be exposed	Could cause fatality/severe injury	Very high risk score 6 or 9

Very high risks require immediate action.

Vulnerable people

Some people are more vulnerable than others, for example, elderly and very young people, people with disabilities and pregnant women. These vulnerabilities need to be considered when organising an activity and also as part of the risk assessment.

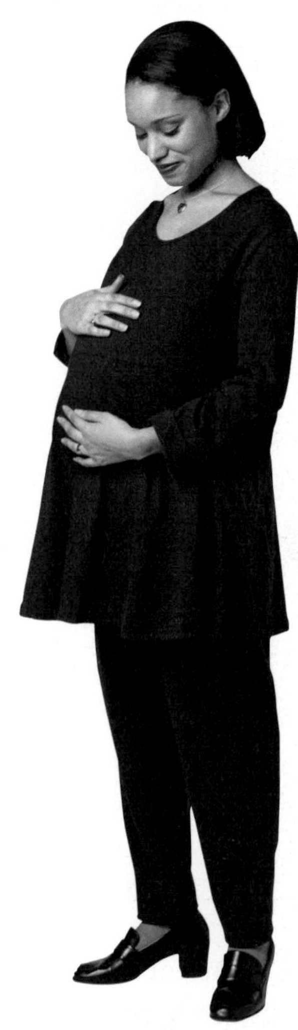

■ *Pregnant women are particularly vulnerable to certain risks*

Dealing with accidents

All accidents must be reported:

- to prevent a more serious incident happening
- in case someone has hurt themselves and it only comes to light later.

Accident report forms

Whenever there is an accident at work, it must be reported, even if no one appears to be hurt. After all, a near miss this time does not mean that next time there will be another near miss – somebody may be badly hurt. Remember, it is everyone's responsibility to report accidents at work.

ACCIDENT REPORT FORM			
This form must be completed in all cases of accident, injury or dangerous occurrences.			
Name of person reporting incident:			
Position in organisation:			
Name of injured person:			
Date of birth:			
Position in organisation:			
Date and time of accident:			
Details of injury/ accident:			
Activity at time of injury/ accident:			
Place of injury/accident:			
Details of injury/ accident:			
First aid treatment given (if any):			
Was the injured person taken to hospital? If so, where?			
Name(s) and position(s) of person(s) present when accident occurred:			
Signature of person reporting incident:			
Print name:		Date:	

■ *Accident report form*

How risks and hazards can be minimised

You have already looked at how you can identify hazards and risks and what to do in the unhappy event of an accident happening. In addition, there are a number of different methods an organisation can employ to help manage risks either in the workplace or arising in work-related activities.

Training

There are two types of health and safety training:

- **Preventative training**: training that is designed to highlight the health and safety risks involved in an activity and how to prevent an incident occurring. For example, cabin crew go through a rigorous training course before they are allowed to fly as cabin crew, and this includes a large amount of training designed to prevent accidents.
- **Reactive training**: this is training in what to do in case of an incident. For example, a hotel will have a complex procedure in case of a fire as there could be a large number of people sleeping in the hotel when the alarm starts and all of these customers will need to be accounted for as well as staff.

Monitoring

It is important to monitor the people and the site as health and safety issues can crop up from time to time. It is important to check regularly that all safety equipment is stored properly and is in correct working order. It is also important to monitor the working procedures to make sure that health and safety precautions are being followed.

What is your school/ college procedure if the fire alarm sounds?

Systems and procedures

All organisations will have a number of systems and procedures for health and safety. These systems and procedures are set so that nothing is missed out. All incidents need to be reported and recorded. In a major incident like a fire, different members of staff will have different responsibilities so that, by working together, the staff in the organisation will cover all the things that need to be done. For example, during a fire, different responsibilities might be to telephone the fire brigade, evacuate the building, turn off gas supply, wait for the fire brigade with the building plans, etc.

Allocation of specific roles and duties

Although the safety of the activity is the responsibility of the organiser, it is also the responsibility of everyone involved in the event. However, within an organisation different members of staff will have different responsibilities. Most organisations will have a member of staff that is the health and safety representative. In a large organisation this might be a person's actual job whereas in a smaller organisation it might be a person's responsibility in addition to their job.

The roles and duties depend on the type of organisation – as you can imagine, the roles and duties would be different on a cruise ship compared to a travel agency.

Notices and reminders

It is a legal requirement to clearly identify hazards and risks so that everyone knows what they are. Signs indicating a hazard or risk should be placed in the appropriate position in the workplace; these are standardised so that they are the same for every workplace. The sign depicts what the hazard is so that if a person cannot read English, he or she can still understand what the sign means.

Corrosive material

Flammable material

Explosive material

Toxic material

No access for pedestrians

Safety helmets must be worn

General danger

Ear protection must be worn

Eye protection must be worn

No smoking

Nearest exit

Nearest fire exit

■ *EU standardised health and safety signs*

It is also not uncommon practice to have notices reminding people of the steps of the procedure that should be followed. For example, you might see next to a fire alarm a step-by-step guide of what to do in the event of a fire.

By reinforcing the health and safety message with notices and reminders, training, monitoring systems and procedures, you might not be able to prevent all accidents but hopefully you will be able to reduce workplace incidences and also be able to respond to them more effectively if they do happen.

Note: If you require further information on health and safety, the Health and Safety Executive has a large number of publications covering all areas. They can be bought or downloaded from their website (a link to this website has been made available at www.heinemann.co.uk/hotlinks by entering the express code 2196P).

Activity

Write a health and safety handbook to be used either for your class or for any educational visit you may go on this year.

■ *How many health and safety issues can you identify in this travel agency?*

Security

Within any travel and tourism industry there are a number of different security issues to identify and address.

Security of finance

As you found out when you were looking at financial procedures in Section 6.1, there are a number of security issues with regards to finance.

The first issue is security of money within the organisation. As you can imagine, some travel and tourism organisations have large amounts of cash going through the business each day. This cash has to be recorded and stored safely before it can be deposited into a bank.

With transactions on credit and debit cards there is increasingly an issue with security of the customer's card details and card fraud. Credit/debit card receipts should therefore be kept as securely as cash.

Security of self

Your personal security is important in keeping yourself, your dignity and your possessions safe; however, the risks are sometimes not so clear.

- You should always make sure that people know that you are on-site and when you leave.
- You should also inform another member of staff if you are visiting a customer off-site and when they can expect you back.
- You must always be aware of the situation that you are getting yourself into.

Security of others

In many travel and tourism situations you could be responsible for others, whether they are customers or members of staff. Some environments are more risky than others and some tourist destinations can be quite dangerous. If you are working in a destination where there are security issues, you must make others aware of these issues for their own personal safety.

You should also be aware that ensuring the security of others can mean keeping information about them secure.

Activity

Different types of customers may have different security needs. In your group, discuss the different security needs the following customers might have:

- a pop star travelling on your airline
- a businesswoman travelling alone and staying in your hotel
- a wheelchair user who is travelling as part of a tour around the UK.

Security of information

Within any organisation you will have a large amount of sensitive information. This information could be about customers, staff, finance, profits, etc., and it needs to be protected and stored securely. This can be done by password protecting computers and restricting access to files.

Security of equipment

Equipment has to be kept secure to prevent theft. There are also issues of health and safety with some equipment. Potentially dangerous equipment should be locked away so that only qualified personnel can have access to it; this is to prevent accidents.

Systems and procedures

As you have already discovered, there are various security issues within the travel and tourism industry. Some working environments have greater security risks than others. Currently there is a huge issue regarding security and terrorism. This has led to increased security at airports and

Activity

Produce a poster highlighting one of the security risks involved in a travel and tourism business.

ports. For security to work effectively it needs to have a set of systems and procedures to deal with any eventuality. These systems can be very complex and involve not only employees of the organisation but also police and in some situations even the armed forces.

In summary

- Health and safety is the responsibility of every employee. You are responsible for the health and safety of yourself, your colleagues and your customers.
- Health and safety awareness is vital to prevent accidents.
- Risk assessment helps to identify risks in the workplace or arising from a work-related activity and gives you opportunities to put preventative measures in place.
- All accidents need to be reported on an accident report form.
- Accidents are prevented by: training, monitoring, systems and procedures, allocation of specific roles and duties, notices and reminders.
- Security is increasingly an issue in travel and tourism, both the security of assets and the security of staff and customers.

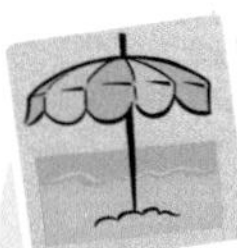

Practice assessment activity

Levels P3/M2/D1

To attempt these tasks you need to research into a specific travel and tourism organisation. Your tutor might organise a guest speaker or a visit to a travel and tourism organisation. Some organisations provide study packs which will give you all the information needed.

P **1** Describe procedures used in a selected travel and tourism organisation to maintain a healthy, safe and secure workplace environment. (P3) Your answer should include mention of some of the following issues: ✓

- *Health and safety awareness*: risks, hazards, risk assessment, training, monitoring, systems and procedures, notices and reminders, and allocation of specific roles and duties;
- *Security*: of finance, self, others, information and equipment; security systems and procedures.

M **2** Analyse the way a selected travel and tourism organisation maintains health, safety and security of staff, customers, equipment and finances. (M2) ✓✓

- Your analysis should include judgments about the systems and procedures and make recommendations.
- Your recommendations should be based on best practice in the industry and your understanding of health and safety legislation.

D **3** Recommend improvements in the documentation used and health, safety and security procedures of a selected travel and tourism organisation. (D1) Your recommendations should be realistic and appropriate for the organisation. They should be written up in a formal report or given in a presentation for your tutor. ✓✓✓

6.3 Know the personal skills and qualities needed to work in a travel and tourism organisation

This section covers:

- personal skills
- qualities.

Personal skills and qualities

There are a number of personal skills and qualities that you need to work within a travel and tourism environment. We will be looking at these skills and qualities one at a time.

Personal skills

Problem solving

Travel and tourism products tend to be very complex and this leads to a number of issues arising on a daily basis. You therefore will require the skill of being able to solve problems. The first solution that you come up with may not be the best idea, so you will need to be able to find a variety of different solutions to any problem and then make a decision on which solution will lead to the best result.

Case studies

David and Gemma Dexter have booked a honeymoon with your travel agency to the Dominican Republic. However, the day before their wedding and two days before they are due to leave on their honeymoon, the Dominican Republic is devastated by a hurricane and the hotel they were due to stay in is destroyed. A very worried David rings you and asks you what can you do for them. You tell David that you will phone back in an hour with some options.

- Think of three solutions that you can give David and Gemma to their honeymoon problem.

Using your initiative

In many travel and tourism situations you will be expected at times to work on your own as well as part of a team. For example, a holiday representative may have sole responsibility for the guest staying in one particular hotel within a resort. This means that when it comes to

Over to you

List the skills that you think are required to make a good team player. Which of these skills do you have? Which do you not have?

problem solving and dealing with everyday issues, you might not always have someone who you can ask for advice. You will therefore need to use your own initiative to solve these issues on your own.

Teamwork

Travel and tourism organisations rely on groups of people working together as teams. This is because a number of people working together can be more productive than the same number of people working separately.

For example, the cabin crew of an airline flying to the United States will have a large number of tasks to complete in the duration of a flight, including safety demonstrations, giving out and collecting two customer meals, showing a movie, serving tea and coffee twice, offering duty-free goods and helping customers fill in their landing cards. If the cabin crew did not work well as a team, all these tasks would not be completed well if at all. (In Section 6.4 you will be investigating different types of teams; see pages 247–250.)

Oral and written communication

To work in the travel and tourism industry you need to communicate well with customers, colleagues and suppliers. This means:

- expressing yourself clearly both in writing and speech
- communicating in a way that the customer can understand
- ensuring that any information you communicate is up to date and accurate.

Case studies

You work as a business travel agent in a large local travel agency. When you return to the office after your lunch break you have the following three messages on your voice mail:

- Mrs P. Montague has a group of 12 Japanese business travellers arriving next Wednesday for an important meeting at her company and requires accommodation and airport-to-accommodation transfer to be organised.
- Mr M. Liu of Foster Racing requires a first-class train ticket to London to arrive at King's Cross for a 10.30am meeting tomorrow. His PA will be around at 5pm today to collect the ticket.
- Mr John Harvey needs you to organise accommodation and flights for a European trip that he is taking next month. He needs to be in Rome on 12th–14th, Prague on 14th–17th and Dublin on 17–19th. He will require business-class tickets and five-star accommodation for himself and his personal assistant, Ms G. Kaur.

Prioritise these three tasks in the order in which you will deal with each booking and explain why you have decided this order.

Time management

At college or school your time is generally organised for you; for example, you are told which lessons to go to and when; you are told what you have to do for each lesson and for your homework. This may not be the case in the workplace and in a lot of travel and tourism jobs you have a lot of freedom to organise and structure your time. For example, a business travel agent may have a number of clients all requiring help at the same time to organise their business trips. Time management is the skill of prioritising both tasks and time in order to complete all the tasks required as efficiently as possible.

Numeracy

Numeracy is a vital skill as most private sector travel and tourism organisations exist to make profit for the owners or shareholders. Numeracy and the use of numbers are vital in many situations, from checking numbers on tours or aircraft, to working out change for a customer after making a purchase, to calculating the cost of the holiday that a customer has booked.

Using ICT

Information Communication Technology (ICT) has rapidly changed the travel and tourism industry since the 1970s. ICT has reduced the costs and time involved in administration in the industry. Most travel and tourism organisations rely heavily on ICT with Global Distribution Systems and Central Reservation systems giving travel agents the ability to book fights and accommodation anywhere in the world. The Internet is also having a huge impact on the travel and tourism industry with more holidays year on year being booked online.

Your development of ICT skills is very important to your success in the travel and tourism industry

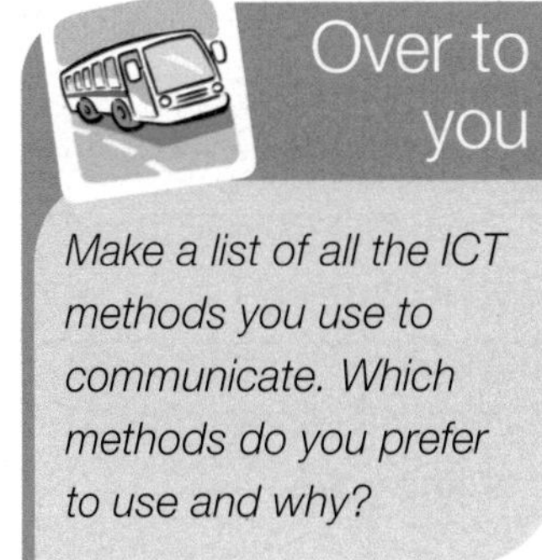

Over to you

Make a list of all the ICT methods you use to communicate. Which methods do you prefer to use and why?

Languages

The ability to speak a foreign language is a great advantage to anybody working in the travel and tourism industry. Even the ability to say a few words in a different language can help put a customer at ease and to feel welcome. In some jobs the ability to speak a particular language is vital, especially if your job involves a lot of contact with foreign language speakers or if you are working in a foreign country.

Interpersonal skills

Large amounts of your working time are spent with customers. Your interpersonal relationship with a customer can make or break the leisure experience for that person.

Over to you

Write down:

- one situation in which you feel that good interpersonal skills added value to the service you received
- one situation in which you feel that bad interpersonal skills devalued a service or experience that you received.

Now share your examples with a colleague. Do your opinions of what constitutes good and bad interpersonal skills differ? If there are any differences, why do you think this is?

Qualities

Reliability

Being reliable is essential if a team is going to work together. Everybody in an organisation relies on each other for the organisation to be successful.

Activity

Create a checklist about your personal presentation to be hung in a staff changing room at an airport.

Personal presentation

How you present yourself reflects on the organisation you work for. Personal presentation is not only about having a clean and ironed uniform but also includes issues such as personal hygiene, body language and how you speak, etc. It is worth remembering that if you have a uniform you represent that organisation whenever you are wearing the uniform, whether you are at work at that moment in time or not.

Personal organisation

Personal organisation is an important quality in the travel and tourism industry. It is not uncommon to have a number of different projects happening at the same time and without being organised you will find that problems can happen and information gets lost, etc.

It is also quite upsetting to a customer to have someone who is unorganised trying to help them. A lack of personal organisation will put across an unprofessional image to the customer of both you and the organisation that you represent.

Self-reflection

Self-reflection, sometimes known as reflective practice, is an important quality as it leads to self-improvement. Self-reflection is the ability to be able to review your own performance and learn from your past experiences, in order to improve your performance in the future. It is similar to how a team would review a project at the end, to see if it was successful and why.

Ownership of tasks

This quality is about accepting responsibility for a task (so that you 'own' the task). This means that once you have taken on or accepted a task you see the task through and complete it by a set deadline. If you have any difficulties in completing the task you need to refer back to your line manager as soon as possible rather than just leaving the problem unresolved. This is similar to completing your coursework for college/school.

Being proactive

Proactive is the opposite of reactive. A person who is reactive will only deal with problems when they happen, i.e. he or she will not take steps to prevent the problem arising in the first place. This approach is sometimes known as 'fire-fighting' management.

A proactive person will identify problems *before* they happen and then put systems or procedures in place to prevent the problem occurring. You cannot predict every problem that will occur in an organisation; however, if a problem does occur a proactive person will learn from this problem and try to put controls in place to prevent it happening again.

The ability to compromise

In work as in life you cannot always get your own way. You need to be able to compromise and find solutions to problems where all involved are happy with the outcome. This is a difficult quality to develop and, to an extent, the ability to compromise comes with experience. The best solution to a problem is called a 'win–win' situation; this is when every party involved feels that they have come out of the negotiations with a good result.

It is worth noting that you should never compromise on your standards at work.

Empathy

Empathy is about the ability to see things from another person's perspective and it requires the ability to really listen to people. For example, if you worked as ground staff at an airport and a customer approached you with concerns that he had lost his luggage, empathy would enable you to appreciate the stress and concern that this situation is causing the customer (even though lost luggage is an everyday occurrence at a large international airport). Empathy will help you to recognise how customers feel and find solutions to satisfy their needs.

In summary

- There are a number of personal skills and qualities that are required in the travel and tourism industry.
- Personal skills required include: problem solving, initiative, teamwork, oral and written communication, time management, numeracy, languages, interpersonal skills and using ICT.
- Qualities required include: reliability, personal presentation, personal organisation, self-reflection, ownership of tasks, being proactive, the ability to compromise, empathy.

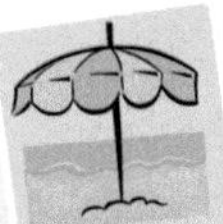

Practice assessment activity

Level P4

Describe, in general, the personal skills and qualities needed to work in a travel and tourism organisation. Your answer should be presented as a career guide and could include examples to demonstrate the skills you are describing.
The following skills and qualities need to be addressed:

- *Skills*: problem solving; initiative; teamwork; oral and written communication; time management; numeracy; using ICT; languages; interpersonal skills.
- *Qualities*: reliability; personal presentation; personal organisation; self-reflection; ownership of tasks; proactivity; compromise; empathy.

6.4 Understand how teams operate in travel and tourism organisations

This section covers:

- types of teams
- teamworking skills.

Types of teams

A team is a group of individuals who work together. All teams fall into three major types:

- formal
- informal
- ad-hoc.

Formal teams

Formal teams are teams that are arranged by the organisation. These teams will have a structure with individuals having particular responsibilities and roles. For example, a resort team is a formal group of holiday representatives that looks after guests in a resort.

Informal teams

Informal teams are teams that form naturally, such as a group of friends that work together. Although these teams are not formal there is a bond between the members. Many travel and tourism organisations encourage informal teams; for example, an ICT-users' group would be people throughout the organisation who use the ICT services, computers and telephones, etc., who meet to feedback to the ICT team. Another example of an informal team is that formed to organise social events for the organisation, such as a charity football match or a Christmas party.

Ad-hoc teams

This is a group of individuals that happen to be working together on a particular task with no structure or pre-organisation. These groups tend to form in situations where something out of the ordinary happens – as the Case study on the next page illustrates.

Where and why teams are needed

Teams are needed in any situation when a task requires more than one person to complete it. There are a number of reasons that travel and tourism organisations need teams:

Case studies

Read the news story below then answer the two questions before discussing this situation with your group.

Baggage handlers' strike threatens Gatwick chaos

By Alan Jones, Industrial Correspondent, PA News

Published: 22 September 2004

Hundreds of baggage handlers and maintenance workers at Gatwick Airport are to strike on Saturday in a row over workloads, threatening travel chaos, it was announced today.

Members of the Transport and General Workers' Union employed by Servisair will also strike on September 30 if the dispute is not settled.

The two stoppages were announced after talks involving the conciliation service Acas failed to break the deadlock.

The TGWU said a row over increased workloads on baggage and cargo handlers, loaders and maintenance staff worsened when a senior union shop steward was 'victimised' and suspended.

Almost 600 workers overwhelmingly backed industrial action in a ballot.

TGWU official Madeleine Richards said: 'Workers are determined to protect their senior steward and to ensure justice. They have voted to strike because they believe their representative is facing trumped-up charges.'

The union said industrial relations at Servisair's operations at Gatwick have been strained over the summer.

The strikes are due to start at 3am on both days.

* Workers who refuel aircraft for dozens of airlines at Heathrow, including British Airways, Virgin Atlantic and Qantas, are set to walk out for 48 hours from Friday in a separate row over pay.

(*Source*: PA News 22nd September, 2004. Reprinted with kind permission of the Press Association)

1 List all the teams you can identify in the news story. What type of team do you think they are – formal, informal or ad-hoc?
2 How do you think these teams performed in this situation?

- when the task is too large for one person to do it in the time frame required
- when the task is too complicated for one person to complete it
- when tasks require more than one person to check that information is correct
- for security reasons (see also Section 6.3)
- when the task physically requires more than one person to complete it
- when health and safety procedures require that more than one person be involved in completing the task (see also Section 6.3).

People

On a personal level, everyone has a need to socialise and have contact with others – people don't only work for money but are also motivated by being with others and the friendships that they form. Many full-time employees spend longer awake with their colleagues than they do with their families and partners. These personal bonds form as strong a structure within an organisation as that provided by the formal structure.

Teamworking skills

As a team is a group of people working towards the same goal, interpersonal skills are vital to the success of the team. There are a number of important issues which help or prevent a team being effective. These include:

- Sharing ideas – after all, two heads are better than one!
- Supporting each other – different people have different strengths so can help each other with different tasks. Also, in the modern working environment people experience different responsibilities and roles as well as different time pressures.
- Listening skills are vitally important within a team for the team to function. Although not every idea may be used, it is important for the members of the team that their ideas are being listened to and considered.

In summary

- There are three main types of teams: formal, informal and ad-hoc.
- Teams are needed in any situation where there is more than one person involved in a task due to the complication of the task or the speed with which the task needs to be completed.
- Skills which are needed for a team to be successful include: interpersonal skills, sharing ideas and supporting each other.

■ *A team meeting*

Practice assessment activity

Levels P5/M3/D2

To attempt this task you need to research two contrasting travel and tourism organisations. Your tutor might organise guest speakers or visits to a travel and tourism organisation. Some organisations provide study packs which will provide the information needed; however, check with your tutor first.

P **1** Describe how teams operate in two contrasting travel and tourism organisations. (P5) Your two organisations need to contrast in some way, i.e. different sectors of the industry (tour operator, travel agency), a different scale (multiple and independent) or different ownership (partnership and PLC). ✓

M **2** Compare the operation of teams in two contrasting travel and tourism organisations. (M3) Using your two organisations from task 1, identify the similarities and differences and comment on why these differences occur, giving reasons. ✓✓

D **3** Evaluate the operation of teams in two contrasting organisations and make recommendations for improvements. (D2) Using the teams discussed in tasks 1 and 2, your evaluation should make clear and detailed judgements and recommendations that are practical and achievable within the context of both teams. ✓✓✓

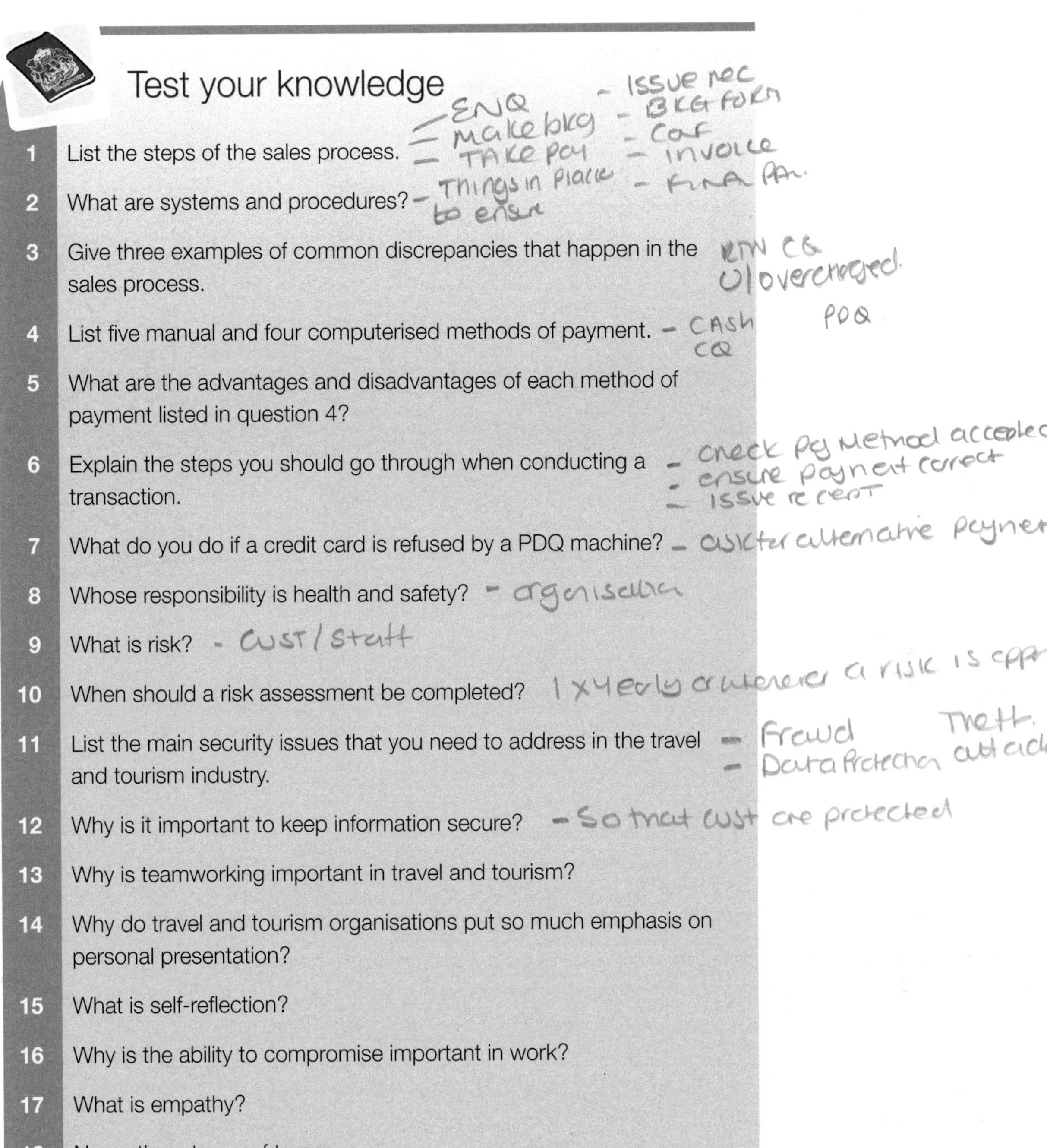

Test your knowledge

1. List the steps of the sales process.
2. What are systems and procedures?
3. Give three examples of common discrepancies that happen in the sales process.
4. List five manual and four computerised methods of payment.
5. What are the advantages and disadvantages of each method of payment listed in question 4?
6. Explain the steps you should go through when conducting a transaction.
7. What do you do if a credit card is refused by a PDQ machine?
8. Whose responsibility is health and safety?
9. What is risk?
10. When should a risk assessment be completed?
11. List the main security issues that you need to address in the travel and tourism industry.
12. Why is it important to keep information secure?
13. Why is teamworking important in travel and tourism?
14. Why do travel and tourism organisations put so much emphasis on personal presentation?
15. What is self-reflection?
16. Why is the ability to compromise important in work?
17. What is empathy?
18. Name three types of teams.
19. Make a list of when and why teams are needed.
20. What skills do you need to work in a team?

7 Developing Employability Skills for Travel and Tourism

Introduction

This unit aims to help you make the most of the opportunities to get a job in the travel and tourism industry. You will be able to develop employability skills in a work-related project within a travel and tourism organisation. You will improve the skills needed in the industry such as customer service, teamwork and problem solving. You will also look at the range of job roles and career opportunities, and how you can start the process of applying for them.

This unit links to *Unit 2: Exploring Customer Service in Travel and Tourism* and *Unit 6: Business Skills for Travel and Tourism*.

How you will be assessed

Unit 7 is assessed internally so the Centre delivering the qualification will assess you against the criteria. On completion of this unit you should be able to:

7.1 understand the skills required to undertake job roles in the travel and tourism industry

7.2 plan and carry out a work-related project in order to develop personal and employability skills

7.3 monitor and review skills development in a work-related project

7.4 undergo a job application process for the travel and tourism industry

Assessment grades

The Edexcel Assessment Grid for Unit 7 details the criteria to be met. In general, to gain a Pass (P) you are asked to identify, plan and prepare material; to gain a Merit (M) you are also asked to explain and complete a work-related project; and to gain a Distinction (D) you are also asked to evaluate and analyse.

7.1 Understand the skills required to undertake job roles in the travel and tourism industry

This section covers:

- job roles, entry and progression in the travel and tourism industry
- matching skills.

Job roles, entry and progression in the travel and tourism industry

You need to know the range of jobs available in the travel and tourism industry so you can choose which ones will be suitable for you.

Travel agents

Travel agents spend much of their time talking face to face or on the telephone to customers as well as to principals (airlines, ferries, etc.). You will need good IT skills and a knowledge of keyboarding and word-processing. There are many different booking systems and you would receive training for the specific ones used. Customers will ask agents for advice concerning destinations, holiday companies, insurance and travel methods, etc.

■ *A busy travel agents*

Agents will need to know how to obtain information from printed and electronic sources, and how to inform customers clearly and accurately. They will then need to process bookings accurately and quickly, so that reservations are confirmed. Some will need to be able to make complex reservations on airline reservation systems, such as Galileo, which will also book car hire and accommodation. Agents must have good customer service skills, and good product and geographical knowledge. Excellent interpersonal skills are essential since the same holiday could be booked via any agency.

Qualifications

Qualifications may include:

- ABTAC (Association of British Travel Agents Certificate)
- IATA Fares and Ticketing qualification (levels 1 and 2)
- NVQ in Travel Services (Retail).

These qualifications could be obtained by working and studying 'on the job' or at college. Some qualifications are also available by distance learning via colleges or the Travel Training Company. Many tour operators and other principals will provide training for organisations, and area or head offices may provide in-house training. Travel agents will often accept students on work placements, so that they can understand how the agency operates.

Progression

Progression is normally as follows:

Trainee travel agent

↓

Travel agent

↓

Senior travel agent/Customer service agent

↓

Deputy manager

↓

Manager

↓

Area manager

Some agencies may have different names for these roles.

Tour operators

Some jobs are based in the UK at Head Office and some overseas.

Head Office

At Head Office there may be many roles required to ensure the holiday goes well. There will be telephone operators who make reservations from agents and the public. There may also be those who deal with problems during or after the holiday. As well as those who deal with customers, there are others who are involved in putting the holidays together, producing holiday brochures and marketing the holidays. Again, the employees who deal with customers need good interpersonal skills and good computer skills.

Progression

Progression could be:

Trainee administrator

↓

Administrator/Telephone operator

↓

Supervisor

↓

Manager of department

Overseas

There are also jobs available overseas in resorts. Representatives work on behalf of the tour operators to ensure the holidaymakers are safe and that all arrangements go smoothly. They also sell excursions to the holidaymakers and supervise transfers from the airport to the accommodation and back. Often they will need to speak the local language. They will also need excellent interpersonal skills as well as considerable stamina for long journeys and late nights. There are opportunities for working with all kinds of customers, from looking after children in clubs, to meeting the entertainment needs of teenagers and young people, to supporting elderly clients.

You may have seen some of the television programmes based on the life of a holiday rep; as these programmes show, reps could be required to do anything from finding false teeth to dealing with a sudden death. They need to have good interpersonal skills and the confidence to deal with groups of people in stressful situations.

Progression

Progression could be:

Children's representative

↓

Resort representative

↓

Area representative

↓

Country supervisor

Qualifications

The qualifications for tour operators could be:

- ABTOC (Association of British Tour Operations Certificate)
- NVQ Travel Services (Tour Operations)
- BTEC qualifications such as the Diploma (Overseas Representative).

These qualifications could be gained from college, and training is done 'on the job' to each operator's specific requirements.

Airlines

There are opportunities both as ground crew and air crew.

Ground crew

Ground crew are responsible for checking in passengers and baggage, helping passengers with particular needs, giving information and checking boarding of aircraft. Good customer service skills are required as well as the confidence to deal with complaints and potentially dangerous situations. The ability to speak another language would be an advantage. There are also administrative roles.

Air crew

Air crew are there to ensure the health and safety of the passengers. They will also, of course, serve food and drinks, provide blankets and sell duty-free goods. The skills required are similar to ground crew, although most airlines require a certain weight–height ratio.

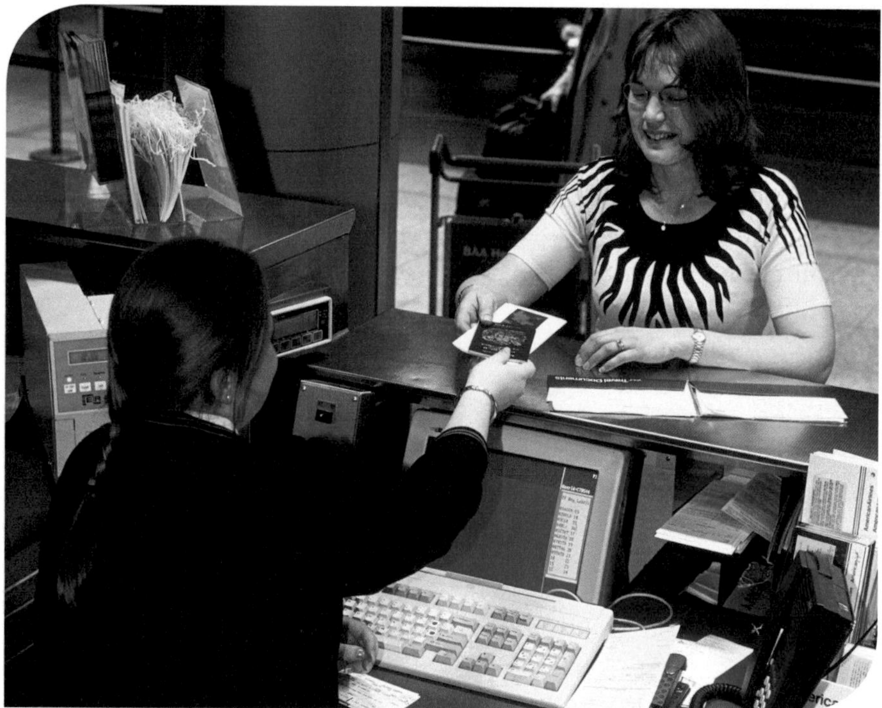

■ *Working at check-in in a busy airport*

Qualifications
There are courses available at college such as:

- IATA Fares and Ticketing
- BTEC Preparation for Air Cabin Crew.

However, most airlines have their own training courses, for which there is often a huge number of applicants.

Progression
Progression could be:

More senior flight attendants will also have the opportunity to travel on transatlantic and worldwide flights.

Accommodation providers

Don't forget accommodation can be anything from 5-star luxury hotels to small bed and breakfast or self-catering cottages. Most of the jobs are in the larger hotels where 'front-of-house' staff deal with customers face to face and 'back-of-house' staff provide the services which make the hotel run smoothly. There can be:

- Reception work, making reservations for customers and checking them in and out of their room. Reception staff may also need to provide information and deal with complaints.
- People who deal with housekeeping – cleaning and equipping rooms or waiting on tables.

Skills for front-of-house may be customer service, another language, computer skills, a good telephone manner and a warm and welcoming

Case studies

Bruce had always wanted to work for a national airline. He was enthusiastic and hard-working but hadn't quite got the academic qualifications to work for the airline immediately. So, he looked at the jobs available at the local airport and went to work as a courier on the inter-airport buses. He was so good with the customers that when he applied a year later to the airline, he was taken on as ground staff. He has since become a trainer and a supervisor – proving that hard work will pay off!

personality. Back-of-house employees may be very organised and have good administrative skills.

Progression

Progression may be:

Trainee receptionist

↓

Receptionist

↓

Supervisor/Shift leader

Front-of-house manager

■ *Working as a hotel receptionist*

Qualifications

There may be opportunities for in-house training, which the hotel industry is particularly good at. There are also many qualifications, such as NVQs and the BTEC National Diploma in Hospitality Supervision. These may be gained at college or at work following an apprenticeship scheme.

Visitor attractions

These can be really varied – anything from large museums to small family-run organisations. There may be staff required to take tickets, guide visitors, produce food and drink or run crèches, etc. Guides for heritage attractions often have a related degree but also include many

■ *A tourist guide introducing tourists to the Ightham Mote manor house in Kent*

volunteers. The skills here are also customer service, giving a warm welcome and the ability to explain information clearly.

Progression and qualifications

There are fewer structures for progression as this depends on the kind of attraction. There are NVQs and the 'Welcome' qualifications – a whole range available under a Certificate in Customer Service. Again, training is available at college or in-house.

Passenger transport

In addition to airlines, ferries and trains (including Eurostar) also employ many staff. These companies often require passenger hosts or pursers, who perform the same functions as air cabin crews, as well as administrators to make reservations, organise supplies and remain at the Head Office or port. Staff who deal directly with customers will have prime responsibility for their passengers' health and safety as well as providing them with information. The same customer service skills and ability to work under pressure will apply.

Training

There are NVQs in Travel Services available which can be studied at college or as an apprentice. On-the job training is given on various different vehicles and procedures.

Over to you

Think about what you enjoy when you go out for the day. Imagine you are going by public transport to an attraction – what do you want from the people you come into contact with? What skills are you looking for when you are the customer?

Practice assessment activity

Levels P1/M1

P **1** For five travel and tourism sectors (choose from those that you have looked at in this unit) identify career opportunities.

- First, list the job roles for each sector.
- Then, from these lists, select and describe two job roles.
- In your description you should include roles, responsibilities and entry requirements as well the personal skills, qualifications and experience required. (P1)

M **2** For your two selected job roles from task 1, identify and explain progression routes into higher positions within the sector or other sectors of the travel and tourism industry. Include the skills, experience and qualifications required, together with the proposed actions for your own development plan. (M1)

Matching skills

So, you have looked at a number of different jobs – how do you know which one is right for you?

Over to you

You can also spend some time assessing your own skills. You can use the form below as a starting point, but remember it is pointless to cheat!

	Don't like (✓)	Don't mind ✓)	Really enjoy (✓)
Working on my own			
Working with people			
Talking on the phone			
Working with computers			
Working in an office			
Doing practical things			
Thinking through problems			
Having the confidence to deal with people who are under stress			
Working shifts			
Having regular office times			
Being creative			

Look at the results and see if you can think of the kind of jobs suitable for you.

Consult a careers professional!

Many schools and colleges have careers or Connexions advisors who can advise you about your career options and progression. Alternatively, you can access the services of a careers office; these have computer programmes which will assess your suitability for different careers. They are not infallible but might be a good place to start.

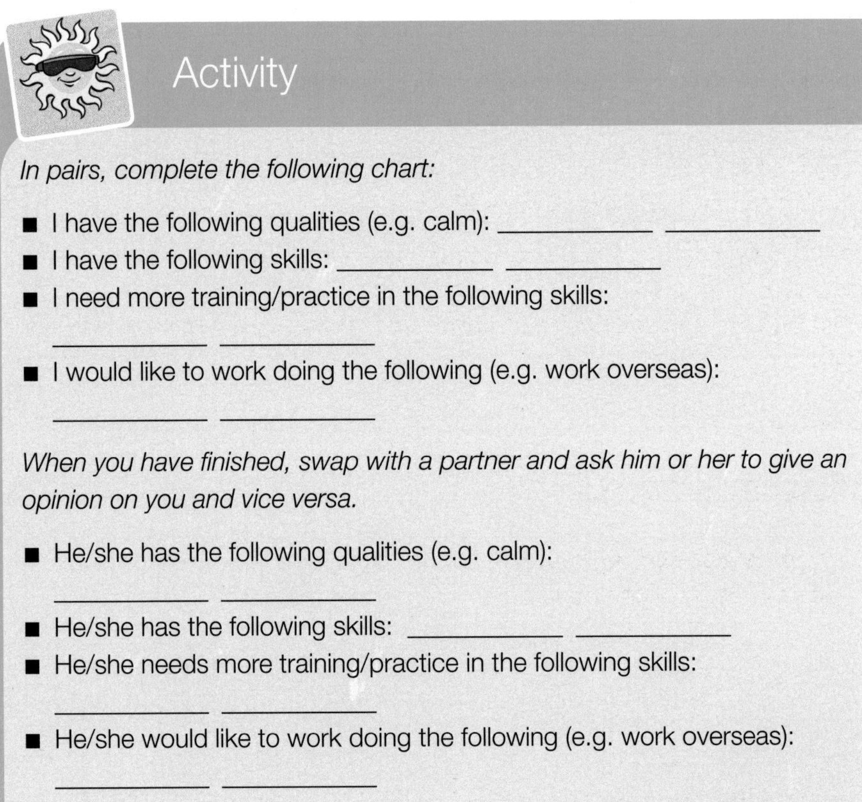

Activity

In pairs, complete the following chart:

- I have the following qualities (e.g. calm): ____________ ____________
- I have the following skills: ____________ ____________
- I need more training/practice in the following skills: ____________ ____________
- I would like to work doing the following (e.g. work overseas): ____________ ____________

When you have finished, swap with a partner and ask him or her to give an opinion on you and vice versa.

- He/she has the following qualities (e.g. calm): ____________ ____________
- He/she has the following skills: ____________ ____________
- He/she needs more training/practice in the following skills: ____________ ____________
- He/she would like to work doing the following (e.g. work overseas): ____________ ____________

When you have both completed your own and each other's forms, you then need to think about how you are going to get to where you want to be in your chosen career.

Activity

Complete a development plan for your chosen career in the travel and tourism organisation, based on the example below.

Skills and qualities	How to achieve	When
Word-processing	Do ECDL course	Enrol in course next term
Confidence in dealing with people	Get part-time job in shop	January

Practice assessment activity

P Level P2

- For the two job roles you described in the previous assessment activity (see page 262), identify and describe the entry requirements. Review your own skills, qualifications and experience against those required. You may do this as a discussion with your tutor, using notes and self-assessment.
- Produce an action plan to develop your skills and experience to achieve the appropriate qualifications for this employment.

7.2 Plan and carry out a work-related project in order to develop personal and employability skills

This section covers:

- planning a project
- skills development within the project
- undertaking the project.

In this section you will need to consider where you could complete a work-related project to improve your skills.

Planning a project

When planning a project, you will first need to think about the skills area of the travel and tourism industry you want to study. This might be a skills area such as:

- customer service
- marketing
- organisational practices
- teamwork
- acquiring new skills and techniques.

Identifying key objectives related to travel and tourism skills areas

For your chosen area of study, you will then need to think of key objectives related to it. For example, if your chosen skills area is teamwork, one objective might be 'Assess teamwork demonstrated by airline check-in staff'.

For each objective you set, you will then need to ask many different questions in order to find the answers and information you need. For example, questions you could ask about the objective 'Assess teamwork demonstrated by airline check-in staff' could include:

- How does the team share roles and responsibilities before, during and after check-in?
- How well do the team members communicate with each other?

Further examples of key objectives and questions relating to them are given below for projects in the skills areas of customer service and marketing.

Project in customer service

Objective 1: Assess practical skills demonstrated in a travel agency

- How do the staff greet customers?
- Do they answer the phone quickly?
- What skills do you think the staff have?
- How do the staff ensure they are reliable?
- How do they work as a team?

Objective 2: Does the organisation know how well (or badly) customers rate its service?

- What monitoring methods does the organisation use?
- What results does it get?
- What does it do with the results – who sees them?
- Does anything happen as a result of this information? If so, what?
- Do the employees think the results are important?
- What improvements could be made?

Project in marketing

Objective 1: Assess the skills needed in marketing

- What qualifications do the staff have?
- What skills are apparent as they work?

Objective 2: Is the marketing effective?

- How does the organisation market its product?
- Is it aimed at a particular market segment?
- Do staff produce or edit 'copy'?
- Do staff in the marketing department have creative visual skills?
- Do they use desktop publishing?

Case studies

Grace had obtained her work placement in a specialist long-haul tour operator. They wanted her to look at the marketing to travel agents, as there had been a decline in the percentage booked. She researched this so well that her findings were used in a training session for the staff and she was offered a discounted flight!

THE OCEAN CENTRE
SPECIAL OFFER
Admit ONE child free when an adult buys a full price ticket
Offer valid until 31 Dec. 2006. No photocopied vouchers.

■ *A marketing tool you may be familiar with*

Meeting needs of own skill development plan

The next step of your project will be to consider your own skill development plan within the project.

Objective setting

Just as for the first stage of your project, you will need to set objectives for your skill development plan. These could be objectives such as:

- Identify what I need to do to prove my own skills.
- Demonstrate improved skills in the work environment.

Qualifications and experience

To develop an effective skills development plan, you will need to think about the qualifications and experience required by the area of the travel and tourism industry you are looking at. The following types of questions will help you to identify what these are:

- What sort of qualifications does the organisation look for?
- Do the current employees have these skills?
- What staff development takes place?
- Do the employees see the benefit of this development?
- Do the current employees have any travel-specific qualifications (for example, NVQs, BTECs, ABTAC, IATA, Fares and Ticketing)?

There are many other kinds of projects and each organisation will be different. However, each project needs to have objectives – that is, what you hope to achieve/find out. It should be quite clear to both the organisation and yourself what you hope to find out and how you are going to do it.

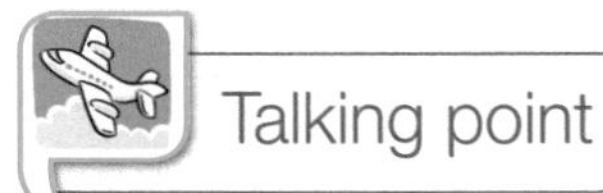

Assume your group has found placements in different sectors of the travel and tourism industry. Find people within the same area, for example, hotels, and brainstorm all the different kinds of projects you can think of for that sector. Present your findings in a spider diagram or mind map.

Skills development within the project

So, now you have your project title and outcome, how are you going to go about it? Tactfully would be one answer! Remember, you are a guest in the organisation and you don't want to be heard saying how amazed you are that nobody in the office has the right qualifications!

Practical research

Ask if you can keep copies of blank customer feedback forms, brochures, development sessions and minutes, etc. Do not just take them; most organisations are happy for you to have them, but some information is sensitive.

Use questionnaires – these will make analysing the answers much easier than a jumble of information. You can produce charts and graphs from the data you receive. Make sure you ask permission if you want to use a questionnaire, particularly if the information may be sensitive.

Timekeeping

Do not leave the project to the last day of the placement or the assignment date. Plan your time effectively so that if one method does not work, you have time to change. You can work on the presentation later!

You can demonstrate how well you can improve your timekeeping skills by following your action plan (see below) and ensuring that you monitor what you achieve by the dates proposed.

Creativity

Perhaps you are lucky enough to be in the marketing department of a tour operator. You can demonstrate your creativity by helping to put together a brochure page or designing a leaflet especially for young people. You could try a marketing campaign for a local travel agency – any of these sorts of projects will improve your skills.

Technical

The kinds of practical skills you could improve may be keyboarding skills, using a spreadsheet, using different software, or use of an EPOS system (Electronic Point of Sale) in a hotel. Your project may help you to improve any of these transferable skills, which can be used in many contexts.

Teamwork

Almost all service industry jobs include working in a team. If you are working as part of a group of people, often of all ages and backgrounds, you will need to expand your 'people skills':

- you will need to be able to judge how people will react to situations and what to say to them
- you will need to be able to adapt to different people appropriately

- above all, you will need to improve your listening skills so that you can judge the way people speak and behave in a professional setting. Some people describe this as having 'emotional intelligence'.

Undertaking the project

Prioritising

It is really important that you prioritise what you need to do. Make sure you do the 'urgent' things first and that you leave time for the 'important' things which might take a bit longer but need some thought and possibly research. In order to do that, planning is essential – there is a saying, 'failing to plan is planning to fail!'.

Action planning

This is essential and should be done well in advance. There are lots of ways to plan, but it is usually better to set down your plan formally. Two types of plan are shown below – the management time plan and the outcome action plan.

Task/Date	14/5	15/5	16/5	17/5	18/5	21/5
Decide on project title						
Draft questionnaire						
Ask permission of manager						
Ask questionnaire in marketing						
Sales						

■ *A management time plan*

Outcome	What do I have already?	What else do I need?	How?	When?	Completed
Completed questionnaire	Project brief List of departments	Word-processed questionnaire	Draft in pencil Get tutor approval	Monday 14 April	Revision needed Completed Thursday 17 April

■ *An outcome action plan*

Key points

Always review your plan regularly and update what needs to be done.

Activity

On your chosen project, draft an outline action plan of how and when you are going to complete it. It does not matter if the action plan needs to be altered as you go along – this is a sign of good monitoring!

Remember that you need to get to and from your placement or part-time job. Check you can do this using public transport, if necessary, and within your budget.

Managing tasks

You will find that using an action plan will really help you to manage the tasks you have to complete. No one expects that an action plan will look untouched – the tasks you start out with are often changed as you go along. However, if you 'tick off' each task as you do it, then you will know exactly what you have to do next. If you have not been able to complete something then use the plan to jot down why this is, and add additional tasks which will get you to where you want to be. The more you can show you have adapted to situations as they arise, the more skilled you will be to work in the ever-changing travel and tourism industry!

Researching

You may need to do research in order to find out about the background to the project. Remember, travel and tourism provides millions of pounds of information in the form of brochures, leaflets and books. These are often written with the purpose of 'selling' the destination to a visitor, so you may like to double-check your information with independent sources, such as the *World Travel Guide* or a good guide book.

The Internet is also a good source of information, but remember that it is only as good as the person who put the information on there and may therefore be just as biased as printed material (although possibly more up to date). Your research skills could be greatly improved if you can demonstrate that you have used many sources to get information, rather than just one.

- Plan effectively – do a plan, refer to it and monitor it!
- Write down your experiences as you go.

Keeping records

You will forget! Always keep records of the interviews and conversations you have. If you are gathering examples of promotional campaigns, write down when and where you found them. This attention to detail will pay off in the end.

Asking questions

When you ask questions, try to use a standard format so that you can ask the same questions of different people – otherwise you will end up with a lot of different information without a structure! You will need to be able to tell when people are busy and to be tactful in your approach. However, if you can improve your ability to gather information from people, this too is an important transferable skill.

7.3 Monitor and review skills development in a work-related project

This section covers:

- monitor skills development
- review skills development.

Monitor skills development

Keeping a log

You will need to make sure that you keep records of all that you are doing as you go along – don't imagine that you will remember what you did at the end! An example of a log is shown below.

Date	Activity	Notes	Initials of supervisor or tutor
17 May	Asked marketing department to complete questionnaire	Sally and Ravi not in. To ask on 19/5	
18 May	Asked permission to give questionnaire to ticketing department	Manager agreed but said to do next week	

■ *A log*

Activity

Draft a log sheet for your placement. You can fill in many of the boxes now, ready to complete on the day.

Research diary

Another way of recording your progress is to keep a research diary (an example is shown below). Don't forget to complete your action plan – in advance – and to monitor where you have achieved your planned activity. You should also remember to take notice of where you have identified that you need to find further information and make sure this appears later in your plan.

Name: ______________________________

Project: ______________________________

Date	Topics	Comments
15/5	Look at customer service records in use	Mr Marti gave permission Collected blank form from reception

■ *A research diary*

Remember – you will be able to monitor your progress against your objectives by using your action plan to its full extent! Make sure that you amend it each time you complete a task or find you need more information. *Write it down!* It really will make a difference if you record everything as you go.

Recording methods

If you are going to interview one or more people, remember that there are other ways of recording what they do and say other than taking notes. For example, you could use an audio or video tape – but remember to ask permission first. Videos can be used to record work practices or marketing events – be creative! You can also use clips or photographs in your presentation.

Witness testimony

You may also like to use a witness testimony to record a particular event; an example of a witness testimony is shown below. It could be used to support audio or visual evidence. Your testimony will have to show more detail of the event; for example, an explanation of the situation, what each person said, the skills and knowledge used, etc.

Name: Laura Bates

Project: Customer service materials

Activity: Role play

Date: 21st May 2006

Laura took part in a training session during which she undertook a role play situation. Laura played a receptionist who had to explain an over-booking situation. She did this well, calming down the client and listening to his point of view before offering an alternative.

Signature: Usha Patel

Name: Usha Patel

Position: Training Manager

■ *A witness testimony*

Review skills development

Formative and summative

You will need to review how well the project is going against the objectives you agreed at the beginning. It is usually best to do this at regular intervals during the project (**formative review**) as well as at the end (**summative review**).

Strengths and weaknesses

Look at what went well and think about what did not go so well and what you would do next time to improve it. Be honest – a clear and objective review with sound suggestions for improvement is far better than saying everything went well and hoping that nobody notices what went wrong (they will!).

Information obtained

How useful was the information you obtained? Was it up to date enough? Was it a balanced view? Could you have found information from a different source which might have been better? Could it have been more visual? Be honest in your evaluation and obtain the views of someone who used your information.

Skills achieved against development plan

Look at the development plan you made earlier. How well do you think you achieved your objectives? Do you feel you have improved your skills? Do you feel that your project helped you to use your skills and will you be able to transfer them to different situations? Ask the people who were looking after you on placement to complete a witness statement describing the improvement in skills.

Review against objectives

Always refer back to your original objectives – how well did you achieve what you set out to do? What might you need to do in the future to fully achieve your goal?

Areas requiring further development and experience

It is unlikely that you will have managed to perfect all of the skills in a short period of time!

- What skills could you improve on? What skills do you feel you might need more experience of? How will you obtain this?
- Was there someone who had really good skills in the workplace? How did they reach this level of skill? What could you do to move towards that level?

Presentation

You will need to present the results of your project in the way requested by your tutor and/or the organisation.

You may be asked to do an oral presentation. Remember to dress smartly, stand up straight and talk enthusiastically to your audience. Use relevant material from the organisation as visual aids, for example, brochures, menus, pictures, videos. Remember to use your data from questionnaires in the form of graphs and charts. If you are able to use PowerPoint® or slides for overhead projectors, then do so – this will give your presentation a professional look.

If you are required to write up your project results then think about how to make this interesting. Use pictures, examples of forms, photographs and charts, etc. to illustrate what you are reporting. Use the organisation's logo on the front – be creative!

Planning how you are going to write your report is really important. Make sure that you refer to the project's objectives and clearly organise your work. Leave enough time to produce a draft and then to proofread this before producing your final version.

Finally – enjoy it! You have spent a considerable amount of time on your project and experienced the world of work. Anybody listening to you or reading your report should be able to understand what it was like and what you have found out. Who knows – you might end up with a full-time job at one of these organisations!

In summary

Record what you do!

- Keep a log or diary.
- Gather leaflets, brochures, posters, etc. during your time at the organisation.
- Refer back to what you are trying to find out (your objectives).
- Be honest in your evaluation and what you have learnt from it.

Practice assessment activity

Levels P3/P4/M2/D1

P **1** Plan a work-related project. Make sure you list the key objectives and the relationship to your own development plan, including timescales and proposed outcomes. (P3) ✓

P **2** Demonstrate that you have monitored and reviewed:

- the project you have undertaken
- your own skills development.

You should report on the project in an appropriate format. (P4) ✓

M **3** Complete your work-related project to the objectives you have set. Demonstrate the ability to monitor and review your skills development, own development plan and proposed outcomes. Include evidence from your supervisors. (M2) ✓✓

D **4** Evaluate your own development of skills, qualification and experience, taking into account performance on a work-related project and recognising and actioning further development needs. (D1) ✓✓✓

7.4 Undergo a job application process for the travel and tourism industry

This section covers:

- documents
- interviews and other selection methods
- preparation for interview
- interview skills.

Now you need to think about how you are going to apply for that dream job!

Documents

Preparing your CV

A CV (curriculum vitae) is a document which has to 'sell' your skills to your future employer. For this reason you should take trouble to make it eye-catching and accurate; it should also be word-processed.

There are three main ways to set out your CV:

- traditional
- skills-based
- individual.

Examples of each are shown below, on pages 276–8.

Talking point

In pairs, look at the three types of CV below.

- Which do you prefer?
- Which do you think is the most effective and why?
- Name two advantages and two disadvantages of each type of CV.

CURRICULUM VITAE

Name: Julie Smith

Date of birth: 22 July 1982

Address: Any Road,
Anytown,
Somewhere,
ANY 1OW

Nationality: British

Email: smith@email.com

EDUCATION
2003–2005: Anytown College of Further Education, Somewhere, ANY 1OW

GCSEs
Business Studies D
Science DD
Maths D
Technology C

WORK EXPERIENCE

Date: March 1999 – present

Company: Cornhill Insurance

Position/Skills used: cleaner (2 hours daily, Monday to Friday)
This job enabled me to further advance my skills as an independent worker. As a key holder my main responsibilities included vacuuming and cleaning of a designated floor.

ACHIEVEMENTS AND LEISURE ACTIVITIES

December 1997
I achieved a high level of attainment in lifesaving and swimming as part of the successful completion of a first aid course.

Sports
I am a fairly sporty person. I enjoy water sports such as swimming and canoeing and I also enjoy cycling.

Interests
Computing takes up a lot of my spare time, whether reading computer books, expanding my knowledge or gaining practical skills.

Leisure
I am a sociable, outgoing person and enjoy meeting people and going to pubs and clubs with friends.

■ *A traditional CV*

CURRICULUM VITAE

Name: Julie Smith

SKILLS

A confident, enthusiastic person who enjoys learning new skills, offering determination and commitment.

- **Customer service** – experience gained at work placement at Eternity Travel where I received commendations on my interpersonal skills.
- **Teamwork** – I have experience of working as part of a lifesaving team. I also take part in team canoe charity work.
- **IT** – I am confident in the use of Word, Excel and PowerPoint, all of which I have used on my College course.

EDUCATION
2003–2005: Anytown College of Further Education,
Somewhere,
ANY 1OW

GCSEs
Business Studies D
Science DD
Maths D
Technology C

PERSONAL DETAILS

Date of birth: 22 July 1982

Address: Any Road,
Anytown,
Somewhere,
ANY 1OW

Nationality: British

Email: smith@email.com

A skills-based CV – note the change in emphasis

CURRICULUM VITAE

Julie Smith

Address
Any Road,
Anytown
Somewhere
ANY 1OW

Date of birth
22 July 1982

EDUCATION
2003–2005: Anytown College of Further Education, Somewhere, ANY 1OW

GCSEs

- **Business Studies – D**
  I was part of a business competition team that sold theatre tickets.
- **Science DD**
  I was particularly interested in Biology and Nutrition
- **Maths D**
  I am currently re-sitting this

SKILLS
I am good at customer service and enjoy meeting people. I am used to working as part of a team to achieve my goals.

An individual CV

Activity

Write a CV and then swap it with a partner. Give each other advice – what is good about the CV? How could it be improved?

Key points

- Make several drafts of your CV in different styles. Ask friends and family which one they prefer.
- Always ask someone to proofread your documents. It is very easy to overlook errors if you proofread your own – you see what you expect to see!

Research shows that people only read the top third of a page properly, so make this part of your CV really stand out. Put the most interesting information at the top.

Letters of application

You may want to apply for a particular job or you may want to work for a particular company. Either way, you will need to send a letter of application. Unless you know someone willing to take you on a placement (friends and relatives are very useful here!) you may need to send many applications in order to get a placement. Don't be discouraged if you receive a refusal – or indeed no reply at all. Don't take it personally and try again!

You will need to write a standard letter which can be adapted for different circumstances. These need to be word-processed and should be set out in a formal business format. An example is shown below. If you have knowledge of mail merge or similar systems, this will be quicker, but cutting and pasting or deleting and re-typing can work just as well.

Your Address

Date

The Manager

Letting Go Travel
42 High Street
Anytown
BG42 1QR

Dear Sir or Madam,

I am studying for the BTEC First Diploma in Travel and Tourism at City College. One of the units is a work placement project and I would really like to work for Letting Go Travel because my family has booked holidays with your branch for years.

The dates would be two weeks from 14 May, and I would need to negotiate a project with you.

I enclose my CV and hope that I will hear from you in the near future.

Yours faithfully,

Laurel Wreath

Laurel Wreath

■ *An application letter*

Tips for completing your application letter

- Write to 'The Manager' if you don't know the name of the person you need to contact, or in the case of a large organisation, write to the Human Resources Department. If you know the manager's name then use it!
- If you don't receive an immediate response, follow up the letter with a phone call or visit. You are much more difficult to refuse if you ask in person.

- Try to give a good reason why you are interested in that particular job or company. Why should they take you? What is special about your application?
- Use 'Yours faithfully' if you have started 'Dear Sir or Madam' and 'Yours sincerely' if you have used the manager's name. (Remember, you can't have two '*S's*' together (Sir/sincerely).)
- Make sure that your letter is word-processed and has correct spelling, punctuation and grammar – read through it carefully to check for any mistakes. Remember to emphasise the skills you have which would allow you to do a job in that organisation.
- Always ask your tutor to check your letter before sending it. Some colleges and schools send out a covering letter explaining more about the project and endorsing your application. This is sometimes a good idea and should stop many students in class applying to the same company!

Activity

1. *Look in your local newspaper or in the* Travel Trade Gazette*. Choose a job and write a letter of application for that job.*
2. *Draft a letter of application to a range of businesses, e.g. travel agent, tour operator, Tourist Information centre. Make sure you state your reasons for applying to each particular organisation.*

Letter of acceptance

Well done! You've been offered a job or placement. You need to accept this by sending out a formal letter, such as that shown below. You must also ensure that both you and the company understand what happens next.

Your Address

Date

Mr H. Smithers
Letting Go Travel
42 High Street
Anytown
BG42 1QR

Dear Mr Smithers,

Thank you very much for your letter of 26 January offering me a placement for two weeks from 14 May.

I am very much looking forward to working with you and would like to arrange an interview to discuss a possible project during next month, if convenient. I will telephone you to arrange an appointment nearer the time.

Thank you for supporting my studies.

Yours sincerely,

Laurel Wreath

Laurel Wreath

A letter of acceptance

Letter of decline

If you are lucky enough to be offered several placements, you will need to decline those that you do not want to accept gracefully or offer them to another student. An example of a letter declining a placement is shown below. When recommending another student, check to make sure that he or she will apply!

> Your Address
>
> Date
>
> Mrs C. Bloomer
> Hotel Saunders
> The Esplanade
> Anytown
> BG42 1PJ
>
> Dear Mrs Bloomer,
>
> Thank you very much for your letter of 31 January offering me a placement from 14 May.
>
> Unfortunately, I have already accepted another placement, but I know that a fellow student, Manjeet Kaur, is intending to apply to you and I hope you would be willing to accept her instead. She will write to you separately.
>
> Thank you for supporting my studies.
>
> Yours sincerely,
>
> *Laurel Wreath*
>
> Laurel Wreath

■ *A letter declining a placement*

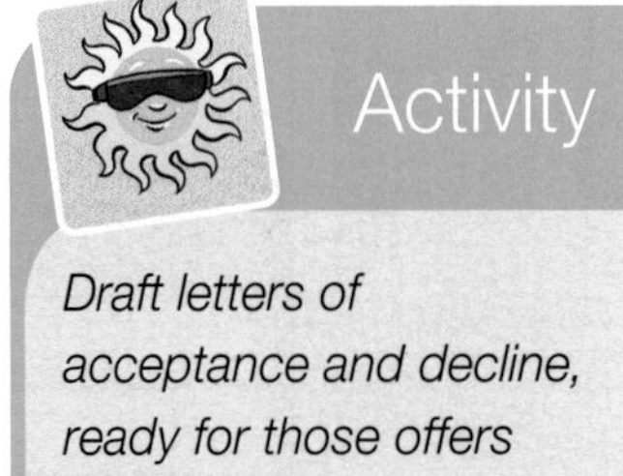

Draft letters of acceptance and decline, ready for those offers coming in!

Application forms

Sometimes organisations prefer applicants to complete a standard form. You need to make sure that you write on these clearly, using capital letters and blue or black ink. Some application forms can be completed on the company's website and emailed to the organisation. In either case, make a copy of the form and practise completing it!

When filling in an application form, it is important that you don't lie or exaggerate – remember what you are applying for and try to reflect the skills and personal qualities needed to do a job in that organisation.

Activity

Copy the application form below and practise filling it in. Remember to sell yourself in your covering letter!

SUNNY TOURS APPLICATION FORM

Please complete form in block capitals

Mr/Mrs/Miss/Ms (delete as applicable)

First names:

Surname:

Address:	Age:	Date of birth:
	Tel no:	Email:

EDUCATION:

Secondary school:	[Dates:]	
	From:	To:

Further education:	Full-time or part-time	[Dates:]	
		From:	To:

QUALIFICATIONS:

Awarding body	Subject	Qualification awarded	Date

Membership of voluntary organisations:

EMPLOYMENT AND WORK EXPERIENCE:

List all previous employment in chronological order, starting with the earliest.

[Date]		Full-time or part-time	Employers	Nature of duties
From:	To:			

■ *An application form*

Interviews and other selection methods

Your offer of a placement or part-time job may be subject to interview. Sometimes there is an interview pre-selection using a telephone conversation. Make sure that you sound enthusiastic and really interested in going to the next interview stage. Smile while you are talking – you will sound 'warmer'.

Sometimes interviews are held in groups. Very often this is to see how you react in a group situation. Make sure that your voice is heard but don't try to dominate the discussion. Listen to other people and take their views into account. You may be seen individually later.

Generally, however, you will be interviewed individually, probably by one or two people from the organisation you are applying to.

Key points

If you are going for a placement interview, bear in mind that you may later want to apply for a permanent job.

Preparation for interview

An interview is the chance to sell yourself, and there are a few techniques that will help you to achieve your potential.

When you go to an interview, a little preparation will make you appear more confident and help to banish any nervousness. Here are some steps to take that will help you to come across in the best way:

- Telephone the organisation and confirm that you are attending the interview.
- Check the time and place and ask for travel directions.
- Check travel arrangements in advance, particularly if it involves a complicated journey by public transport. Do a dummy run so you are sure how long it will take you to get there.
- Arrive early! Even if you have to wait around for a while, it is better than arriving late or flustered.

Over to you

Why do you want to work in travel and tourism? The hours can be long and the pay can vary – what is it that draws you to this industry?

Knowledge of the organisation

Find out as much as you can about the organisation – what it does, how big it is, what its image is, etc. Ways in which you can do this include:

- visiting the organisation's website
- finding a copy of its company report in the local library and reading the introduction
- talking to people who have worked there or used their services.

Interviewers are always impressed if the candidate has done some background research and you will feel more confident that you know what you are letting yourself in for!

Knowledge of the job role

You should also find out as much as you can about the job role itself. You could do this by looking closely at the job description and comparing it to what you are used to doing yourself. There is very often a 'person specification' which will describe the sort of person they are looking for and their skills and attributes. Look at this and see if you can understand why the person doing the role would need those skills.

If it is a job role which is dealing with the public, such as check-in at an airport or guiding visitors, go to a similar place and watch what is happening – is this the sort of thing you would like to do?

Write down questions you want to ask at the interview, particularly about the project, job role or working conditions. Interviewers are always impressed by candidates that are genuinely interested in the role they are applying for.

Dress code and personal appearance

You will need to be clean and smart for the interview. Try to find out what the people who work there are wearing – if they wear smart suits then you should aim for a similarly formal look. If you are going to an organisation which deals with student backpackers then smart casual should be appropriate.

Whatever you wear, you must make sure that everything about you is clean and tidy, with neat hair and clean hands and nails. Most organisations in the travel and tourism industry have a 'customer focus' and need to employ staff who would impress their customers.

Key points

- Be confident – or at least look confident! You can do this by making sure you leave plenty of time for getting to the interview, have done your research, and look well-presented and unhurried.
- Do your research into the organisation. This will impress your interviewers and give you confidence.
- Don't say you are only there because your tutor says you have to do a project.

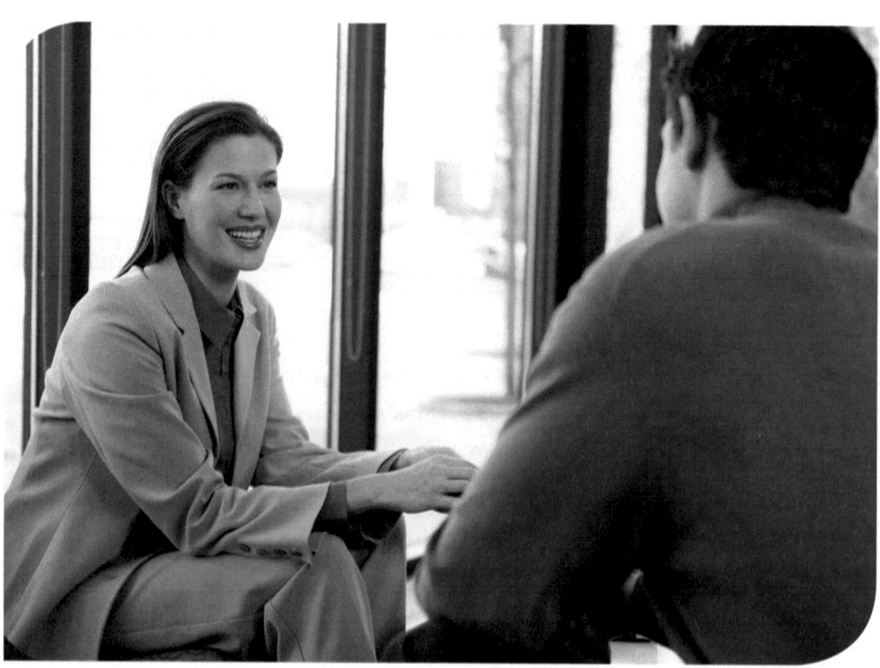

Your appearance should be clean and smart for any interview

Interview skills

Body language

You know when someone you are talking to is bored or not listening – so does the interviewer. It is therefore very important that you remember to sit up straight, with your arms comfortably placed at your side and not crossed, and look interested.

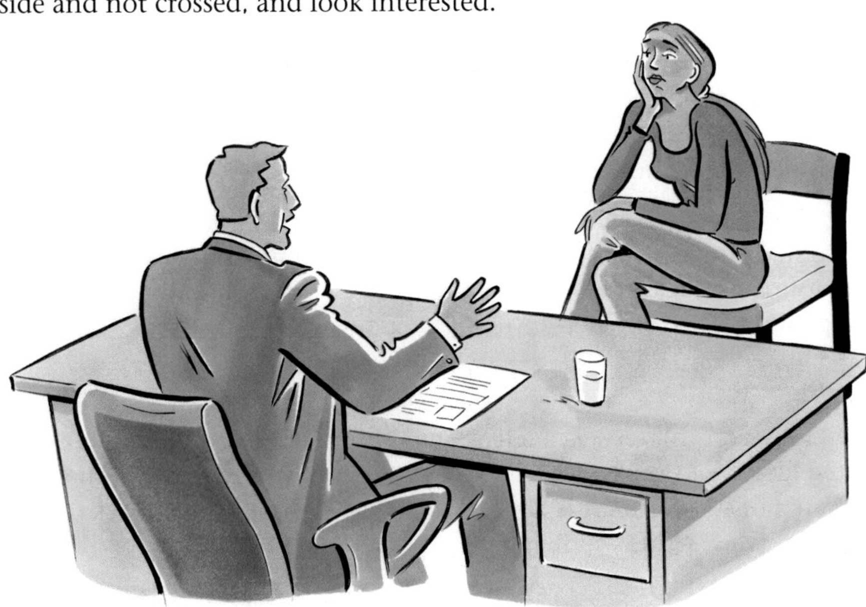

Activity

In pairs, take it in turns to convey a feeling through body language not words. Try to guess what the other person is feeling. Then write a list of the most common ways of expressing emotion without words.

Social skills

An interview is a formal situation and you need to act formally:

- Wait to be asked to enter the room – knock if the door is closed and wait for an answer.
- Wait to be asked to sit down.
- You may be asked to shake hands. Make sure you offer your right hand and grip firmly (but not too hard!).
- Say thank you and goodbye on leaving – remember the organisation is doing you a favour not the other way round.
- Remember to smile and look enthusiastic about working there.
- Respond to questions positively – if you don't understand the question then say so. You can always say 'Do you mean...?' and rephrase the question, to show your understanding of it.
- Repeat the question in your own words if you are not sure how to answer it.
- Make sure you ask questions yourself. You should have written down some questions before arrival and you may have thought of more questions during the interview. Jot these down on a notepad – it will jog your memory.

Group interaction

You may be interviewed by a panel, either formally sitting behind a desk or informally as a group situation. When people are to be working in a team, interviewers will often watch what happens when they are in a group situation. Make sure that you:

- listen to what the others have to say – look at them and make sure your body language is alert
- ask questions and ensure you listen to the answers
- value what others have to say, even if you don't agree – for example, don't say 'You're wrong' or 'You're joking' but use phrases such as 'That's interesting, but in my experience...'; 'Can you give some examples of why you think...'; 'Can you explain why...'

Make sure you leave everyone in the group feeling that you value their opinion, but that you also have an opinion of your own, which you are happy to explain. Be assertive but not aggressive!

Confirmation

Hopefully you will receive a telephone call the same day or within a stated length of time to confirm whether you have been offered the job or were not successful. It is always worthwhile to ask for feedback on your interview – this will help you next time!

Case studies

Tamir had looked forward to the interview and had done a lot of research on the website as well as looking at brochures. Unfortunately, she was so nervous that she kept cracking jokes during the interview, even though she knew about the company. When she asked for feedback, the panel had decided she was a very happy person but not committed enough to the hard work needed in the office. At her next interview Tamir made sure she smiled, but looked as though the interview was important to her – and she got the job!

Key points

The whole of the job selection procedure is shown in the diagram (right).

Advertisement for vacancy (may be internal and/or external)
↓
Applications sent to company (by letter/form/CV)
↓
Interviewers select those to call for interview
↓
Interview (by individual or panel)
↓
Offer of position
↓
Acceptance or decline of position

■ *Job selection procedure*

In summary

Prepare for the interview:

- Find out where it is and when, and plan your journey in advance.
- Research the organisation you want to go to and find out about the job role.
- Prepare some questions to ask your interviewers.

Develop good interview skills:

- Take pride in your appearance.
- Appear confident and enthusiastic during the interview – and remember to smile!

Practice assessment activity

Levels P5/M3/D2

For this assessment, your tutor may want to arrange 'mock' interviews or give you experience of the real thing, perhaps with a local employer.

P **1** You will need to prepare a suitable word-processed CV and application form for a specific job. You will need to undertake a job interview, demonstrating appropriate interview skills. It would be useful to use the jobs defined in P1 (see page 262). (P5)

M **2** You need to explain how the CV, application form and interview have created a positive image. You must refer to:

- the layout and content of the CV and application form
- how you prepared for the interview
- the interview skills you demonstrated. (M3)

D **3** Analyse your own performance though the application process, making sure you are honest about your strengths and areas for improvement. (D2)

Test your knowledge

1. Name three vocational qualifications which you could obtain at work or at college.
2. List four skills which are useful for those working in the travel and tourism industry.
3. Name three ways of recording information for your project.
4. What is the dress code for a formal interview?
5. How should you address a letter if you have signed it 'Yours sincerely'?
6. Why should you always copy an application form before you start completing it?
7. Where can you find information about an organisation?
8. Name two ways in which you can demonstrate that you are listening to someone?
9. What is the difference between assertive and aggressive?
10. Why should you ask for feedback on your interview if you are not successful?

8 Planning Visits for Travel and Tourism

Introduction

When working in the travel and tourism industry it is important to be able to plan travel and tourism visits so that you can understand what is involved and how that affects the work you do. It is essential that you know:

- where to look for information
- how to use the available sources accurately
- how to meet the needs of a wide range of customers
- how to review itineraries and visits.

This unit will enable you to do so and to experience how the many and varied components of the travel and tourism industry fit together. Your tutor may link this to an actual visit your group is organising.

Throughout this unit you will read about the experiences of students at Oak College as they planned, operated and reviewed an event. Think about their experiences and what you can learn from them as you progress through the unit.

How you will be assessed

Unit 8 is assessed internally so the Centre delivering the qualification will assess you against the criteria. On completion of this unit you should demonstrate that you:

8.1 can use different sources of information when planning itineraries

8.2 know how to plan itineraries for different customer types

8.3 understand the planning process involved when organising a visit

8.4 are able to review travel itineraries and visits.

Since Unit 8 has a substantial practical element to it, in that you will be planning and evaluating a visit, you should keep a diary of events as they happen. Ask your tutor to give you five minutes at the end of each lesson to write in your diary what you have learned, what action you have got to take and how you are feeling. Also make entries whenever there are meetings or other key events.

Assessment grades

The Edexcel Assessment Grid for Unit 8 details the criteria to be met. In general, to gain a Pass (P) you are asked to create itineraries or describe aims, objectives, constraints, sources and processes; to gain a Merit (M) you are also asked to explain and participate; and to gain a Distinction (D) you are also asked to evaluate.

8.1 Use different sources of information when planning itineraries

This section covers:

- brochures and timetables
- Internet
- travel directories
- reference materials.

As a travel and tourism professional you will be expected to have a comprehensive knowledge of the industry, to help customers plan their itineraries. You cannot be expected to know all the answers, so where are you going to find the information which will help you design and recommend visits? In this section you will look at some of the sources.

Definition of itinerary

- An **itinerary** provides the details of a client's travel arrangements, such as destinations, dates, times, transport and accommodation.
- Supplementary information might be added to the itinerary including: passport and visa requirements; health recommendations; national currencies; key contact names and addresses, for example, the British Embassy and the travel organiser.

Brochures and timetables

Brochures

You will be familiar with the brochures and leaflets which can be found in places like travel agents, hotels and tourist offices. Sometimes tour operators' *Inclusive Holiday* brochures contain information on destinations, weather, health recommendations, and passport and visa requirements.

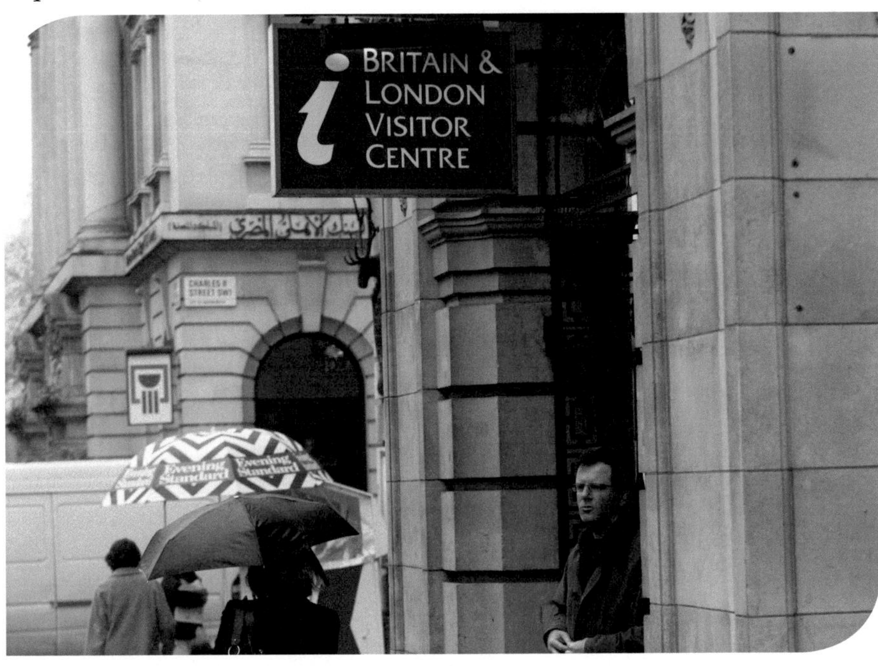

■ *Visitor Centres are a good source of information*

Activity

Visit a local travel agent. Browse through some Inclusive Holiday *brochures and make a note of the main categories of information they provide.*

Compare your findings with the rest of your group.

National, regional and city/town tourist information offices are also great providers of information about destinations and visitor attractions. Visitor attractions also produce their own brochures, as do hotel and restaurant chains and transport operators.

Timetables

Timetables are a vital source of information when planning an itinerary. Publications include:

- *The OAG Flight Guide,* which is published monthly and is found in most travel organisations. It lists all scheduled flights for the current and upcoming season for every airline and every commercial airport in the world, as well as key flight connections. The directory also provides key airport information such as minimum check-in and flight connection times and ground transport information.
- *The OAG Rail Guide* is a similar publication timetabling UK train services.
- Thomas Cook produce overseas rail timetables.
- Timetables are also produced by airlines and coach companies, although they increasingly depend upon their websites to communicate such information.

Timetables need careful reading and accurate interpretation because wrong information can result in your clients missing their transport and travel connections. It can be annoying if you've told clients that their bus leaves 15 minutes earlier than it does, but imagine the consequences of telling clients that their flight leaves at 9pm instead of 9am. A mistake like this could cause them to miss the cruise ship they were supposed to join! (This is a good reason for ensuring that you always use the 24-hour clock, so 9am and 9pm become 0900 and 2100.)

Over to you

How would your business client feel if you misinterpreted a country's local time as a result of which they arrived late for their meeting?

Activity

Look at the following coach timetable.

1 *A passenger has to catch a flight that departs from Terminal 2, Garwood Airport, at 1230 and she must check-in at the airport no later than 45 minutes before departure. Which coach would you recommend that she catches from Harlsford?*

Harlsford coach station	0920	0940	1000	1020	1040	1100	1120	1140	1200
Garwood Airport (Terminal 1)	1005	1025	1045	1105	1125	1145	1205	1225	1245
Garwood Airport (Terminal 2)	1015	1035	1055	1115	1135	1155	1215	1235	1255

Which coach did you recommend? Did you allow time to cope with delays en route or a check-in queue at the airport?

2 *The same passenger will return on Friday 21st March, and is scheduled to arrive at Terminal 1, Garwood Airport, at 2100. She has no hold baggage.*

a) What time would you expect her to leave Garwood Airport and arrive at Harlsford?

b) At what time does the last bus leave Garwood Airport (Terminal 1)?

Garwood Airport (Terminal 2)	2040	2100(1)	2120(2)	2140	2200	2220(3)
Garwood Airport (Terminal 1)	2050	2110(1)	2130(2)	2150	2210	2230(3)
Harlsford coach station	2135	2155(1)	2215(2)	2235(4)	2255	2315(3)

Notes:
(1) Operates 01 Jan–28 Feb and 01 Apr–31 Jul
(2) Only for airport staff
(3) Operates weekends only
(4) Operates via Clinksville Road on Fridays, arriving Harlsford coach station 2245.

Activity

Have a look at the websites of the following organisations:

- Galileo International
- Amadeus
- Sabre Holdings Corporation
- Worldspan
- (Links to these websites have been made available at www.heinemann.co.uk/hotlinks by entering the express code 2196P.)

For which areas of the industry do they provide Global Distribution Systems?

Internet

An increasingly common source of information is electronic. Travel agents and tour operators have dedicated systems to access industry information, including Global Distribution Systems (GDS) which provide booking facilities for inclusive holidays, accommodation and transport, etc.

Many Internet sites are available for the public when planning itineraries, including tour operators, airlines, train operators, coach companies, hotels and tourist attractions. They are the source of much information and most of them provide online booking facilities.

There are other websites which provide support information and advice for travellers. An important one is the Foreign and Commonwealth Office's website (a link to this website has been made available at www.heinemann.co.uk/hotlinks by entering the express code 2196P). This provides up-to-date travel advice on such issues as entry requirements, health recommendations and safety (country by country).

Look at the Foreign and Commonwealth Office website (a link to this website has been made available at www.heinemann.co.uk/hotlinks by entering the express code 2196P). Which countries does it advise travellers not to go to?

Travel directories

There are a number of well-respected travel directories which are the source of valuable travel and tourism information. These include:

- *World Travel Guide*, published annually by Columbus, which contains country by country details on a large number of subjects including: useful contacts; maps; general information such as population, language, government and religion; passports/visas; money; public holidays; health; climate; internal travel; accommodation; recreation; calendar of events; social and business profiles; and time zones.
- *Hotel and Travel Index* is an Internet-based guide which provides hotel information, contacts and rates as well as travel advice.
- *Coaching Venues and Excursions Guide* is an annual guide to group travel destinations. It provides contacts for visitor attractions and tourist offices in the UK and some European countries.
- *Travel Information Manual* is produced monthly by IATA. It details passport and visa regulations, health requirements and recommendations, and currency information, country by country.

Reference materials

Customers will often be unsure of just where they are going and inquisitive as to their destination. They will look to you to know the answers. It is important, therefore, to have access to atlases, maps and guidebooks.

Activity

Help these customers by answering their questions. You can use any trade publications available to you or any other library resources, but do not use the Internet:

- Mrs Lindsay needs to travel to the capital of Jordan but doesn't know what it is called.
- Mr Hooson wants to know what the currency is called in Thailand.
- Mr Cohen has to travel to Ulaanbaatar but doesn't know which country it is in.
- Mrs Khan is going on holiday to Mauritius and wants to know what the national language is.
- Mr Lee needs to join a ship at the main port in Belgium and needs to know the name of that port.
- Miss Jennings wants to know which is the hottest month in Cyprus.

The publications you refer to need to be up to date. Even those published as little as two years ago will almost certainly now be inaccurate. For example, country names may have changed; smoking in public places may no longer be allowed in some countries; distances and speed restrictions may now be in metric; licensing hours may have changed; new attractions may have opened and old ones closed, etc.

In summary

- Many types of information are required when planning itineraries, including information on countries, destinations, visitor attractions, laws, distances, availability of inclusive holidays, transport and accommodation, as well as detailed timetable information.
- Information sources will also be wide ranging and will include Inclusive holiday brochures, visitor attraction leaflets, timetables, travel directories and other reference books and maps.
- Information is also available from support organisations like tourist offices and the Foreign and Commonwealth Office.
- Increasingly, information is available via the Internet.
- Information must be up to date and must be interpreted accurately.

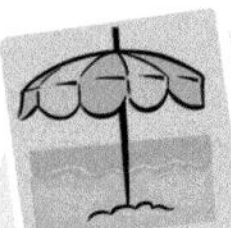

Practice assessment activity

Level P1

1 Describe the sources of information you might use when planning itineraries for:

a) a school group wanting an educational day out in a city within 50 miles (80 km) of their base

b) a family wishing to book an independent walking holiday in Switzerland

c) a businesswoman who has to visit India, Thailand and Hong Kong in a single business trip from the UK.

Make sure that in your total answer you have covered at least two sources from each of the four main groups of sources covered in this section.

Over to you

Are you keeping your diary up to date?

8.2 Know how to plan itineraries for different customer types

This section covers:

- itineraries
- customer types
- considerations.

Itineraries

Before you can create itineraries, you must understand what they need to include.

- An itinerary provides the details of a client's travel arrangements, such as destinations, dates, times, transport and accommodation.
- Supplementary information might be added to the itinerary including: passport and visa requirements; health recommendations; national currencies; key contact names and addresses, for example, the British Embassy and the travel organiser.

Activity

Imagine your group is going on an educational day visit.

- On your own, decide where you will visit and how you will get there.
- Decide how you will show this information in a useful itinerary and write it down.

Perhaps your itinerary looked something like the one below.

Visit to Alton Towers, Tuesday 15th May 2007	
0915	Meet outside college main gates
0930	Depart college by coach
1030	Stop at motorway service station
1100	Depart motorway service station
1200	Arrive Alton Towers
1215–1245	Lunch
1700	Meet at main gates
1715	Leave Alton Towers by coach
1815	Stop at motorway service station
1845	Depart motorway service station
1945	Arrive at college main gates

An itinerary should include:

- the destination
- transport details
- dates
- departure and arrival times
- any other timings the client needs to know.

Notice that an itinerary is set out in chronological order (i.e. time order). Using the 24-hour clock is much preferable to using the 12-hour clock as it avoids confusion as to whether the time is *am* or *pm*. However, it is important to ensure that your clients understand the 24-hour clock system.

Over to you

What other information might you include on the Alton Towers itinerary?

Don't try to make the itinerary too tight – allow time for traffic jams, roadworks, etc. Remember that coaches travel more slowly than cars – ask the coach company for advice.

The Alton Towers itinerary also includes some information about lunch. Remember that the definition of an itinerary mentioned that you might want to include other information in it. Usually that would include any activities that have been arranged and the cost of the itinerary.

You may wish to explain what will be happening at the destination and what to do if there are problems, so that everyone knows the arrangements. For example:

> Please bring a picnic lunch. We will eat this on arrival at Alton Towers. If it is raining, there will be a room provided.
>
> You will be free to go on the rides but please stay in pairs or small groups. There will be a rendezvous point at 1500 at the main gates for assistance. Please contact the tutor on her mobile phone number (show tutor's mobile number) in an emergency.
>
> The cost will be £24.00 per person, payable by 1st May. This includes the cost of the coach transport between college and Alton Towers, the entrance fee and all rides.
>
> Please bring enough money for food, drink, souvenirs and any other expenses you may have. Make sure you keep your money safe at all times.

Information like this means that everybody knows exactly what is going on.

Customer types

You have already covered different types of customers and their needs in *Unit 2: Exploring Customer Service in Travel and Tourism* (see pages 47–89). Understanding customer types and their needs is particularly important when designing an itinerary.

Your clients may be travelling for business or pleasure or for other specific reasons like visiting friends and relatives, education, health, religion or sport. They may be young or elderly; families, couples or singles; in a group where the members know each other or in a group where the members have only just met. In every case, the content and style of the itinerary you design should be tailored to meet their needs.

Activity

Think of your relatives, friends and other people you know. Using the customer types in the previous paragraph and any others you can think of, put those people into categories most suited to them. Of course, some people may fit into more than one category, depending upon their reasons for travel.

Considerations

Specific needs

All clients have their own set of needs and preferences. Some will have very specific needs; some of these are described below.

Some of your clients may have a physical or learning disability. This may or may not be obvious by looking at the person – for example, it may be easy to recognise a blind person but not somebody who is deaf. The disability may be major or minor. Parents travelling with small children will also have special needs that will need to be met.

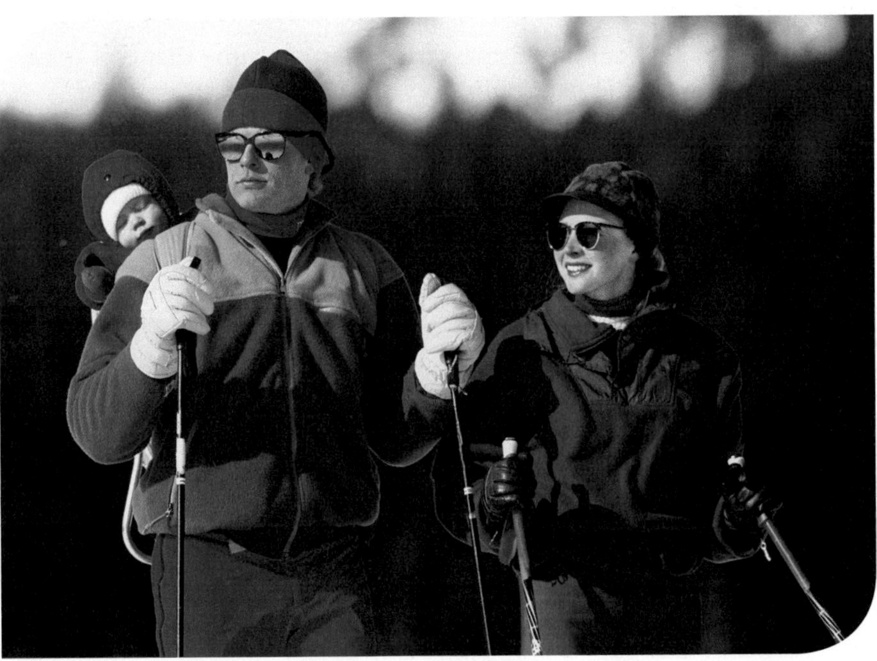

■ *Small children and their parents will have special needs*

Over to you

Could only speaking English be considered a disability in some countries?

Talking point

In small groups, discuss what special needs young children and their parents might have:

a) during the journey

b) whilst at their destination.

How might you meet those needs?

Time constraints

Time constraints may also affect the itinerary. For example, you may have to choose between places to visit and activities to do if:

- there is only a limited amount of time available
- the transport connections are tight
- your clients need more time, perhaps because they are disabled or elderly.

Budgets

Wouldn't it be great if you didn't need to consider the cost of the visit? Unfortunately for most people, the budget will influence where and when they go, the quality of accommodation they stay in and the method of transport they use.

Low cost

Much of the growth in air travel in recent years has been on budget airlines. They have made air travel much less expensive and changed travel patterns, with people going to places they haven't been to before and taking more frequent and shorter breaks.

Exclusive travellers

Towards the other end of the range, there are the luxury visits for those who have larger budgets. Increasingly, people are making the trip of a lifetime, perhaps to celebrate an important milestone like a honeymoon, birthday, anniversary or retirement. This might be a cruise or round-the-world tour, or an exclusive luxury visit to an event.

Business expenses

Companies pay for staff on business trips. Don't assume that cost does not matter for such clients. Companies closely monitor the cost of business trips and look for good deals. They often insist that their staff travel economy class if the journey is under 4 hours. They will want competitive hotel rates. For domestic or European trips, they will aim to bring their staff back the same day, so that they can save on accommodation costs, even if that means a very long day for the staff.

■ *Business travellers checking into a hotel. This type of customer is also cost-conscious*

Day visit costs

One of the biggest costs may be the transport. If by coach, the cost will include the driver's time, the use of the coach, petrol and parking. All this is usually given as a total cost. Rail fares are often good value for students under 18 years travelling together to and from the destination. Minibuses are normally costed the same way as coaches and may be cheaper if the group is small.

Costings usually show both total cost and cost per participant. The cost needs to be clearly calculated and labelled, as shown in the table below.

Item	Number	Cost	Total cost
Cost of coach	**1**	**£250.00**	**£250.00**
Entry price			
■ Student entry	18	£14.00	£252.00
■ Wheelchair user	1	£10.50	£10.50
■ Helper	1	FREE	–
■ Adult (student)	1	£20.00	£20.00
■ Adult (tutor)	1	FREE	–
Car parking; tolls		£27.50	£27.50
Grand total:			£560.00

Total cost (£560.00) divided by total number of students (20) = £28.00 per person.

(It might be decided to charge the wheelchair user less and the adult student more, when sharing costs.)

Residential visit costs

These are more complex since you are adding a further component – the accommodation. This will add to the cost considerably, particularly if food is included.

Activity

Complete the missing amounts to calculate the cost of an overnight trip for 20 people.

Item	Cost	Number of	Number of rooms or people	Total cost
Twin room per room (including breakfast)	£30.00	2		
Single room per room (including breakfast)	£35.00	2	2 staff	
Evening meal	£5.50	2	20 people	
			Grand total:	
			Price per person (equal shares for all 20 participants):	

(It might be decided to share the total cost of the trip just between the students. How much would that cost for each student?)

In summary

- An itinerary details a client's travel arrangements such as destinations, dates, times, transport and accommodation. It may also include other key information.
- There are many different types of customer and that will shape the itinerary.
- All customers have their own set of needs. Some have specific needs, like those with disabilities and parents with young children.
- Cost will be a consideration when creating the itinerary.

Practice assessment activity

Levels P2/M1/D1

P **1** Using at least three different sources of information, create an itinerary for:
- **a)** a businessman travelling on a day trip from Birmingham to Edinburgh
- **b)** a family with two children aged 3 and 7 years, who want a two-week beach holiday
- **c)** a low-cost weekend in Europe for a hen party group of 10, two of whom are visually impaired. (P2)

✓

M **2** Provide a list of the sources you used for task 1. For each source, explain how you used that information to help in planning the itineraries. (M1)

✓✓

D **3** Evaluate the itineraries you designed in task 1, identifying the specific needs of those clients and explaining how the itineraries meet those needs. What improvements could you make to the itineraries? (D1)

✓✓✓

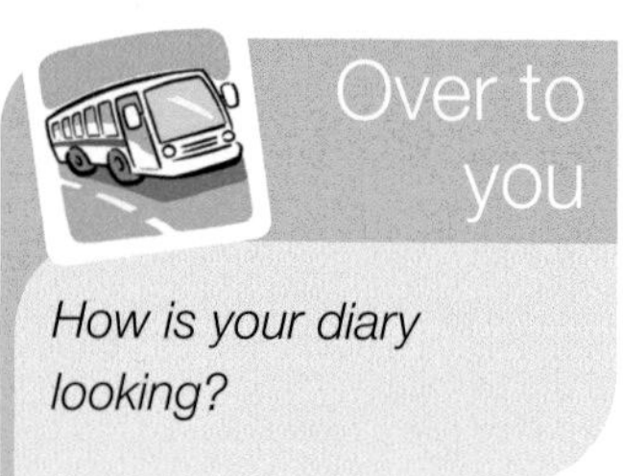

How is your diary looking?

8.3 Understand the planning process involved when organising a visit

This section covers:

- aims and objectives
- constraints
- plan
- itinerary.

Aims and objectives

You do it every day! You decide what your objectives are and you plan to meet them. You may not do it in a very conscious, organised way – but you do it. For example, your objectives may be to meet friends in the evening to exchange news and enjoy each other's company. Then you plan how to meet those objectives. Do your friends want to meet you and are they available tonight? What time shall you meet and where? Do you need to book anything? How will you get to and from the venue? What will you wear? How much money will you need? What do you want to talk about?

Even the biggest event goes through the same process, although on a much larger and longer scale. The objectives of the event have to be decided and planning is needed to meet those objectives.

This is a whole group exercise. As the first stage in planning a visit for your group, decide whether you are going to be looking at a day or a residential visit.

Take your tutor's advice.

Don't go any further yet in deciding where you will go.

Think about your objectives for doing this travel and tourism course.

Case studies

The Olympic Games are planned many years in advance. First, cities clearly establish what their objectives would be if they were to host the Olympics. These are likely to include providing employment and attracting international businesses and tourists in the long-term. The International Olympics Committee announces the shortlist of candidates eight years before the event. In May 2004, Paris, New York, Moscow, London and Madrid were shortlisted for the 2012 games. In July 2005 it was announced that London would be the host city! It may become the biggest travel and tourism event for the UK for decades.

Once selected, there are seven years of intensive preparation. Projects will include:

- building sporting venues and accommodation
- creating transportation and communication systems
- planning events and entertainment
- obtaining funding and negotiating many marketing contracts
- creating itineraries for visits to the Games by the participants and spectators.

Each of these projects will need objectives to be set before the planning starts. Planning and preparing for the Olympics requires many resources, for example: funding; staffing; expertise; equipment; liaison with governments, sporting bodies, participants, transport organisations and the media. All this has to be achieved by a set deadline – the date cannot be changed! Imagine the hard work and headaches, but also the satisfaction and pride, in being involved in such a venture!

Years of objective setting and planning ensure the success of the Olympic Games

Converting aims into objectives

You may have a set of general aims for your group, for example:

- to gather information for *Unit 5: Exploring Marketing in Travel and Tourism*
- to have an interesting day out
- to look at customer service at a hotel
- to get information from a theme park location
- to work together as a team to organise and operate the visit.

These aims need to be converted into objectives. If you do not set objectives, how will you know what visit to arrange or if that visit has been successful? By setting objectives all the team members will know what they are aiming to achieve so that they work together with a single purpose. Once your objectives have been set, decisions can be made about the visit you want to arrange.

SMART objectives

Your objectives must also be SMART (see *Unit 5: Exploring Marketing in Travel and Tourism*, pages 177–8, for information on SMART objectives). Too many plans fail because people are eager to get on with the action rather than creating SMART objectives and putting careful planning into place. Tasks get missed or duplicated, deadlines get missed and resources such as money and people are wasted. Team members are not clear about what the team and individuals in the team are supposed to be doing. People become demotivated and the results are varying degrees of failure!

Objectives must be SMART:

Specific
Measurable
Achievable
Realistic
Timed.

With regard to the five aims described above, your objectives might be:

- to collect five leaflets from the shop for my marketing assignment
- to help organise a day out which 90 per cent of respondents enjoy
- to complete a questionnaire for customer service at the Garden Hotel on Wednesday
- to take notes from Alton Towers' marketing officer during her presentation
- to gain feedback from the other group members to demonstrate that the team was at least 90 per cent successful in working together.

Over to you

Later in this unit, you will evaluate the success of your event. You will only be able to do this well if you started with a set of SMART objectives.

Stakeholders

Stakeholders are people or organisations that may be affected by your objectives. They might include:

- **Your customers**. Who will come on the visit? It may be other students on a day trip or residential visit. Why would they want to take part? What would they want to do? You might find out by talking informally with potential customers or gathering a group of

Key points

Stakeholders include:

- your customers
- your organisation
- parents/guardians
- sponsors.

them together to discuss their wishes, or distributing a questionnaire asking for their views.

- **Your organisation**. This might be your school or college, because what you are planning may impact upon the curriculum, the availability of school/college time or resources, or the image of the school/college.
- **Parents/guardians**. They will have an interest in what their children are going to do. They may also be financial stakeholders.
- **Sponsors**. You may have individuals or organisations that have agreed to provide you with funds, resources, accommodation or advertising space, etc.

You will need to identify all of your stakeholders and ensure your objectives and plans are designed to meet their needs.

Talking point

Hold a brainstorming session to suggest objectives for a visit you would like to organise and operate. At this stage do not think about what that visit will be.

In your team, consider each of the objectives suggested in the brainstorming session.

- Do they match the SMART criteria?
- Do they meet the needs of all stakeholders?

Personal or study-related?

The objectives of the visit may be work- or study-related, or personal.

For example, in planning a college visit you will have study-related objectives, such as visiting somewhere which has relevance to your course or providing research opportunities which help you to meet the assessment criteria of the unit you are studying. You may also want the visit to help with your career development.

You may want to visit the destination for personal reasons, perhaps because you have never been there before or your grandfather was born there. The desired outcome of the visit may be an assignment paper you need to write or the personal satisfaction of tracing your grandfather's birthplace.

■ *Once you have your objectives, you can brainstorm ideas for the visit*

Activity

Use a flip-chart sheet to brainstorm ideas about destinations for your visit. Just say whatever comes to mind. The visit should require a significant amount and range of planning across several weeks. Your tutor will give you guidance.

When no more ideas are forthcoming, consider each of the suggestions and evaluate them for viability, measuring them against your SMART objectives.

The following questions may help you to make your decision:

- Does it meet the objectives?
- How long will it take to get there?
- Is it easy to access (train, coach parks, etc.)?
- What is the cost of (a) transport, (b) entry, (c) accommodation?
- What is there to do at the location?
- Are there worksheets, study rooms, speakers?
- Is the visit dependent on good weather?
- Are there facilities for food/drink/toilets?
- Is any special equipment needed?
- Do any of the group have particular needs which must be taken into account?

If you are still left with too many options, try awarding points to each of the above.

Over to you

Are your objectives comprehensive? Do they pass the SMART test?

Case studies

Oak College – objective setting

As part of their course, six travel and tourism students were tasked with planning and running a four-day overseas visit for their college. Their tutor asked where they had been before, as one of her objectives was for them to experience a different country and culture. She also measured the proposed destinations against the learning value to the course. The students were given a choice of destinations and they chose Prague.

The students individually created objectives and discussed them. They were pleased to find they had many common ones but also some which others had not thought of. They agreed their objectives were to:

- enable each student on the project to pass the course
- use the skills and techniques described in the course
- develop team skills
- learn about another country
- promote the college image
- financially break even (neither make a profit nor a loss)
- meet the needs of all stakeholders
- have fun!

The students checked each of their objectives against the SMART criteria and the visit for feasibility. They felt it would require a substantial amount of planning but this could be achieved within the ten weeks available.

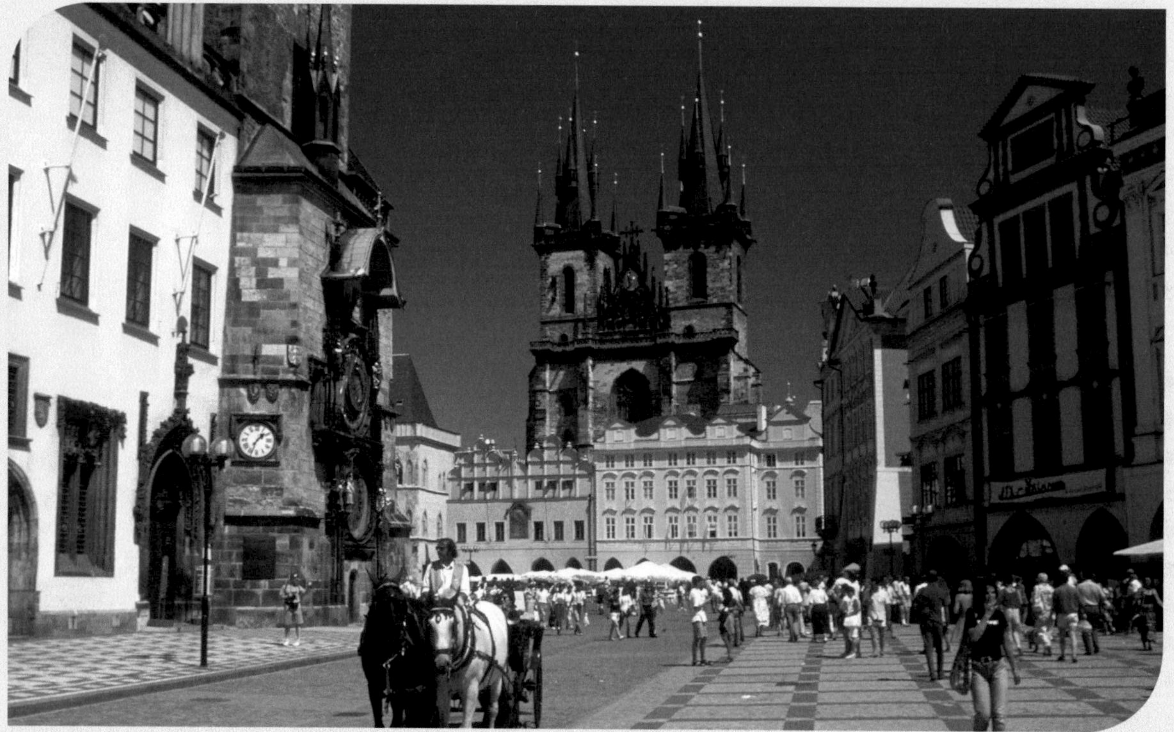

The Oak College travel and tourism team chose Prague as the destination for their event

Managing the process

Having established your objectives, your team must organise itself to manage the planning process. Agree who will be involved. Make a list of the main groups of tasks which need doing. Share the tasks amongst the group, using the group members' skills, knowledge and interests. For example, you may want to select colleagues who will be:

- transport manager
- accommodation manager
- activities and local visits manager
- social events manager
- finance manager
- administration manager
- public relations and advertising manager.

It is a good idea to have two people per task, in case the workload is heavier than expected or one person is not available for a meeting, etc.

Communication is vital

It is important that the team members keep each other well informed so that the team works in an integrated manner. Planned meetings with agreed agendas issued before the meetings and minutes distributed after them, provide opportunities to create and discuss ideas, resolve problems, make decisions and communicate progress. Unstructured meetings waste time and will not produce the outcomes that are needed.

Always be honest – if you've hit a problem, say so. Someone else may be able to help and some of your colleagues may need to know that you have a problem, so they can adjust their own plans.

Talking point

In your team, discuss and agree who will take on which roles. This may require some negotiation. Record and distribute the list of jobholders to every member of the team.

Over to you

How would you feel if you went to a meeting not knowing what was going to be discussed?

How would you feel if someone hadn't told you they had a problem which could affect you?

How would these affect your effectiveness at and after the meeting?

■ *Meetings should be business-like*

Activity

Select one of your group to be Meeting Secretary and one to be Chairperson.

- At least one week before the meeting, issue an Agenda for your first meeting (produced by the Secretary with input from the Chairperson. Any member can propose a subject for discussion).
- Hold the meeting. Agree actions, who will take them and by when.
- Agree on the date of the next meeting(s) (at which members will report on progress made and any problems, and agree action).
- Produce and distribute the Minutes (an action for the Secretary). (The group might like to have a different Secretary and Chairperson for each meeting.)

Key points

A **constraint** is something you cannot do because of a limit or objective you have been set.

Constraints

The more you think about the task, the more complex it seems to become and the more constraints there appear to be. There seems to be so much to do and it is difficult to 'see the wood for the trees'. How can you make sense of it all? Sharing tasks between team members and sharing news and problems at meetings will help.

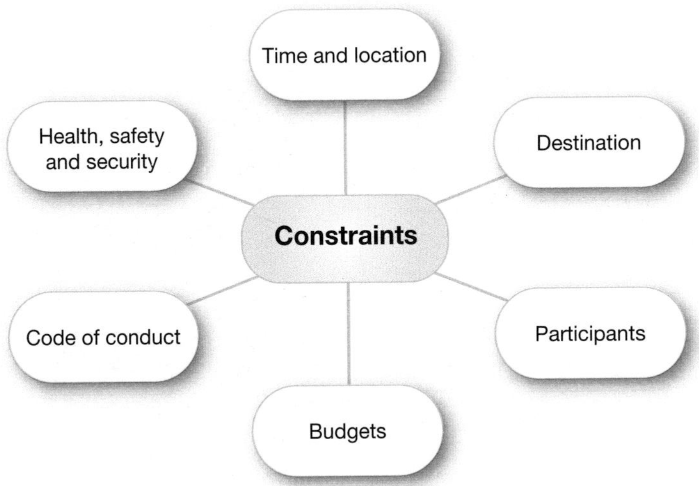

■ *Recognising and organising the constraints is the first stage to managing them*

Time and location

Make sure you set the date of your visit at a point in the year when you will have time to complete the preparations. It may need to be at a convenient time for your other studies too. Talk to people who might have an interest in the timing. Think also about where you are going to do your planning work and hold your meetings, and whether it has the facilities you need.

Destination

Suggestions for a day visit might include:

- a theme park, e.g. Alton Towers
- a city, e.g. Edinburgh
- a castle, e.g. Warwick Castle
- a large shopping mall, e.g. Bluewater
- a museum, e.g. Science Museum
- a seaside resort, e.g. Brighton
- an outdoor museum, e.g. Ironbridge Gorge
- a theatre visit.

Your choice of destination will depend on where your clients are based. A day trip by coach should not be more than two hours' drive in each direction. Many attractions supply worksheets, talks or information sheets. This will give a focus to the day.

Residential visit

If the plan is for a residential visit, an early decision needs to be made about whether that will be to somewhere in the UK or to another

■ *It's up to you where you visit!*

country. Journey times, time differences and length of stay will need to be taken into account. If the journey is going to take more than half a day, then a minimum of three days should be allocated for the overall trip, as most of the first and last days will be given over to travelling. If there is a big time difference between countries, allow for time to recover from jet-lag. A visit to the United States, for example, preferably should be at least five days overall.

Travelling abroad

If a visit to another country is suggested, remember that participants will need a current passport – it is advisable to have a minimum of six months left to run on the passport from the date of return (inspect all passports at least a month in advance and take a note of the passport number in case of loss). They may also require:

- a visa (this applies to some countries outside the European Union – check with the country's embassy)
- vaccinations and health advice, depending on the country you are planning to visit (check the Department of Health website for health advice to travellers – a link to this website has been made available at www.heinemann.co.uk/hotlinks by entering the express code 2196P).

Particularly careful attention needs to be given to those with non-UK passports, as they may need visas which are not required by the rest of the group, and these may take some time to obtain. The Foreign and Commonwealth Office has a useful travel advice section on its website (a link to this website has been made available at www.heinemann.co.uk/hotlinks by entering the express code 2196P).

Activity

Design a questionnaire to ask people who may come on the visit their thoughts on:

- how far they would be prepared to travel
- how much they would be prepared to pay
- the type of destination they would like to visit – give them a choice of five or so different types of destination, for example, city or seaside
- their own suggestions.

Measure the responses against the objectives you have set for the visit and select the suggestion which meets the SMART criteria.

Participants

You must take the age of the participants into account. You may think a visit to a nightclub would be enjoyable, but the nightclub is unlikely to accept a group where any member is under the age of 18 years. Equally, a visit to a puppet theatre might not be appropriate for 17-year-olds!

Those with special needs

If the group includes a participant with special needs, this must be planned for. The Disability Discrimination Act (1995) requires destinations (unless exempt) to make 'reasonable adjustments' to accommodate those with a disability; for example, the provision of ground-floor bedrooms, flashing fire alarms, ramps, appropriate toilet facilities, etc. You will need to:

- ask the participant exactly what his or her needs are
- inform everyone involved, e.g. the coach company, the attraction, the hotel, and confirm this in writing.

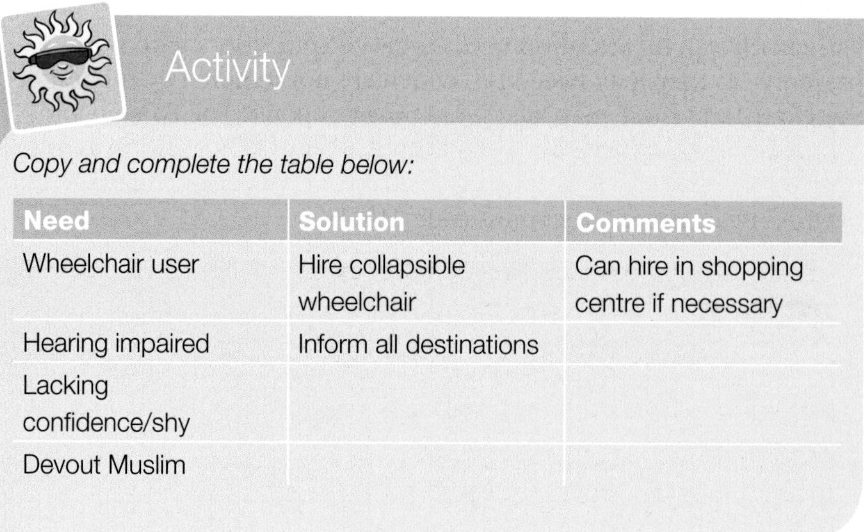

Activity

Copy and complete the table below:

Need	Solution	Comments
Wheelchair user	Hire collapsible wheelchair	Can hire in shopping centre if necessary
Hearing impaired	Inform all destinations	
Lacking confidence/shy		
Devout Muslim		

Most organisations are only too happy to help. Wheelchairs may be available on loan, and many town centres have mobility centres where equipment is for hire.

Gaining written permission

If you are arranging a visit for students you will need to make sure that you have the necessary written permission for the visit from the college or school authorities as well as the parents or guardians. If participants are under 18 years (or older if 'vulnerable'), the party leader has to be an adult and will be *in loco parentis* (taking the place of parents or guardians). Below is an example of a parent/guardian consent form.

Consent form

I agree for ______________________ to travel and take part in the visit.

I accept liability for full payment.

I understand that those supervising ______________________ are acting *in loco parentis* and will exercise a standard of care that would be expected of a reasonably prudent parent. I also understand that during any free time he/she will not be under direct supervision.

The College/School will not be responsible for personal injury or any other damage or loss unless due to negligence of the staff.

I agree to all the items above.

Signed: ______________________ Date: __________

Name: ______________________

■ *Parent/guardian consent form*

Key points

You must consider the needs of the participants in terms of their age, needs and constraints.

Budget

The budget is also important. You saw some basic costings earlier in this unit (see page 301). It is always wise to add on a small amount for contingencies such as tolls, tips, money to buy brochures, etc. Do you need to add a profit margin or is your aim just to break even?

Code of conduct

Specific codes of conduct are normally prepared for school and college visits and are intended to ensure:

- the safety of each individual and the group
- that the visit runs smoothly and to time
- that the public image of the group is protected or enhanced
- that everyone gets the maximum value and enjoyment from the visit, in a responsible manner.

A code of conduct can be more effective if it is the group which agrees on what is acceptable behaviour. There are usually some negative instructions but positive phrases are much more likely to have positive outcomes! Your group's code of conduct might include the following:

- All behaviour should benefit the reputation of the school/college.
- Any participant found under the influence of or in possession of drugs or alcohol will be severely disciplined.
- Dress should be appropriate on all occasions.
- All participants should arrive at all meeting points punctually.

Activity

This is a group activity.

- Design a Code of Conduct for your visit appropriate to the participants in your group and the place(s) which will be visited.
- Obtain a copy of your organisation's Code of Conduct for visits and ensure those issues are included in your Code of Conduct.

Health, safety and security

Medical considerations

When going on a residential visit it is sensible for each participant to provide a list of his or her medical conditions and/or prescribed medication, dietary needs, allergies, etc. This means that should a participant fall ill or an accident happen, the tour leader or tutor can give this information to a doctor. Below is an example of a medical information form.

Medical information form

Student's name: ______________________

Tutor: ______________________

Medical conditions/other	Delete as appropriate	
Medical conditions (give details)	Yes	No
Allergies (give details)	Yes	No
Medication prescribed (give details)	Yes	No
Dietary needs (give details)	Yes	No
Asthma/medication	Yes	No

I declare this information to be correct.

Signed: ______________________
(Student or parent/guardian if student under 18 years old)

Name: ______________________ (Printed)

Date: ______________________

■ *A medical information form*

Unless medically qualified, tutors are not allowed to dispense medicines, so participants should be encouraged to bring patent medicines such as paracetamol if they think they will need them.

Contact details

For student groups and other groups which may require particular support, the tour leader or tutor should ensure that he or she has a list of mobile telephone numbers so that stray members of the group can be contacted. The tour leader should also have emergency numbers for parents/guardians. The group members should have the tour leader's or tutor's mobile phone number.

Key points

Health and safety must always be of prime importance and should override all other considerations.

Risk assessments

All transport providers and attractions should have their own risk assessment, but you will also need to do one for the trip. A risk assessment looks at possible hazards and at the controls put in place to avoid them or minimise the effect. How the controls manage to offset the hazards will result in the assessed grade of risk. An example is shown below (see also *Unit 6: Business Skills for Travel and Tourism*, pages 213–251).

Hazard	Precautions	Risk
Travelling by coach	Comply with level of staff–student supervision Ensure students are seated Ensure seat belts are worn Ensure behaviour is appropriate	Low
Slipping/tripping/ falling	Keep to pavements and footpaths Follow instructions	Low

■ *A risk assessment for a day visit*

Activity

Using the example on this page as a model, work in pairs to create a risk assessment for a visit by you to your local shopping centre, travelling by bus.

Your school or college is likely to have a similar assessment which will need to be completed.

The plan

Now the detailed planning starts! This is when your objective setting, allocation of tasks to specific people and meetings will start to be useful. That preparation means:

- you all know what has to be achieved and by whom
- you have created a shared, balanced workload
- you are going to meet regularly to check on progress and overcome any problems.

Time schedules should be created. These will identify what has to be done, by when and by whom. They will help the team members meet their deadlines and keep track of what should be happening. There are two main types of plan that you could use:

- Key Events Plan
- Gantt Chart.

Key Events Plan

This type of plan specifies the overall framework so that everyone can fit in their work to meet the events and deadlines listed. A Key Events Plan does not identify all of the tasks which need to be done, it only highlights key events along the way and key tasks which need to be completed before those events. In the example below, the dates of some key events are shown in the planning of an overseas trip. Also shown are the main tasks which have to be done for those key events.

Case studies

Oak College – Key Events Plan

Date	Key event	Tasks to be completed before specified key event
10 February	Overseas trip announced to college	Decision made on dates, destination, method of transport and outline costs. Posters and explanatory leaflets prepared.
24 February	Provisional bookings made with tour operator	Deposits received.
10 March	Parents/students evening	Presentations prepared. Information packs produced. Invitations sent by 3 March. Hall and equipment booked. Refreshments arranged.
17 March	Final balance paid to tour operator	All payments received.
24 March	Meeting of those going on visit	Briefing packs produced. Rooming arrangements agreed. Tutors briefed.
31 March	Visit begins	All planning completed.

Talking point

What will the key events be in your plan? Work as a team to create a Key Events Plan.

Gantt Chart

A Gantt Chart is a rather more complex but very useful technique. This lists tasks in more detail and shows when they need to be done. The length of the task line also indicates how long that task will take and enables readers to recognise which tasks cannot start until others have finished (see page 319).

Destination

You have decided on this already, so detailed work can be done on how to get there and arranging entrance fees and/or accommodation. Many tourist information centres are happy to arrange a talk before the visit and often supply information or task sheets linked to the curriculum. A lot of attractions welcome a visit prior to the group arriving.

You will need to make sure that for every destination, you have a set timetable of activities, otherwise the group will not get good value from the visit and you will have unhappy people who may become difficult to control! Set times to gather all participants together at meeting points throughout the day would be helpful, to check that objectives are being met.

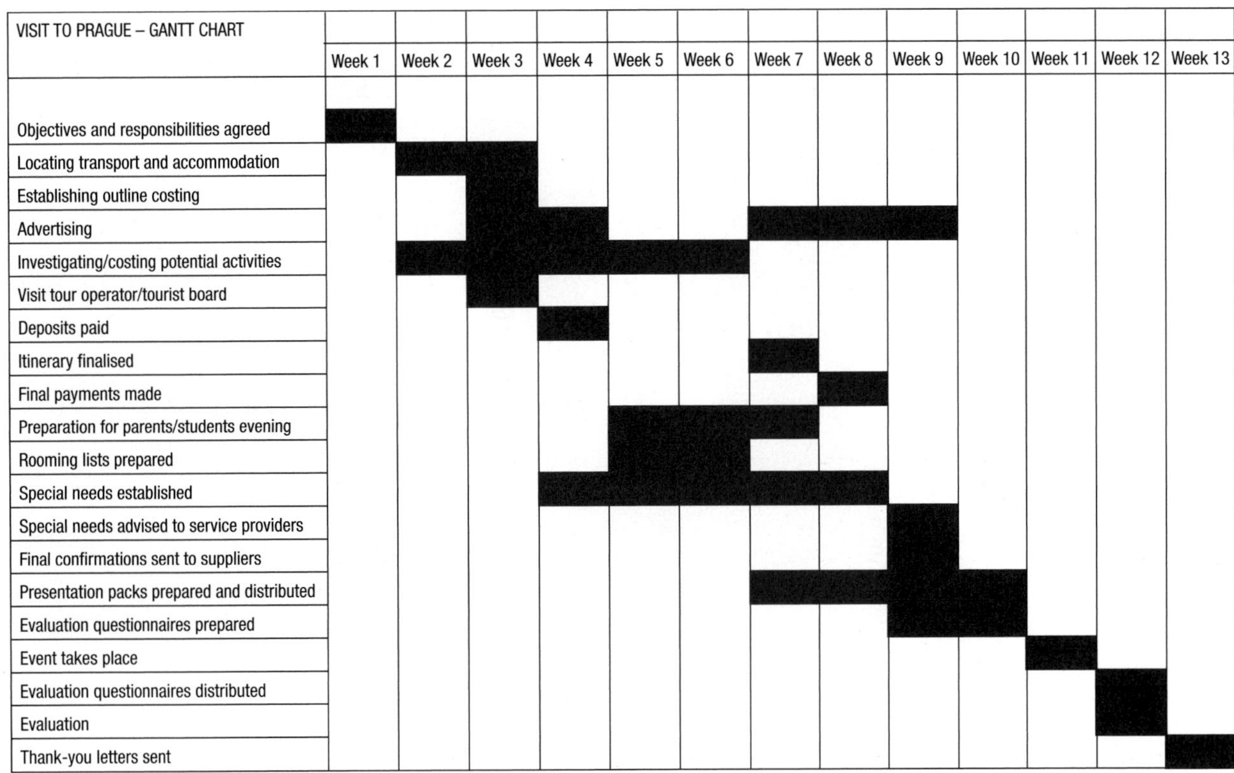

■ *A Gantt Chart for the Oak College overseas visit*

Time

Once you have decided on the time of year for the visit, you will need to decide on the best day of the week. This may depend on:

- your tutor's availability
- the length of the visit
- how many other classes it may affect
- opening times of attractions
- cost of transport and accommodation (which may vary by month and day of the week).

Departure and arrival times are important – try not to travel in the middle of the rush hour; an hour earlier or later may save almost as much if you can avoid traffic jams. However, don't start the day too early – remember, people have got to get up and get to the departure point! Always arrange a meeting time 15 minutes before you must depart, as there are bound to be people who arrive late. Don't forget the timing of the return journey. Can people get home from the arrival point? Try not to cut transport times – be generous in your estimations. Ask for advice – it is far easier to arrive in good time than have to hurry at the last minute.

Comfort breaks are important, particularly for young children and older folk, so make sure you build them in every couple of hours or so. Ask for advice about service stations and public toilets, etc.

■ *Make sure you allow plenty of time to get to your destination*

Transport

Is the transport you are selecting appropriate to the needs of all group members? Is anyone likely to have difficulty with it? If so, what arrangements do you need to make? If using public transport, does the group know exactly where to go and what the check-in times are? Are there are any special arrangements for groups? What baggage allowance does the group have? What facilities are there on board? If you are visiting a city or attraction by coach, check where the coach could drop-off/pick-up the group.

Accommodation

You will need to decide on the type of accommodation, the location and whether rooms will be shared (and if so, by how many). Is catering to be included? Are there any special diets required? A tour operator may be able to get attractive rates for your transport and accommodation but do your own research as well – look at brochures, try the Internet, call the transport operator or accommodation provider.

Research and education

If you are arranging a study trip, what opportunities are there for research and education? What arrangements can you make for the group to visit suitable tourist locations, factories, museums, etc? When are they open and what is the entrance fee? Can you arrange guest speakers and behind-the-scenes visits which will really add value to the visit? If you are going to arrange a talk, make sure the speaker understands what information you need – send a copy of the assessment criteria or assignment questions. If participants are going to an attraction without a set information session, a questionnaire or 'treasure hunt' might be helpful.

Activity

Choose a large attraction near you and find out if it has an education officer. Most English Heritage properties or those which belong to large groups, such as Madame Tussauds, will have someone responsible for education. Ask them to send you a pack so that you can see the kinds of services they offer.

Attractions and entertainment

It may be that your group will visit attractions and entertainment locations as part of their studies. Do some research on venues:

- Are they suitable for the group (remember age constraints and disabilities)?
- Do they cater for different interests or needs? (If not, you should ensure the group members have a choice of attractions and entertainments to go to.)
- What is the cost?
- What feedback can you get about the attraction in advance?

Variety

Make sure that the trip or visit provides a variety of things to do, to cater for the differing interests of the group members. Some people like to try new things and be adventurous, whilst others prefer things which they have tried before and enjoy a quieter life. Respect these differences and provide for all tastes.

Contact details

Do all members of the group have all the contact details they may need, including the addresses and/or telephone numbers of:

- the places they will visit
- the tour operator or group leader
- emergency contacts?

Does the tour leader have the contact details of the group members, as appropriate? (It may also be necessary for a tutor to have the contact details of students' next-of-kin, although this information is probably not appropriate for a tourist guide escorting visitors on a day trip.)

Activity

You could also produce a brochure for your trip, based around the formal itinerary but using pictures and photographs as well as colour and varied fonts to make it look really interesting – sell it!

Talking point

In a small group, collect three or four tour brochures. Discuss how they encourage people to go on their holidays, e.g. added information, maps, etc.

What can you learn from these that you can use in your own brochure?

Itinerary

You have done the detailed planning – now for the final documents! You might like to produce a formal itinerary – like the Alton Towers one on page 297. On a residential visit you may need several sheets of daily schedules. Below is an example of an itinerary for one of the days of a residential visit.

It might be helpful to present your ideas to the rest of the group and other stakeholders and really sell the visit. Obtain leaflets and brochures from the destination so you can explain exactly what it is like. Show a DVD or video or use PowerPoint® slides to give more details and photographs. Hand out leaflets, information sheets or brochures to your audience. Make sure you have included contact details for the locations the group will visit and the group leader, and emergency numbers.

Travel and tourism visit to Bruges, 8–11 May

Itinerary for Wednesday 10 May	
0830	Breakfast
0930	Meet in foyer
0940	Depart for Bruges Diamond House
1000	Arrive at Diamond House
1015	Presentation
1045	Tour of Diamond House
1215	Picnic lunch in Grote Markt
1400	Walk to Brewery De Halve Maan
1415	Visit brewery
1600	Free time – shopping
1800	Evening briefing – main lounge
1900	Evening meal

Hotel Sint Michiel: Walplein 38, Bruges. Phone 3250 339901

Brewery De Halve Maan: Cordoeanierstraat 26, Bruges. Phone 3250 333545

Bruges Diamond House: Langestraat 5, Bruges. Phone 3250 341189

Tour leader: Chris Pritchard. Phone (show number here)

Emergency: If any problems call Chris Pritchard.

For fire/medical assistance also call 100. For police call 101.

Activity

This is a group exercise for your visit.

- Go through all of the activities for each day and check that decisions have been recorded.
- Make a file with plastic pockets containing each day's attractions and transport arrangements.
- Ensure you have letters of confirmation, joining instructions, phone numbers, maps and any other correspondence in your file.

In summary

- Start the planning by clearly stating what the aims and objectives are of the visit.
- Make objectives SMART and take into account the interests of all the stakeholders.
- Allocate group members to be responsible for specific tasks and hold regular meetings to track progress and overcome problems.
- Identify and address constraints. They may arise because of the time and resources available; the type of participant; the destination; budgets; health, safety and security.
- Do some detailed planning to consider such issues as the destination; time of visit; transport; accommodation; opportunities for research and education; attractions and entertainment; and contact details.
- Use planning techniques including Key Events Plans and Gantt Charts.
- Produce detailed itineraries. They can be supported by making presentations and creating brochures.

Over to you

That was a long section! I hope you are up to date with your diary – the time is coming when you will need it!

Practice assessment activity

Levels P3/P4/M2

M **1** Participate in the planning of a visit. Explain what roles and tasks you undertook and support this with evidence. (M2)

P **2** Describe the aims, objectives and constraints that were identified for this visit and how they relate to the organisation and planning of it. (P3)

P **3** Describe the processes used to plan the visit. Create an itinerary for it. (P4)

8.4 Review travel itineraries and visits

This section covers:

- itineraries
- organisation of visits
- personal and career development
- evaluation techniques.

Itineraries

Adapting your itinerary for unforeseen events

Although your itinerary has been prepared, unforeseen events may mean it has to be changed. Perhaps the flight times have been changed or the hotel can no longer accommodate the group and another hotel has to be found. Perhaps another group will be joining you and they are studying a different course and need to visit different venues. Your team will need to be prepared for such events and be flexible, speedy and good at communicating.

Always be prepared for disruption and have contingency plans ready. What will you do if the coach fails to arrive, if it rains during your walking tour, or if someone becomes ill or gets separated from the group? Always have written contingency plans for each part of your event and make them known to everyone who may need to know them.

■ *The weather may be something you have to plan for!*

Oak College – Contingencies

The Oak College team discussed what to do if the flight home was delayed or cancelled. They decided on the following:

- If the participants would still arrive on the same flight on the same day, parents/guardians would be asked to use Teletext/Ceefax, the airline or airport websites, or phone the airline to check the arrival time.
- If the flight was cancelled or delayed overnight, a cascade system would be used to tell the college and parents/guardians of the new arrangements. One person on the tour would call two college managers who would each contact three parents/guardians, and each of those parents/guardians would call two more. Anyone who did not wish to take part in the cascade system would receive a call from the college instead.

Adapting your itinerary for people with different needs

Perhaps your itinerary proved very successful and you have been asked to operate it again, but this time for visitors with different needs. Could you do it?

What contingency plans have you prepared? Who needs to know what they are?

Activity

As a group activity, review your itinerary. What changes would be needed to make it more appropriate for:

- A group with different educational interests to the group in your first visit?
- An elderly group with the same educational needs as your first group but travelling in a different season of the year?

Remember to collect evidence as you go – it's too late when you come back!

Organisation of visits

Your work is not complete until you have reviewed and evaluated the visit.

Reviewing your objectives

Remember, before you started planning this visit, your team created a set of objectives. Now it is time to discover how well each objective was met and what could be done better next time. The review should consider whether:

- the itinerary itself was appropriate and offered value for money
- the routes and timings were suitable
- the time allocated to each event and location was appropriate
- there were amendments to the itinerary and, if so, whether they were handled well
- whether there should have been any other amendments
- the quality of the destinations, attractions, features, entertainment, facilities, catering, transport and guides
- whether anything added value to the visit, for example, a guest speaker, behind-the-scenes visit or surprise bonus.

Personal and career development

Organising this visit should also have benefited you. In reviewing and evaluating your performance and the benefits you gained you should consider your personal and career development.

Your personal development

- How did you perform as a team member and as someone with specific responsibilities?
- How good was your timekeeping?
- How well did you communicate with others?
- Did you show respect to others?
- Did you help others?
- How good were your organisational and problem-solving skills?
- Did you behave and dress professionally?
- What skills and knowledge did you gain?
- What were others' views of you?

Your career development

- How has the organisation of and participation in this visit enhanced your knowledge of the travel and tourism industry?
- What skills have you developed to assist you in your career?
- Has your career path been clarified or strengthened by this event?

Evaluation techniques

This visit is not just for fun – it should also be contributing to your studies! You will need evidence of the planning and operation of the visit, what the team did and what your involvement was.

Sources of information

How are you going to know what happened and how well things went? There are four key sources of information:

- your diary
- other written evidence
- audio/visual evidence
- customer and other stakeholders' evaluation.

Your diary

Your diary should have recorded:

- the actual activities
- your involvement in them
- the involvement of others
- any problems and how they were resolved
- any other comments and observations you made (for example, how motivated you felt)
- your views on your performance and the performance of other individuals and the team as a whole.

Other written evidence

This should include:

- copies of all the correspondence (including emails)
- records of conversations
- agendas and minutes
- risk assessments
- check sheets
- financial and other records
- leaflets, brochures, guidebooks
- research completion (notes from talks, etc.)
- log sheets
- statements from your tutor or group.

Examples of a log sheet and skills assessment are given below.

Log sheet

Visit to: ______________________________ Date: __________

Activity	My contribution	Outcome
2 people late	I phoned on my mobile	We waited 3 minutes
Briefing	I handed out the resources	All had them

■ *A log sheet*

Visit to Magma

Person observed: ______________________________ Date: __________

Demonstrated skills	Activity
Body language	Smiled and looked interested during briefing
Interpersonal skills	Ensured all participants paired/in a group
Personal effectiveness	Made file of all organised attractions available
Problem-solving	When student late, found phone number and called
Time management techniques	Always arrived five minutes early
Teamwork	Helped unwell colleague by typing booklet
Communication	Talked on microphone on coach effectively

■ *Example of skills assessment*

Audio/visual evidence

Audio/visual evidence includes photos, videos and audio tapes (of briefings, etc.).

Customer and other stakeholders' evaluation

It is important that you get the customers' views on how the visit went and how you performed. After all, the visit was for them! You can discover customers' views:

- by informal methods such as asking them verbally during or after the visit or having team members listen to customers discussing the visit with others

- by formal methods, for example, a customer questionnaire, a witness statement, or a feedback presentation from your customers.

If possible, gather customer opinion by more than one method. Don't forget to get feedback from your other stakeholders. What are their opinions? You may also be able to get feedback from the coach driver, attraction guide, hotel manager, etc.

The Oak College team produced a questionnaire which they distributed to participants on the flight home and collected as the participants got off the aircraft – that way they hoped to get a higher response than if they asked participants to return questionnaires later.

Prague visit, March 2006

1 = Excellent, 2 = Good, 3 = Satisfactory, 4 = Poor

	1	2	3	4
Before the trip				
1 Rate the amount of information you received about the trip.				
2 How well did your class representatives keep you informed?				
3 Did you attend the parent/student evening? If yes, go to Q4, if no, go to Q5.				
4 How useful did you find the evening?				
5 Did your parent/guardian attend that evening? If yes, go to Q6, if no, go to Q7.				
6 How useful did your parent/guardian find the evening?				
Sunday				
7 How informative/enjoyable was the sightseeing tour with the Czech students?				

Oak College's feedback questionnaire for the Prague visit

Activity

Produce a clear questionnaire for your visit, to include yes/no boxes plus comments for areas such as:

- the journey: route, amendments, method of transport, timescales
- destination: attractions, features, entertainment, facilities
- extras: guest speaker, tours, information packs
- value for money: what's included, overall cost.

Distribute it to all who went on the visit.

State on the questionnaire the date by when it should be returned and the name/address of the person to whom it should be given.

Activity

This is a group exercise.

1. *Collect and summarise the feedback data (your tutor can advise you how to do this).*
2. *Compare the results with your objectives. Which objectives were:*
   - fully met
   - partly met
   - not met at all?
3. *How would you do things differently next time, to make the trip even more successful?*

Personal evaluation

You may receive feedback from your tutor and you should also ask your colleagues for feedback on your performance. Ask them for examples for every statement they make about you. Compare their comments with how well you think you did and what you have learnt. Be honest! If you are not, the only person you are being dishonest with is yourself, and that doesn't help you!

This cycle of organisation – visit – evaluation is a pivotal part of travel and tourism. Well done – you have now experienced what happens every day in the travel and tourism industry!

Talking point

In a small group, discuss your assessment of yourself and take notes of how the rest of the group sees your contribution and whether this agrees with your own viewpoint.

Assess whether you now know more about:

- the travel and tourism industry and how it works
- how well you work in a team
- your own role in a group situation
- how effective you are at solving problems
- how organised you can be
- anything else, for example, your ability to stay calm in a crisis.

In summary

- Itineraries need to be adaptable to cope with unforeseen circumstances and different types of customers.
- Written contingency plans should be prepared and available for each key event.
- Itineraries, visits and personal performance should always have a post-event evaluation.
- To evaluate effectively it is essential that records are taken of events as they happen throughout the process and that the views of stakeholders are obtained.
- Feedback can be obtained using a range of oral, written or presented information.
- Seek feedback on your own performance. Be honest with yourself. Use that feedback to further improve your performance.

Practice assessment activity

Levels P5/M3/D2

P **1** Describe at least three techniques used to review the visit you organised. (P5)

M **2** Explain how the visit contributed to your personal and career development. What further and/or different involvement in the visit could have added more to your development? How? (M3)

D **3** Evaluate the planning and organisation of the visit using input from a range of sources. Make justified recommendations for future visits. (D2)

Note: In your assessment, you will be asked to produce evidence of your evaluation either in the form of a presentation or as a discussion, or possibly a written report. Ensure you include all your sources of evidence and any visual aids such as photographs and leaflets, etc. If you needed to obtain any leaflets or other material, make sure you have these available for evidence.

Test your knowledge

1. Name three travel directories.
2. Name two groups of people who have special needs.
3. Why is it important to set objectives?
4. Why does a party leader have to take particular care if a group contains people under 18 years of age?
5. Give three reasons to have a student code of conduct on visits.
6. What contact numbers should be provided and to whom?
7. What should always override any other consideration?
8. Name two ways in which you can prove you participated effectively in a study visit.
9. Give two methods of obtaining customer feedback.
10. Should you write your diary and evaluation (a) before, during and after the visit or (b) only on the night before your assignment is due?

Appendix

Links to all websites have been made available at www.heinemann.co.uk/hotlinks. Enter the express code 2196P.

Unit 1

References and further reading

Books, magazines, journals:
Travel Trade Gazette
Travel Weekly
Thomas Cook – the holiday maker. Jill Hamilton (Stroud, Sutton Publishers 2005)
Grand Tours and Cook's Tours. Lynne Withey (London, Aurum 1998)
United Kingdom Tourism Survey
International Passenger Survey

Websites:
Transport Salaried Staff' association
Civil Aviation Authority
Office for National Statistics
Association of British Travel Agents
UKInbound
Highlands of Scotland Tourist Board
Belfast Visitor and Convention Bureau
Butlins Institute of Tourist Guiding
Federation of Tour Operators (FTO)
Guild of Travel Management Companies (GTMC)
Foreign and Commonwealth Office
Department for Culture, Media and Sport
First Choice
European Union
Countryside Agency
CAA – ATOL
Office of Public Sector Information

Unit 2

References and further reading

Books, magazines, journals:
Moments of truth. J. Carlzon (Cambridge MA, Ballinger Publishing 1997)
Crowning the customer. Feargal Quinn (Dublin, O'Brien Press 1990)
Complete idiot's guide to great customer service. Ron Karr and Don Blowhowiak (1997)

BTEC First Travel and Tourism (first edition). Dennis Brombley, Malcolm Jefferies, Andy Kerr, Christine King (Oxford, Heinemann 2005)
Travel guides (for international cultures)

Organisations and websites:
Institute of Customer Service
CSM – e-magazine
Health and Safety Executive
British Airways
Easyjet
Virgin Atlantic
Ryanair
Biz Help

TV programmes:
Airport (BBC)
Airline (ITV)

Unit 3

References and further reading

Books, magazines, journals:
Group Leisure
Travel Trade Gazette
World Travel Guide
World Travel Atlas
Travel guides e.g. *England: The Rough Guide*. Jonathan Buckley and Rob Humphreys (Eds.) (London, Rough Guide Travel Guides 2000)
Tour Operators brochures

Websites:
VisitBritain
County Council websites
Town/city websites
National Trust/National Trust for Scotland
English Heritage etc.
Local Tourist Information Centres

TV programmes:
Holiday (BBC)
Wish you were here (ITV)

Unit 4

References and further reading

Books, magazines, journals:
Travel Trade Gazette
World Travel Guide (Columbus Travel Publishing – annual publication)
Travel Guides e.g *Lonely Planet France*, 3rd Edition. Steve Fallon, Daniel Robinson, Nicola Williams (Eds.) (Lonely Planet 1999)
Tour Operators brochures
CD Roms e.g. *Encarta*, geography resources

Websites:
Country Tourist Offices sites e.g. Italian State Tourist Office
Car Hire companies e.g. Avis
Insurance companies
UK Passport Office

TV programmes:
Holiday (BBC)
Wish you were here (ITV)
Holiday Reps (BBC)

Unit 5

References and further reading

Books, magazines, journals:
Principles of Marketing. F Brassington and S Pettitt (London, Pitman 1997)
Essentials of Marketing. 3rd Edition. J Bythe (Harlow, Prentice Hall 2005)
Marketing for Leisure and Tourism. D Field (London, Hodder & Stoughton 1997)

Websites:
Biz.Ed Guide
VisitBritain
National Office for Statistics
Air Miles
Marketing Virtual Library
Business Marketing Association
Wikipedia – marketing entry
Institution of Direct Marketing

DVDs/Videos:
Marketing for Leisure II, TV Choice (2004)
Marketing a Theme Park, TV Choice

Unit 6

References and further reading

Books, magazines, journals:
BTEC First Business. C Carysforth and M Heild (Oxford, Heinemann 2004)
The Business of Tourism. J Holloway (Harlow, Pearson 2002)
Complete A–Z Business Studies Handbook. D Line et al (London, Hodder & Stoughton 2003)

Websites:
Biz.Ed Guide
Air Miles
Statistics on Tourism and Research
Association of British Travel Agents
Passenger Shipping Association
World Tourism Organization
World Travel and Tourism Council

DVDs /Video:
Systems in Travel, TV Choice
Inside a Travel Business, TV Choice

TV programmes:
Back to the Floor (BBC)
Trouble at the Top (BBC)
The Apprentice (BBC)

Unit 7

References and further reading

Books, magazines, journals:
Travel Trade Gazette
Local and National newspapers job vacancy pages
The Perfect CV. Max Eggert (London, Arrow Business Books 1992)
Writing a Winning CV. Julie-Ann Amos (Oxford, how to books)
Perfect Job Search Strategies. Tom Jackson (London, Piatkus 1994)

Websites:
Connexions, young peoples Careers Advisors
People First
Springboard
Edexcel
British Airports Authority
Tour Operators
Ferry companies
Airlines

TV programmes:
Airport (BBC)
Airline (ITV)
Holiday Reps (BBC)
Back to the floor (BBC)
The Apprentice (BBC)

Unit 8

References and further reading

Books and periodicals:
World Travel Guide (Columbus Travel Publishing -- annual publication)
Coaching Venues and Excursions Guide (Milton Keynes, Yandell Publishing – annual publication)
OAG Flight Guide (OAG – monthly publication)
OAG Rail Guide (OAG – monthly publication)
Travel Information Manual (TIM) (IATA – monthly publication)

Websites:
Foreign and Commonwealth Office
Department of Health

Index

Locators with k, e.g. 125k, signify a 'key point'

D

E

F

G

H

I

J

K

L